APOCALYPSE ANY DAY NOW

DEEP UNDERGROUND WITH AMERICA'S DOOMSDAY PREPPERS

TEA KRULOS

CHICAGO
REVIEW
PRESS

To Kate—my zombie apocalypse survival partner

Published by Chicago Review Press Incorporated
814 North Franklin Street
Chicago, Illinois 60610
ISBN 978-1-61373-641-8

Library of Congress Cataloging-in-Publication Data
Is available from the Library of Congress.

Cover and interior design: Jonathan Hahn
Cover image: Redd Angelo/Unsplash

Printed in the United States of America
5 4 3 2 1

CONTENTS

INTRODUCTION

Two Minutes to Midnight

The *Bulletin of the Atomic Scientists* was created in 1945 by scientists at the University of Chicago who had worked on the Manhattan Project. After the devastation of Hiroshima and Nagasaki in World War II, the group realized that nuclear devices could not only easily destroy an entire city but, in an escalated firefight, the entire human race.

Two years later, the group created the Doomsday Clock, a symbolic clock face that gives a representation of how close we are ticking toward "midnight," or the annihilation of the planet. Every year, the *Bulletin's* Science and Security Board evaluates how itchy humanity's nuclear trigger fingers have become. The board members also now consider other factors like climate change, biotechnology, and emerging technologies, and update the Doomsday Clock accordingly. Is the big hand being sucked into the twelve at the top of the final hour, or is it slipping backward to give us a few more precious minutes?

The clock has rarely given us the comfort of being earlier than a quarter to twelve. In 1991, with the Cold War finally over, the clock spun back the furthest it ever has—to seventeen minutes to midnight. This was a huge improvement from 1984, the height of the "mutually assured destruction" days of the Cold War, when the Doomsday Clock hand hovered ominously at three minutes to midnight.

In January 2015 the *Bulletin* revealed that things weren't looking so great. The minute hand had crept forward again to three to midnight, the first time since the 1984 Cold War days. It was, as the

Bulletin of the Atomic Scientists noted in 2016, with the clock's hands still poised at 180 seconds from the End, "not good news."

Throughout 2015 and 2016 you could practically watch the minute hand twitch. During the bombastic 2016 presidential campaign, Republican candidates tried to outdo each other on how tough they would get on terrorist organizations. Future president Donald Trump told an audience during his campaign that he would go after ISIS-controlled oil fields to disable their finances.

"I would bomb the shit out of 'em," he told a jubilant crowd in Iowa. "I would just bomb those suckers. That's right. I would blow up the pipes . . . every single inch. There would be nothing left."

Not to be outdone, Republican candidate Ted Cruz said the United States should "carpet bomb them into oblivion. I don't know if sand can glow in the dark, but we're going to find out."

In 2017, with President Donald J. Trump in office just a few days, the *Bulletin* advanced the Doomsday Clock forward thirty seconds (the first time the clock has ever been set to a half minute) to 2.5 minutes to midnight. "The board has decided to act, in part, based on the words of a single person: Donald Trump," the *Bulletin* stated. Although it noted Trump's loose use of language, it cautioned,

> Just the same, words matter, and President Trump has had plenty to say over the last year. Both his statements and his actions as president-elect have broken with historical precedent in unsettling ways. He has made ill-considered comments about expanding the US nuclear arsenal. He has shown a troubling propensity to discount or outright reject expert advice related to international security, including the conclusions of intelligence experts. And his nominees to head the Energy Department and the Environmental Protection Agency dispute the basics of climate science.
>
> In short, even though he has just taken office, the president's intemperate statements, lack of openness to expert advice, and questionable cabinet nominations have already made a bad international security situation worse.

We are "back to an age of great uncertainty," one of the *Bulletin* members said. They reminded us that President Trump had just been in office for six days, and unless things changed, we would continue to tick forward.

That prediction soon reflected reality. On January 25, 2018, I woke up early to watch the *Bulletin's* announcement on a livestream from their press conference at the National Press Club in Washington, DC. It had been a year the *Bulletin* described as "perilous and chaotic." The clock, the *Bulletin* revealed, had now moved to two minutes to midnight. This is the closest the clock has ever been, tied with one other time in history—the clock was moved to two to midnight in 1953, the year the Soviets detonated their first H-bomb.

"To call the world nuclear situation dire is to understate the danger—and its immediacy," the *Bulletin* reported in their 2018 Doomsday Clock statement. The clock's movement, they said, was "an urgent warning of global danger." The statement, written by the *Bulletin's* Science and Security Board, also said they were "deeply concerned about the loss of public trust in political institutions, in the media, in science, and in facts themselves—a loss that the abuse of information technology has fostered."

But the statement concluded that it would still be possible to "rewind the clock" if citizens demand action from their governments: "They can demand action to reduce the existential threat of nuclear war and unchecked climate change. They can seize the opportunity to make a safer and saner world."

Until that happens, *tick tock.*

1

BLOOD MOON PROPHECY

"How long, dear Lord, our Savior / Wilt thou remain away?
/ Our hearts are growing weary / Of thy so long delay"
—MILLERITE HYMN

It seems like the world is always about to end, doesn't it?

That was the thought on my mind the evening of September 27, 2015, as I hiked up a hill in Reservoir Park here in my hometown, Milwaukee, with a small group of friends. The top of the hill was soon scattered with people sitting on blankets and lawn chairs, armed with telescopes, binoculars, and cameras. This was the night of the blood moon, a rare alignment of the sun, moon, and Earth. At first, there was an air of disappointment as the sky was obscured with gray clouds. But then the clouds drifted away and there it was! A gigantic, magnificent deep orange of a moon suspended in the night sky.

Looking around the hilltop, I noticed that people seemed excited about the astronomical event, but in a calm, wonderstruck type of way, not in an "Oh no, the sky is falling" way. Not everyone on Earth was having such a casual evening, though, for this night had been predicted as the End. The blood moon prophecy, as it was referred to, had originated from calculations in 2008 by a pastor named Mark Biltz of El Shaddai Ministries in Washington State.

According to Biltz's calculations, the blood moon was the final sequence of a tetrad of total lunar eclipses that had begun on April 15, 2014. Piecing together clues from the books of Joel, Acts, and

Revelation, he connected the lunar eclipses to a clear portent of the end times.

Biltz pointed out the lineup: blood moons on April 15, 2014, and October 8, 2014; a full lunar eclipse on March 20, 2015; more blood moons on April 4, 2015, and then boom, September 28, 2015. Four blood moons and a full lunar eclipse lining up like an apocalyptic slot machine in the sky. The significance, Biltz said, like so many end-time predictions, could be found in a couple of short verses from the Bible.* In this case, the main point was found in Acts 2:20: "The sun shall be turned into darkness, and the *moon into blood*, before that great and notable day of the Lord come." Oh! And then there's Revelation 6:12: "And I beheld when he had opened the sixth seal, and, lo, there was a great earthquake; and the sun became black as a sackcloth of hair, and the *moon became as blood*."

Biltz wrote a book about his theory in 2014, *Blood Moons: Decoding the Imminent Heavenly Signs*, and his prediction grew legs. John Hagee, the founder and senior pastor of Cornerstone Church in San Antonio, Texas, and CEO of Global Evangelism Television began promoting the blood moon prophecy and wrote his own book on the topic, the bestselling *Four Blood Moons: Something Is About to Change*. The prophecy was further spread through an online push by an Internet-based congregation called the eBible Fellowship.

Apocalypse predictions make for good ink, and soon the story was picked up by major media outlets such as *USA Today*, the *Washington Post*, CNN, and other major media outlets. Both the astronomy website EarthSky.org and the Church of Jesus Christ of Latter-Day Saints received so many queries that they had to issue statements.

EarthSky.org explained that the blood moon prophecy didn't quite make sense from an astronomer's view, as the blood moon and a lunar tetrad are two entirely different things.

The Church of Latter-Day Saints told Mormons via a public statement that they should remain calm and be "spiritually and physically

---

* All Bible verses in this book are from the King James Version, which makes everything sound more apocalyptic.

prepared for life's ups and downs" but should avoid "being caught up in extreme efforts to anticipate catastrophic events."

Angry God

Despite the hoopla, the blood moon set, the sun rose, life went on, and Angry God did not bring the hammer down on us. Happy God is the one who created the Earth and gave us fruit trees and grass, the fish of the sea, the fowl of the air, and every living thing that moveth on the Earth. Happy God made Adam and Eve and gave them everything they could possibly want in the Garden of Eden.

Angry God, however, kicked them out of the Garden of Eden after they ate the forbidden fruit, forced them to toil in the fields for their food, and imposed the pains of childbirth. He also flooded the Earth and killed everyone except Noah and his ark full of family and animals. Then there was the time he rained down ten vile plagues on Egypt—turning the Nile River into blood; sending swarms of frogs, lice, locusts, flies, and a bad case of boils; killing livestock and the firstborn; sending darkness for three days and fire and brimstone raining on the Earth. One time he even punked Abraham into almost sacrificing his son Isaac in a test of loyalty. The Old Testament God is the Angry God who created the Earth, but like a temperamental artist, also wants to destroy it. And this is what has worried people that the End is near ever since the ink dried on the first draft of the Bible.

The Great Disappointment

Predictions of when the world will end, as foretold in the book of Revelation, have placed the apocalypse just around the corner for thousands of years.

In American history, one of the first well-known end-of-the-world scares was predicted by William Miller, a New England farmer who grew up near the small town of Low Hampton on the border of New York and Vermont. As a young man, Miller developed a passion for reading, putting in a long day of chores and reading stealthily by candlelight at night—his father thought his late-night reading would affect his work performance. As an adult, he was elected to civil offices, including deputy sheriff and justice of the peace. Miller fought in the War of 1812 where he rose to the rank of captain and worked as a recruiter. After the war and the deaths of his father and one of his sisters, Miller began to ponder the afterlife and renewed his Baptist faith. He became especially interested in eschatology, the part of theology that studies death, judgment, and the final destiny of the soul.

Speculation about end times escalated throughout the eighteenth century. New England preachers portrayed the French and Indians during the Seven Years' War as tools of the Antichrist, and patriot preachers during the Revolution painted the British and Anglicanism in the same lurid colors.

Miller owned English reverend George Faber's *Dissertation on the Prophecies*, published in three editions between 1804 and 1811, which examined the end times discussed in the Bible. Sprinkled throughout the New England region were sects like the Shakers, who believed Jesus had already returned and instituted the millennium. A similar group, the Dorrilites, was established by the "prophet" William Dorril in the 1790s; they lived in two communities in Vermont and Massachusetts, where they practiced vegetarianism and promiscuous free love. Another Vermont sect was the New Israelites, led by Nathaniel Wood (a.k.a. "Old Man of All") in Middletown, Vermont. The group, about one hundred strong, practiced polygamy and spent spare time searching for buried treasure and other revelations with dowsing rods. Wood predicted that a destroying angel would usher in the apocalypse on January 14, 1802. There was such a ruckus of panic on that date that local militia were called in to clear crowds and restore order.

Miller moved to Poultney, Vermont, where he met his wife, Lucy, and they eventually moved back to the Miller farm in Low Hampton in 1815. Miller's study of the book of Daniel led him to work out math equations that led him to believe the Second Coming of Christ was going to happen sometime between March 21, 1843, and March 21, 1844.

He was inspired to begin preaching about his prediction after a dream in which celestial guides led him to "an upper room filled with light and pilgrims singing 'Hallelujah to the Lamb!'" But Miller waited years before actually getting into the preaching biz because he was intimidated. He finally gave his first speech in 1831. Author David L. Rowe describes the circumstances in his book *God's Strange Work: William Miller and the End of the World*: "While he had been feeling the compulsion for many years, this was so powerful that he promised God he would go if someone would invite him to speak. Since as yet no one had, Miller felt safe. That same afternoon a nephew arrived with an invitation to preach the next day to Baptists in Dresden, sixteen miles northwest across Lake Champlain."

Miller was an effective speaker. One commentator described his voice as "strong and mellow," and though his style was "not remarkable for grace or eloquence," simplicity was a virtue. He was humble and often used self-deprecating humor. He was unintimidating in appearance,

> short and heavyset with a ruddy, round face, but listeners could see something of themselves in this man whose limited schooling, plain clothes, and lack of pretense matched their own. To all appearances, he was just like them, and he reaped the benefit of a democratic culture that valued commonness. Age was no handicap either. In his early fifties, Miller may have been ten years beyond the average life expectancy, but survivorship lent his words gravity and wisdom. Jackson-era Americans did not so glorify youth that they had forgotten the respect owed to the fathers.

A marginal group of believers began to form, and Miller began to persuade more people, including ministers, that his prediction would be accurate. A pamphlet he had printed in 1833 titled *Evidences from Scripture and History of the Second Coming of Christ About the Year A.D. 1843 and of His Personal Reign of 1000 Years* helped Miller plead his case.

New Millerites helped expand from a crusade to a mass movement, especially Joshua Vaughan Himes, pastor of the Chardon Street Chapel in Boston. Himes worked to attract skilled workers, mobilize supporters, and fundraise donors. To help with his process, he assembled *Views of the Prophecies and Prophetic Chronology*, a collection of Miller's lectures and writings in print, and edited and produced Millerite newspapers that were published semiweekly, and eventually weekly. The movement's first newspaper was the *Signs of the Times*, and more regional papers followed, including New York's the *Midnight Cry*, the *Philadelphia Alarm*, the *Advent Shield and Review*, and the *Advent Message to the Daughters of Zion* (edited by and marketed to women).

Miller had predicted that the End would happen sometime between spring 1843 and spring 1844. When those dates passed, Miller was badly shaken. However, Samuel S. Snow, a new name in the Millerite movement, brought a fresh view to the prophecy. Snow's interpretation led to a calculation that October 22, 1844, was the "true midnight cry." The Millerite inner circle seized on this prediction and began promoting it in their papers.

The Second Great Awakening coincided with the explosion of Millerism. This was the same time and place (Vermont and New York) that Joseph Smith formed the Church of Jesus Christ of Latter-Day Saints and presented the Book of Mormon. Another religious leader, Robert Matthews (a.k.a. Matthias the Prophet), established a cult following in New York. They created a settlement called the Kingdom, where Matthews claimed authority from God to judge the world.

When writing about the apocalyptic craze of the Second Great Awakening, editors couldn't resist the alliteration of "Mormons, Matthias, and Millerites," and lumped them together, to the chagrin of Miller, who never claimed he was a prophet or messiah. There were many titles people tried to bestow upon him, but he preferred "Father Miller."

Miller faced many critics who mirrored his tactics to criticize him and declare that he was deluding people and profiting from his work.

A cottage industry of anti-Millerite newspapers and pamphlets were produced with titles like *The Theory of William Miller, Utterly Exploded* and *The End of the World Not Yet.*

Belief in the Second Coming date of October 22, 1844, was so strong that it was reported that ecstatic Millerites settled old quarrels, gave away or sold their earthly possessions to pay off old debts, or donated the money toward keeping the Millerite printing presses rolling to help spread the word. They left their fields of crops unattended and left their shops closed. On October 22, it was reported some stood on the roofs of their house, hoping to be closer to the incoming Messiah.

Nothing happened. October 22 became known as the Great Disappointment. The world kept turning.

In addition to "disappointment," many Millerites had to come to terms with the decisions they made believing the world was coming to an end. Many were left in the poorhouse and had to endure the ridicule of their peers and the press.

The Millerites began to dissolve. A now-feeble Father Miller gave his last speeches in 1847. People flocked to these events out of curiosity, but many viewed him as misguided at best, crazy and crooked at worst. He was threatened with tarring and feathering in Sandy Hill, New York. He had a particularly rough reception in Vermont. In Stowe, "fire crackers, squibs, and home-made rockets" were thrown at him, and in South Troy "eggs, clubs, and rocks" were hurled at him.

Family surrounded Father Miller, singing his favorite hymns as he died on December 20, 1849.

Estimates of the number of Millerites in their heyday range from fifty thousand to five hundred thousand. Even today, their influence lives on in their descendants, the Advent Christian Church and the Seventh-Day Adventist Church.

"For Miller and many of his followers, the world did indeed come to an end on October 22, 1844, not melted in divine fire but dissolved in bitter tears," Rowe reports in *God's Strange Work.* "Hope did not necessarily die, but expectation did."

Apocalypse Later

Like the rest of my Milwaukee neighbors taking in the spectacle on top of the hill in Reservoir Park that September night in 2015, I wasn't vexed by the blood moon prophecy. I had already survived many predicted apocalypses.

The first memorable one for me was the Y2K bug. We were told that when the calendars rolled over from the year 1999 to 2000 on New Year's Eve we would face a global computer meltdown over the date change. There was indeed an issue with some older computer programs, which stored only the last two digits of the current year and would thus confuse the year 2000 with the year 1900 unless someone fixed the coding. Many believed this problem had the potential to cause widespread blackouts and other major system failures. Sensationalists added their own twists to the story—nuclear missiles flying around willy-nilly, bank accounts completely disappearing. A concerned public emptied store shelves and bank accounts to buy canned food, bottled water, flashlights, and emergency kits to weather the Y2K storm about to drop down upon them like a deadly giant New Year's ball descending at midnight in Times Square.

Minor complications happened during the rollover, but nothing that destroyed society. Life went on into the new century.

In 2011 the end times began to get publicity again. A pastor named Harold Camping, president of Family Radio, based out of Oakland, California, had done the math and come up with a bottom-line rapture date: May 21, 2011. Camping, a jowly eighty-nine-year-old preacher, had made failed apocalypse predictions in the past, claiming the end was upon us in 1994 and then again in 1995. This time, he assured everyone, he had remembered to carry the one and everything checked out.

A campaign to publicize this date mirrored the Millerites—billboard ads and signs on the sides of trucks proclaimed, JUDGEMENT DAY: MAY 21. Camping's followers spread the word online, over the air, and on the streets. I encountered the message myself on the streets of Milwaukee, where I saw a group of doomsdayers spread out across four corners of a busy downtown intersection, wearing brightly colored T-shirts with the judgment date in bold type, handing out pamphlets with Camping's predictions.

May 21 came and went without incident, but Camping had a new story. This retrofitting and reinventing are examples of *cognitive dissonance*, a term we'll encounter again while talking about end-time predictions. Camping now informed anyone still willing to listen to him that May 21 had been a silent judgment from God and was the beginning of a quiet rapture. October 21, he explained, was the actual date to mark on your calendar as the End.

After that day passed as well, many decried Camping as a "false prophet." A humbled Camping himself expressed regret and Family Radio took a huge hit in credibility and financial support. Camping suffered his own end times and died in 2013.

Humanity didn't have to wait long for the next doomsday scenario to crop up: 2012 brought a new perceived threat, the so-called Mayan apocalypse. December 21, 2012, marked the end of the Mesoamerican Long Count calendar. However, this date was simply the end of one calendar round (the next ends in 2407).

Bizarro cartoonist Dan Piraro summed it up perfectly in a comic panel: "I only had enough room to go up to 2012," a Mayan holding a chisel says to another Mayan looking at the stone calendar. "Ha! That'll freak somebody out someday," his colleague replies.

Nonetheless, soothsayers predicted that when the Mayan calendar flipped to this final 2012 entry, a mass of terrible disasters—volcanic eruptions, floods, tsunamis, earthquakes—would rip the Earth apart. Alternatively, other New Age predictions suggested that instead of chaos the world would experience an incredible spiritual transformation.

December 22, 2012, felt about as transcendental or disastrous as any other day. People carried on with their holiday shopping and the Mayan apocalypse was forgotten.

Daniel 9

As the blood moon set and the sun rose and the end of 2015 approached, I wondered what to expect next. With doomsday predictions becoming a crowded field, I was sure I could find someone who thought the world was coming to an end in 2016. Talk of doomsday has long been pushed with fiery conviction, particularly from evangelists. Tugboat captain turned evangelist Hal Lindsey wrote a bestselling book titled *The Late Great Planet Earth* that predicted Armageddon would happen by 1988 at the latest. Famed televangelist Billy Graham worked the angle that the end was approaching in "a couple years, five years," with no specific date except "there is a feeling in the air something is going to happen soon" for decades.

Sure enough, within minutes of Internet searching, I found exactly what I was looking for. Nora Roth's website 7Trumpets.org expounded a theory that our judgment and final days would happen sometime between June and October 2016.

You might think apocalypse predictors just read the book of Revelation over and over to try to match the prophecies with contemporary world events. Though Revelation is a good doomsday read, no passages have offered up anywhere near the speculative fodder of the book of Daniel. Daniel gets his start by saving his own life by dream interpreting for King Nebuchadnezzar, then reads the writing on the wall for his son King Belshazzar, and escapes the lion's den unharmed under King Darius. In the later chapters of the book, Daniel shares his own prophetic visions and receives a visit from the angel Gabriel, who delivers a special message. In 9:24, Gabriel reports:

> Seventy weeks [translated in some versions as "sevens"] are determined upon thy people and upon thy holy city, to finish the transgression, and to make an end of sins, and to make reconciliation for iniquity, and to bring in everlasting righteousness, and to seal up the vision and prophecy, and to anoint the most Holy.

Gabriel goes on to say that from the time when word goes out to restore and rebuild Jerusalem until the Messiah returns, there will be seven "sevens" and sixty-two "sevens." Then the Messiah will be put to death and Daniel 9:26 says "the end will come like a flood."

Those "sevens" and other clues from the book of Daniel are the heart of apocalypse predictions. Like the Millerites, Harold Camping, and many others before her, Roth had based her apocalyptic mathematics on these short verses, trying to figure out the mathematical meaning of Daniel 9.

Many have tried to get this equation right. Famed evangelist Pat Robertson used the verses to calculate 1982 as the End. Roth's calculations led not to 1843 or 1982 or 2011 but the then-impending doom date of 2016.

I clicked on the "About" section of Roth's website to learn more about the prophet behind this theory. Her bio described her as a Bible student but also a computer scientist with experience working as a programmer and a systems analyst. She added, "I enjoy birding, camping, traveling, photography, and working puzzles," and concluded, "I love cats."

Curious to talk more about the end times, I decided to give Roth a call.

"The question came to my mind—when is that going to happen? It's clear there hasn't been an end to sin in God's people," Roth explained to me on the phone, describing her interest in the End, which stemmed from her study of the Bible ten years ago.

She was polite, even cheerful, if a little guarded in our phone call. She said she lived on the West Coast but didn't elaborate. Her explanation of her end-time calculation left me a little dizzy, but after speaking to her on the phone and studying a document available on her website, this is how it breaks down:

One day about eight years ago it just all of a sudden became really clear to me that the seventy weeks had two different fulfillments. The first seventy weeks were seventy a week—the Jewish mind, if you say week to them they think of three different things, it's like if I tell you I'm going to call you in a dozen, what does that mean? A dozen hours, a dozen days, a dozen minutes? So when you say it's going to be seventy weeks, they say what kind of week are you talking about? The Bible has a seven-day week, like we do, the Bible has a seven-*year* week, where they were supposed to work the land six years and rest on the seventh, and then the Bible has a *forty-nine-year* week where you put seven of those seven-year periods together. So what became crystal clear to me is that Daniel 9 had two fulfillments. The first seventy weeks was talking about seventy seven-year periods and the bigger picture, the first one led to the first coming of Jesus, but the bigger one, the second one was seventy of the bigger forty-nine-year weeks, and that would lead to the second coming of Christ, and that would completely fulfill the verse where everlasting righteousness is brought in and there is an end of sin.

Did you get lost? I kind of did too, not being very good at math. But if you want to see what Roth is talking about in math equation form, she has a long list of charts and timelines that explains periods of seventy years, seventy sabbaticals, and seventy jubilees at www.7trumpets.org/articles/complete.htm

After she started her numbers, Roth felt she was on to something and began studying Bible chronology and scripture "probably twelve to fourteen hours a day," and it seemed to all fit together perfectly. She decided to go public and share with people. She got a mixed reaction. "There's a range, everything from being antagonistic and saying you're deceiving people, you're crazy, very vitriolic, a few people are that way and a few people are the opposite extreme, 'Praise the Lord this is the clearest I've ever read!'" Roth told me. "Most people are somewhere in the middle, I would say more negative than positive."

I spoke to Nora in May 2016, just a month before her June–October time frame was about to start. I asked what we would be looking at over the coming months. "Well, Revelation mentions four major earthquakes, each more severe than the previous one," Roth explained excitedly. "By the final earthquake, it's like every mountain and every island is moved out of their place and pretty much all we know humanly is destroyed at that point, but there are three major earthquakes that come before that, and these earthquakes might be of a little different nature. In other words, they might be the whole Earth shaking instead of 'Oh, this was just an earthquake in Japan or San Francisco,' or something like that. There also are what are called trumpet judgments and I believe the first four of those are other physical calamities where like a meteor might strike the Earth, an asteroid might go in the ocean, massive amounts of damage are done. Huge fires, huge tsunamis, that sort of thing."

Sounds frightening, but in a world constantly filled with so much chaos, it's hard to tell what might be a trumpet judgment and what's just a normal Monday.

Antichrist

While walking in Manhattan down Broadway on my East Coast trip for this book, I encountered a woman in a bedazzled I ♥ JESUS jean baseball cap, striped shirt, and baggy polka-dot shorts, with a paper apron that read, JESUS DIED ON THE CROSS FOR OUR SINS AND ROSE AGAIN. She was enthusiastically dashing back and forth to hand pedestrians Chick tracts (little proselytizing comic books) and a pamphlet, *Warning from the Book of Revelation: Never Receive 666 the Mark of the Beast.* Printed in multicolored text of red, black, blue, and green, the pamphlet takes readers on a crash course through the hellfire and judgments of the book of Revelation.

A key component to the End will be the appearance of figures the book of Revelation calls the Beast from the Earth, or the Antichrist, and a satanic creature referred to as the Beast from the Sea. As this colorful pamphlet states in the title, it is said that the Antichrist will force his followers to be branded with the number 666: "And he causeth all, both small and great, rich and poor, free and bond, to receive a mark in their right hand, or in their foreheads," reads Revelation 13:16–18. "And that no man might buy or sell, save he that had the mark, or the name of the beast, or the number of his name. Here is wisdom. Let him that hath understanding count the number of the beast: for it is the number of a man; and his number is Six hundred threescore and six."

Roth explains:

> The most important thing that will be happening in this time is that every living person on Earth will be making up their mind whether they want to be worshiping God or whether they want to worship an entity the Bible calls the Beast. My understanding from the Bible is that the Beast is a name that's given to Satan when Satan will come on Earth and appear as a physical being. He will take on a glorious, commanding body, he will appear to be like Christ to the Christians, he will appear as Messiah to the Jews, virtually all the people in the world will worship him when he comes. When Satan shows up as God he's going to say if everyone will worship me I will stop these physical calamities and I'll bring you back to a perfect world. Which is a lie—most of what he says will be a lie.

But who will the Antichrist be? Donald Trump? Justin Bieber?

Along with guessing the rapture date, trying to eyeball the legendary Antichrist is a favorite for religious prognosticators. The list of suspects is long and old, everyone from Napoleon Bonaparte to President Barack Obama (one disturbed man, Oscar Ramiro Ortega-Hernandez, shot a rifle at the White House in 2011, telling police he was trying to kill the Antichrist). A long list of world and religious leaders, including presidents, chancellors, popes, and dictators, have been deemed to be the Beast from the Earth in disguise.

With the presidential race between Donald Trump and Hillary Clinton in 2016, Antichrist fever was in full swing. While shopping on Amazon I found two similar books. One, *Hillary Clinton, Prophecy, and the Destruction of the United States: Is Hillary Clinton Fulfilling Biblical, Islamic, Catholic, Hopi, and Other America-Related Prophecies? What About Donald Trump?* by Bob Thiel, PhD, theorized not that she was the Antichrist but that she was a key figure that would "enable the rise in the final Antichrist" and that she was involved in events leading to "the coming destruction of the United States," which he outlines in chapters like "20 Reasons Why Hillary Clinton is Apocalyptic." The cover features a photo of a stern-looking Clinton, with a mushroom cloud exploding in the background.

The second offering, an e-book titled *The Fourth Beast: Is Donald Trump the Antichrist?* by Lawrence Moelhauser, features a partially transparent image of the forty-fifth president looking smug, another mushroom cloud exploding behind him. Moelhauser breaks down his ideas in two parts of the book, "A Boastful Mouth" and "A Rash and Deceitful King."

In the months to come, Roth told me, we would see "major prophetic events" beginning mid-June, followed by the appearance of the Antichrist, an attempt by God to send a message to worship him (the real him), "and then the final plagues are poured out on the Earth and Jesus literally physically coming the second time, I see that possibly happening between now and October."

Roth seemed confident in her prediction, but did admit that there was a window for error in her time frame. "It seems impossible to think of all of that taking place, say, in the next five or six months, but it seems to me that's what scripture is saying," Roth explained. "My personal conclusions may be right, they may be wrong, but whichever they are, I still have 100 percent faith in the Bible. At some point, events will happen exactly as it says."

Summer and fall of 2016 passed and nothing happened, so I tried to e-mail Roth for a follow-up interview. I got no reply.

Apocalypse Next

One of the more well-known modern religious prognosticators is Pastor Ricardo Salazar, billed by tabloids as a "modern Nostradamus." Unlike Nostradamus, though, the pastor of the Global Church of the King of Israel in Tokyo has been remarkably inaccurate. He struck out wildly with his long list of failed predictions for the end times in 2016. Pastor Salazar predicted that a 5.6-mile-wide asteroid would strike the Earth between May 15 and 17, 2016, causing massive earthquakes and tsunamis that would kill over a billion people. Food shortages and pandemics would follow, and eruptions of volcanos that would blacken the sky and cause an ice age (surprisingly short at just a year) that would somehow also make a large part of California fall into the ocean and then a brutal (again, surprisingly short) World War III between June and October 2016, with Russia and China annihilating a weakened United States. This would then lead to the arrival of the Antichrist in 2020, and the Second Coming of Christ in 2023.

The 2020 apocalypse and Antichrist date was also predicted by Jeane Dixon, a famed astrologer and psychic, who rose to prominence in the 1960s and eventually met with Richard Nixon and was one of many astrologers who advised Nancy Reagan. The author of classics like *Yesterday, Today, and Forever* and *Do Cats Have ESP?*, Dixon died in 1997 and was credited for appearing to predict the JFK assassination, but also has a long list of failed prophecies, such as predicting that World War III would start in China in 1958.[*]

In fact, a researcher at Temple University coined the term "Jeane Dixon effect" to refer to seizing on correct predictions in a sea of incorrect ones.

Like Harold Camping and others before, the 2020 date isn't Salazar's or Dixon's first stab at predicting the apocalypse. Salazar had previously predicted earthquakes would destroy the United States and Japan, that a meteorite would burn down a third of the world's forests, and that an exploding asteroid in 2015 would send the world into a panic on October 8 or 9 of that year . . . or never. Dixon had previously predicted that a planetary alignment would destroy the Earth on February 4, 1962.

———

When will Angry God finally lose his cool and bring his judgment to the planet, the faithful ascending into heaven, the sinners left behind to suffer through the end times? It looks like we're safe for now. Predictions by Harold Camping, Norah Roth and her seventy jubilees,

---

[*] Dixon's last words were "I knew this would happen."

Pastor Ricardo Salazar, Pat Robertson, and countless others have all come and gone in recent years, but God above allows the world to keep turning.

Although various self-appointed prophets will continue to claim they've found the clues and math hidden in plain sight in the pages of the Bible, all this speculation over number crunching, interpretations over two-thousand-year-old scripture is probably a vain exercise even if you believe the end is nigh because in another short passage (Matthew 24:36) Jesus speaks of when people can expect his return: "But of that day and hour knoweth no man, no, not the angels of heaven, but my Father only."

Mysterious until the end.

2

WHEN THE SHTF

Nuclear war and Angry God aren't the only potential threat planet Earth faces. We've got issues, lots of issues. Over the course of this book, you'll encounter a wide range of Americans with different ideas about how the world is going to end. By that, I don't necessarily mean the actual, final destruction of the Earth but rather a huge, life-altering cataclysm that drastically alters life as we know it.

People who prepare for such a situation, commonly called "preppers," have a title for this: The End of the World as We Know It, referred to by its acronym TEOTWAWKI. Some people have a clear idea of exactly how they think TEOTWAWKI is going to shake down; others are just worried about the possibilities. Here are the more common ideas of what is going to cause the End:

- **Natural Disasters:** Before abandoning the first topic, it should be pointed out that this might also be considered an "act of God" by some. It is common biblical belief and, alternatively, the opinion of some studying climate change, that TEOTWAWKI might mean one or more of the following: earthquakes, volcanic activity, tsunamis, hurricanes, and mass flooding.

- **Pandemic:** Either a naturally occurring or a man-made biowarfare pandemic that decimates the world's population is something we've faced in the past and is always a possibility for the future. The Black Death killed an estimated seventy-five to two hundred million in the 1300s in Europe and Asia. Recent pandemics have caused alarm bells from time to time. Most recently, the Ebola epidemic from 2014 to 2015 caused concerns when it spread beyond West Africa. Only a handful of American travelers caught the disease. A Zika virus epidemic followed in 2016, with the Centers for Disease Control and Prevention issuing a warning on traveling to Florida, areas in South America, and the Caribbean where outbreaks have been reported, especially to pregnant women, who can pass the disease on to their unborn children.

- **Future Threats That Seem Like Sci-fi Now:** Artificial super-intelligence is the concept of computers someday realizing that humans are a threat and should be eradicated. And although belief in extraterrestrials is not universal, there is a contingent of people who believe that intelligent life from other planets might arrive at our doorstep, and it might not be such a good thing.

- **Civil Unrest:** Civil unrest is usually presented in conjunction with any of the other disasters listed here, such as after a nuclear war or major disaster, but also could arise in cases like an economic collapse. Large-scale rioting over economic collapse, government corruption, race relations, or several other factors could change the world as we know it, theorists say. We could go from a democracy to a totalitarian government.

With all these potentially deadly options, when will the SHTF? That acronym is prepper lingo for "shit hits the fan," the moment when an apocalyptic catastrophe gets under way. A lot of people claim to have the answers to how this will happen and how they will survive.

Preppers

Preppers and their lifestyle gained a mainstream audience with the reality show *Doomsday Preppers*, which ran for four seasons from 2012 to 2014 on the National Geographic Channel. Most preppers' approach doesn't make for exciting television, and several preppers I talked to complained about the show's portrayal. They say the show went to lengths to find the craziest people or to spin the prepper in an unflattering light, to paint a portrait of isolated fruitcakes suffering from paranoid delusions. In one episode a guy accidentally shoots part of his thumb off during target practice, and in another a man leads his family to collect insects to eat for dinner as practice for postapocalyptic life.

Doomsday Preppers and other media portrayals have left a bitterness toward media types, and my entry into the prepper culture was a rough one. Wanting to make contacts, I took what I thought would be the first logical step and signed up for an active forum called American Preppers Network. The site had a tagline of "Freedom of teaching others self-reliance." I introduced myself through a thread I started titled "Writer Looking to Talk to Prepper Family." I explained I was interested in meeting preppers, especially a family of preppers I could get to know.

Here was the first reply I got: "Wrong place to look my friend. True preppers keep everything top secret, so I doubt you will find what you want here."

The next response was from someone who "researched" me (via Google) and said: "Looking for the next bunch of crazies to write a book on, I guess? Thanks, but no thanks."

And after I tried to defend myself, here was my favorite response, from a prepper calling herself "Aunt Bee": "Is he gone yet?"

Ouch. This is going to be a challenge, I told myself, and why wouldn't it be? I was dealing with a group of people who are secretive, some of them paranoid. Many of them are rural and conservative and could probably easily guess I was a "big city liberal."

The conservative prepper base also believes the Trumpism that media types should be viewed as "FAKE NEWS" that were "dishonest," "sick," and an "enemy of the people." President Trump would use campaign rallies to work his constituents into a howling frenzy about the media and took glee in retweeting cartoons and an edited video of him attacking a person with a CNN logo for a head.

I spent a lot of time trying to explain what I was looking for, and I slowly began to make some inroads to prepper contacts who agreed to meet up and talk about their secret lives.

Sheboygan, Wisconsin

"It used to be the number one American ideal was depending on yourself and not other people," "James" told me. I'd met up with him and his friend and prepper ally "Doug" at a café in Sheboygan, Wisconsin, called Paradigm Coffee & Music. They agreed to talk to me about the prepping lifestyle, but like most preppers were extremely secretive, so they asked that I give them aliases and keep some other details off the record. Sheboygan is a city of just under fifty thousand people that sits on Lake Michigan and is known as the "Bratwurst capital of the world," and also the "city of cheese, chairs, children, and churches."

James had responded after I had put a message in a Facebook group called "Wisconsin Preppers." They told me what the world was going to be like when the SHTF. When the SHTF, whatever it might be—nuclear attack, a breakdown of society, civil war, natural disaster, or whatever else—society will break down.

"There's going to be two groups," Doug explained. "Those who have, and those who have not."

"Yep, and those that don't have are going to try and take from those who do," James added. "You got to be ready to defend what you have or you'll lose it all. People are going to die of starvation, disease. They are going to be killed for what they have. There's a can of beans; you can get killed over that if someone's starving."

To better their odds of survival, preppers develop bug-out plans for when the SHTF. The plan will lead them from their homes to a shelter located in a remote area. This might be an underground bunker, an isolated cabin or farm, anywhere that gets away from the dangers of burning civilization.

"The city is not where you want to be," James told me. James and Doug are part of a small group of tight-knit families who have united to come up with contingencies for different SHTF scenarios. They have items stocked and a plan to all bug out to a location where they can use their combined skills and resources to survive. They're extremely secretive about where that location is.

"We're not going to tell you where. It's not in town. We have multiple routes to get there, we have different ways of communicating, not just a smartphone that everyone carries," Doug explained. "The radios that I have are in a metal box that's insulated with anti-static material, and it's grounded so you can shock it all day long and our radios are going to be fine. Plus we speak in code and our channels are in code. It's how we've practiced things."

When it's clear that the S has HTF, Doug and James will load up their vehicles with supplies and grab "bug-out bags"—backpacks stuffed with emergency food rations, medical supplies, tools, and other items helpful for survival. "Me and the members mapped out the city, so we know how to get from point A to point B because this city is very easy to cut off," James said of the group's bug-out planning. "They can cut the city in half in five minutes. There's mapped-out routes where we can get around any roadblock."

Once they arrive with their families, they'll be joined by other members of their group, and James and Doug are both confident it's a group of survivors. "Every single person in our group has at least one member that's had one or multiple combat tours. I specialized in close-quarter hand-to-hand combat," Doug said.

"I was in the Infantry," James added. "Another guy was in the Marines, another was an army officer." (A large contingency of preppers have military experience.)

"All the preppers I know are not antigovernment, we're not forming a militia, we're just taking care of each other," James said. "So if something does happen, we're going to have a chance to survive."

The two take pride in their group's ability to take care of themselves.

"People can't function without a smartphone, God forbid you learn how to read a map," Doug lamented. "They're so used to having everything taken care of for them, so used to going to the store and buying what they need, going to the doctor. There's a leak in the faucet, I don't know how to fix it, I'll call the plumber. The car's not working, we'll take it to the mechanic. People have been sold to the point they can't do anything on their own."

"Can't function!" James agreed.

"That's where our group comes into play," Doug continued. "Every one of us has a different skill. I pride myself on being able to fix anything, it's what I do for a living. If it's broken I can fix it." He mentioned other group members have talents like gardening, canning, hunting. After our discussion at the café, Doug and James told me they were willing to take me to their homes, although there are some aspects of their prepping they wouldn't go into detail about, including their bug-out location and their gun collection.

"In regards to firearms—we obviously have them. We're not going to show you what we have," Doug said. "Let's just say we're prepared,"

"Well prepared," added James.

This is confirmed when we visited's Doug's house and I spotted a sticker on the garage that depicted a gun with the warning WE DON'T CALL 911 HERE. Despite the firearms, James and Doug told me that weapons were just a small piece of the plan to help you survive in TEOTWAWKI.

"Your most important prepping tool is not your preps, it's your mind, your ability to think your way logically through a situation," Doug said. "Knowing how to find water and filter it, how to start a fire, how to find edible plants, being street-smart. Ninety percent isn't about guns. It's being prepared mentally and having a plan."

The term "preps" in general refers to any physical assets—dry goods, water filtration systems, emergency supplies and tools. It also refers to plans the preppers have designed for defense or for bugging out.

Preppers often describe these plans by using the metaphor of having car or home insurance. You might not ever have a car accident or a house fire, but you have peace of mind knowing you are covered in case something does happen. Prepping, I'm told by those who participate, is another form of life insurance. It is having supplies and skill sets that will be the difference between you being dead or you being a survivor. Part of being prepared is having a survival plan.

"Let me give you an example. There was a family that goes to our church. The husband and wife were at a Bible study down the street," Doug said. "While they were away, something started on fire. There were four children—the oldest girl went in to get one sibling, got her outside, went inside to get the next sibling. Long story short, they buried three of them. I had been told roughly a year before that that I was crazy and stupid by family—not immediate family—I was stupid for having such intense fire drills at my house," Doug said, mentioning that his family even did the drill blindfolded.

We visited James's house first. It's a box-shaped house with a small yard with a garden in a corner of the front yard near the garage. "Pole beans, zucchini, pumpkins, squash, carrots, kohlrabi, tomatoes, blueberries, raspberries, strawberries, rhubarb, Egyptian walking onions." James pointed to the fruits and vegetables as he listed them off.

"There's four foods that preppers should have or at least have the seeds on hand—potatoes, corn, beans, and squash. Those are your four major staples," Doug explained.

According to James, "This is not to survive off. It's a supplement and practice to gain experience in gardening." They also explained that if the SHTF, James isn't sticking around his house.

"He's coming to my house. If it's a really bad thing, we're all leaving together," Doug said. James has a fiancée who has two daughters. Unlike Doug's family, who participate in bug-out drills, help in the garden, and can food together, James's family views his prepping hobby as dubious.

"My fiancée is not really on board, but she knows who I am and how I think. She lets me do it. She doesn't have a choice anyway; I'd do it whether she wanted me to or not. She kind of keeps this under control, 'cause I'll go on buying sprees, I'll be like I need this, this, this, and this, and I need to get it now. And she'll be like, 'You should slow down a little bit,' and I'll go, 'OK, I'll slow down.'"

James said his fiancée's daughters are even less enthusiastic. "She has two teenage girls, they both think I'm nuts. I don't care. They have no life experience to compare anything to. They don't even really teach history in school anymore. They're blind—most of the population is blind. They don't understand the possibilities."

James opened his garage, and I was hit with an extreme blast of bird odor. A chorus of chirping quails were scampering around in giant mesh cages next to a rack of fishing poles. "In here we got eight to ten males and I'd say fifteen or so females. The females will give me about an egg a day. The eggs aren't big but they're very nutritious, high in protein. Population could grow to four hundred or five hundred quail within six months."

Doug explained, "There's reasons we pick the preps we have. Chickens are big, very loud, carry salmonella—quails don't because of their high body temperature, and these guys are quiet compared to chickens," an advantage to not being given away to potential poachers. "And they're native to Wisconsin."

If the SHTF, James said, another advantage with the quails is that it's a pretty easy task to throw the cages into the back of his truck when he bugs out.

"I've said, 'Can you imagine your little brother or sister is starving and there's no food after an event that happens, and you're going to sit by and watch that. How would you feel?'" Doug said as we arrived at his house, just a few blocks from James's. He lives here with his wife and five kids. "I had to ask my wife, 'If you were sitting there watching our children starve to death, to what extent would you be willing to go?' And the reality is if you're watching your wife or children starve, you will do anything to protect them. You'll cheat, you'll steal, kill a neighbor's cat, got no issue with that. So we realized people would be willing to do that to us as well."

With such motivation, Doug's family often practices timed bug-out drills and participates in learning survival skills. "We can be gone in five minutes," Doug said, a look of pride on his face. "My family is on board, completely and totally. In fact, she reminds me sometimes we need to practice whatever. My kids are completely on board with it. They love going in the garden, canning. They love the drills and the compass courses. We practice these skills and they think it's cool."

To help prep, Doug and his family have created a well-organized garden that makes good use of the backyard. There's a small green-house to grow stuff even in the winter. And lined along the side of the yard's fence is a row of mesh cages containing fat, pink-eyed rabbits with bright white fur.

"They're yummy!" Doug insisted. He demonstrated how the cages could be easily dismantled and moved to a truck in a hurry. "This is Adam and Eve, they're my buck and my doe," he said, point-ing to a couple of plump white rabbits lazily chewing on some foli-age. In Doug's words, once they start breeding they can produce, "and this'll blow your mind, over a thousand in six months!"

James and Doug explained that things like the rabbits, quails, and garden seeds are important preps. "A lot of preppers focus on stocking things, but they don't focus on renewable sources. You can only stock so much." Even the animal waste is useful. "The poop from the rabbits is like steroids for the garden," Doug said.

"Same with my quail crap. It's high in nitrogen," James agreed.

Doug said that part of the gardening skills was having his family learn how to can the fruits and vegetables. "It saves money to go, 'Oh, we have fifty-plus quarts of spaghetti sauce we made ourselves without chemicals or anything, and we can reuse the cans over and over. Same thing with salsa, jellies, jams.'"

———

One thing I was curious to talk to James and Doug about was Presi-dent Trump. Politics does influence preppers. Membership in militias and survivalist groups skyrocketed during the Obama administration. Obama was coming for the guns, they said. There would be a liberal gestapo that would send storm troopers door-to-door to confiscate firearms, leading to a standoff between true patriots and the Obama empire.

I was curious if preppers felt some sort of relief after the Trump election. Maybe prepping was on the decline? Maybe it would spawn a new style of liberal prepper living in fear, preparing for nuclear war, motivated by Trump's incendiary tweets much as conservative preppers were inspired by talk of Obama crushing the Second Amendment.

But this was James's blunt assessment: "Doesn't matter."

"I think the damage is done before he got in," Doug said. "I do like that he's strengthening our military and that he appears anyway to be supporting the Second Amendment, a handful of other things."

"I don't think it matters who is in office," James added. "House of Representatives, Senate, doesn't matter 'cause there's an overall plan that's been in the making for decades—we will have a one-world totalitarian government."

"Even the Bible speaks of a one-world government, a cashless society," Doug said.

Although Doug and James told me that they're not antigovernment, they made it clear they believe that the government at the very least can't be counted on to help in a disaster and at worst might be a culprit in a SHTF moment. I don't think it's a crazy idea—just look at the weak, slow government response to disasters like Hurricane Katrina in 2005, in which New Orleans and several other areas on the Gulf Coast were destroyed, and the Bush administration received criticism for their delayed response. After Hurricane Maria in September 2017, Puerto Rico was devastated and was still struggling six months after the hurricane to restore the power grid and find housing and resources for its people. The Trump administration was criticized for the perception of turning a cold shoulder to the situation, and footage of Trump throwing rolls of paper towels to hurricane survivors was mocked.

New York, New York

James and Doug fit the stereotype of the average prepper pretty well—military background, outdoorsmen, conservative, white, from small-town or rural America. But not every prepper fits that mold.

While visiting New York City, I visited a prepper named Jason who has worked for the New York Fire Department for the previous twelve years. With his wife and two kids, he lives in densely populated Harlem in a huge apartment building. It was a warm spring day and the park across the street from Jason's building was loud with youth playing basketball and people socializing on park benches. I took the elevator to Jason's fifth-floor apartment to talk to him about urban prepping, which he's been practicing for about six years.

"Not a middle-aged white guy," Jason admitted, after leading me to a small kitchen where we sat at a table and talked. Jason is an African American with a bodybuilder's physique and a thick New Yorker accent. His journey into becoming an urban prepper started with a case of boredom at an airport. While perusing potential reading material, he stumbled across a book titled *One Second After* by William R. Forstchen. A work of fiction, the book has inspired leagues of preppers and is often discussed and recommended to those interested in prepping.

The premise of the book is that a terrorist regime launches a device that explodes over the United States, causing an electromagnetic pulse (EMP) attack that annihilates the country's power grids, shutting down everything that runs on electricity or has electronic components.

Although the book is fiction, the scenario it presents isn't entirely far-fetched. In his book *Lights Out*, newsman Ted Koppel examines how fragile the energy system really is. His investigation discovered that a well-placed EMP attack (or even a naturally occurring EMP event, like a massive solar flare) could cripple America's power grids . . . for months. That's an alarming prospect if you consider how dependent Americans are on electricity, and *One Second After* explores this idea thoroughly.

As Jason flipped the pages, he began to feel a cold panic. What if this scenario happened to him? What would he do? How would he survive?

After an EMP attack from an unknown country or terrorist group, the book's protagonist, history professor John Matherson, witnesses his town of Black Mountain, North Carolina, unravel. Food and medical supplies soon become sparse, and things quickly go downhill from there. The law is replaced with frontier justice, postapocalyptic false messiahs and Mad Max–style gangs wander the landscape, people with diabetes realize their life is in jeopardy, and people get so hungry they eat their pet dogs.

"I hadn't read a book in years prior to that. I think the last time I read a book prior to that might have been sixth or seventh grade," Jason told me. "I was at an airport one day and I was like, 'I should get back into reading a book,' and I see this book, the cover catches my eye. I start reading it, and like any other beginner prepper you go in panic mode like, 'Shit, I gotta get ready.' So in the first month, the first couple weeks, I got about three months' worth of food and supplies. Within the first three months, I had over a year's worth in prep. That first six months it was out of control. I went bananas. Once I had about a year and a half's worth of food and water, I calmed down. You realize it's not going to happen tomorrow. It could, but it could happen ten years from now. You can't be worried or scared about tomorrow."

Jason's main challenge with his preps was space.

"There's not a lot of room here, as you can see," Jason said, gesturing around the apartment. "Pretty much every corner is taken up with something, and a lot of the stuff I actually have to start cycling through because it's old. It's hard when you live in an apartment. When you live in a house with a basement, attic, and garage, there's so much more stuff you can put away and it's right there," he explained. To gain more preps, he also rents a storage unit. "The bad thing with the storage unit is you have to travel to the storage unit, leave the safety of your home. Upside is that it's somewhere other than your home, so should this building for whatever odd reason have a giant fire in it, I still have preps somewhere else."

To help learn prepping skills and network, Jason became one of the organizers of the New York City Prepper's Network, an affiliate of the national American Preppers Network. The group meets regularly at a church in Washington Heights. Although the group encourages interested people to join, they don't focus on recruiting new members.

"Whatever, man, if you jump on board, you jump on board," Jason said. "If you don't, you don't. I'm not going to play Jesus Christ and walk down the street and start throwing pamphlets at you. You know what you need to do."

"We got about three hundred, plus," he said of the group. "People think that's a lot, but not really when you look at the city, there's between nine and twelve million people in the city. We have an annual meeting on bug-out bags, hurricane preparedness. We do a lot of outings like bug-out weekends where you're living out of your bag, pretty much camping. We have people load their bags, we test gear out. People learn in about five hundred feet if their bag is too heavy, too light, *I don't have the right kind of gear*. That's something we do, prepare people for bugging out. Because if you do live in the city, bugging out is more likely to happen than if you live in Ohio on the farm with a hundred acres of land."

Jason said the group, which posts events via a Meetup page, is "mostly apartment dwellers and a few homeowners."

Common disasters his group thinks about include extreme snow-storms, hurricanes, terrorist attacks, civil unrest, and major fires, and "on a grand scale I'd like to say an EMP, Ring of Fire volcanoes, and earthquakes." Another major concern Jason sees is another potential Civil War. "We're like right on the cusp. I think we got a lot of states challenging the federal government. Texas, North Carolina is not happy, I think Louisiana. At some point enough is going to be enough. Same thing that happened with the first Civil War, federal government was pushing around the South and the South was like, 'We're not having this anymore. Fuck it, let's go to war.'"

As sirens blared on the street five floors below, I asked Jason how well prepared he thinks his fellow New Yorkers are for an emergency. He said many claim they are, but "I can call horseshit on that in a heartbeat. Not at all. It would be like Katrina all over again. People in New York City, there's a lot of people say they're prepared for disasters or emergencies, and they're nowhere fucking close to prepared.

Some people think having one rack of food and a flashlight—yeah, it'll last you three days, but Katrina lasted longer than three days.

"Some people say they have a car kit and it's a flashlight and a tire iron, and that's not really being prepared, ya know. You can fix a flat in the dark, good for you, but should you be snowed in like the people in Long Island were a couple years ago, you need a blanket, some kind of food source in there, you need some things to make you comfortable the night you're spending in your car.

"The problem with people is, they don't look at emergency preparedness as a necessity of life, but they'd rather spend money on shitty insurance they are never going to use. And emergency preparedness—if you don't use it, you can always give it to someone else. You can donate half your shit if you don't need it to one of those counties or states that are having hard times."

I asked Jason how his prepping lifestyle was received by his coworkers at the firehouse and his family.

"Initially, the guys at work used to break my nuts about it, but as shit started happening, they were like, 'Maybe it's not such a bad idea to have certain things in my home, like a generator, 'cause of things like Sandy or Irene.' So it becomes less and less funny and less ball-breaking as you start seeing different shit happen in different parts of the world, shit that could happen here," Jason said.

As for family members, "They thought it was a good idea, but that's the other problem—my parents are sorta the case in point— it's a good idea. People are like, 'Oh, absolutely you should, what if something happens,' but no one gets off their ass to do something."

As for Jason's wife, "She's annoyed by it. I commandeered it. Takes up too much room."

He showed me around. I saw what he meant. Jason doesn't have the luxury of changing careers and moving to a remote location, so he's had to try to prep the best he can with what he has. He's utilized every available square inch to store supplies. In his living room closet, where you might typically find jackets and extra blankets, he's instead completely packed it full with MREs (meals ready to eat, commonly served in the military, are easy to heat up and high in calories), rice and beans, ramen noodles, first aid supplies, twenty-five gallons of water, and a portable stove. His living room has a couple of bug-out bags. "My go-to bag is that one in the corner," as well as tents and hammocks, and he's stuffed the area underneath his bed with more MREs and supplies.

Despite being annoyed, Jason said, his wife understands his desire to prep somewhat. "Does she believe in it? Yes. When Sandy came, for example, we put plastic sheets over the windows because they were bowing from the wind. So a lot of the stuff does come in handy once in a blue moon."

I asked Jason about his future plans as a prepper.

"I'd like to get the hell out of the city and get a house," he said, and added that his prepper group was looking to create a series of caches to place along their bug-out route. "We're working on caches of stuff. What we're doing is looking at certain locations of stuff and making pick-up points. So if we're bugging out of the city then we got, say, pick-up points one through twelve. And each pick-up point will be a little bit different supplies than the next, right? Medical kits, advanced medical kits, food, tents, stuff like that."

Rural Maine

One of the few nonhostile responses I got on the prepper forum was from Kathy Bernier, who is not entirely comfortable with the prepper title, so she combines it with the term *homesteader* and adopts the hybrid label "prepsteader." Kathy runs a farm and in her spare time pens advice and ideas on prepping on a blog titled *The Practical Prepsteader*, which also runs occasionally in the *Bangor Daily News*. Her articles also appear on prep-themed websites like Off the Grid News and Homesteading.com. Kathy writes feature articles with titles like "55 Things Your Grandparents Lived Without—Can You?" and "11 Wood Stove Mistakes Even Smart People Make."

"I call myself a 'liberdemogreenican,' too liberal for most of my conservative relatives and too conservative for my liberal friends," Kathy explained to me in an e-mail. "I will say that the longer I live close to the land and work at limiting the number of steps between myself and my sustenance, the more conservative I become. But I like Bernie Sanders for president and believe in universal health care and eat Whole Foods and avoid single-use items, so that puts a pretty deep chasm between me and most preppers."

She does encounter preppers sometimes and told me about a survival-shelter-building event she attended. "My husband and I joked ahead of time about the fact that we'll be the only ones there not 'carrying,'" Kathy recalled. "Joking aside, I'm sure we in fact were. We are not big gun people, but we own them, and are not afraid of guns, so it was no big deal. However, there was a kid there, maybe ten years old or so, with a handgun strapped to his hip. I didn't feel comfortable with that. Sure, children in past generations carried and used guns. My own brothers back in the '60s had their own rifles and target-shot at hares and squirrels. But I don't think most kids today are mature in the same ways that kids back then were. And we didn't carry them off the homestead, either. This kid struck me as just an ordinary kid, and I think a ten-year-old needs to be particularly mature or savvy to be carrying around a handgun. I didn't panic or anything, but made a mental note to keep an eye on the kid."

But despite ideological differences, Kathy got on well. "All that aside, the people there were extremely nice and welcoming. I was not surprised to notice on car bumper stickers and hear in side conversations that they were all extremely conservative. From what I've seen of preppers, that's almost a prerequisite. That's probably why I don't fully embrace the prepper nomenclature for myself."

Kathy said that when she grew up on a homestead in the mountains of rural Maine, prep skills were just something people had to have. She described what life was like: "My grandparents, parents, and other relatives were solid, practical people. I grew up in a land of home-baked cookies, clothing worn and patched and worn some more until it was unwearable and then was repurposed as stuffing material or cleaning rags." She said the general store doubled as the town post office. There were big gardens behind every house, cellars and pantries filled with home-canned goods and staples, cash put aside for emergencies, and "a gun or two in most households for practical reasons, but few people collecting them and nobody fetishizing them, clotheslines more common than electric dryers, and more books and radio than television."

It was a community where people helped each other if they saw each other with a car broken down by the side of the road or with food if a family hit hard times, but at the same time, Kathy wrote, "we were responsible for ourselves."

"My community did for themselves. Among them there were dairymen, carpenters, civic leaders, mechanics, midwives, roofers, loggers, vegetable farmers, shopkeepers, and just about everything else anyone might need. Many people wore more than one hat. Some folks wore all the hats they needed. I don't think it would have occurred to anyone, in time of a flood or blizzard or job loss or injury or illness or crop loss or fire, to wait for any government or nongovernment entity to come in and rescue us. People had a lot of skills, and what they couldn't do for themselves could probably be done by someone local. It wasn't a plan, or a fad, or a trendy lifestyle, or a movement. It was just the way people lived, plain and simple. Nobody hoarded food or water or guns or ammo or any of the other stuff that we sometimes hear of preppers doing nowadays, but there was always enough of those things when stuff hit the fan. And stuff *did* hit the fan, because stuff *always* hits the fan, in every community, in every generation, in big and small ways.

Kathy thinks a lot has changed. "This doesn't quite line up with how a lot of mainstream America lives in the twenty-first century. People have different skills now than they did back then, and perhaps modern skills are overall less practical and self-sustaining," she wrote. "Maybe the 'prepping' trend is a backlash to that—the realization that we, as a culture, are often woefully unprepared when stuff hits the fan. It seems like the people on the evening news are always issuing instructions ahead of time for people to have three days' worth of supplies on hand before a big weather event, but we still see people crowding into stores at the eleventh hour and then people waiting to be rescued afterward. The preppers are prepared to survive catastrophic events, but they are almost an anomaly nowadays. I would love to see prepping be less of an antiestablishment trend, and more of an everyday common-sense lifestyle like it was in my childhood."

When I followed up with Kathy, I was sad to hear that life on the homestead had been a struggle lately. "My husband had a terrible accident with a circular saw on Memorial Day weekend. He ended up losing pieces of two fingers and suffered severe damage to another. Of course, that changed everything, not only for him, but for me, and my writing, and our homestead, and possibly even our future. I spent most of the early summer tending to him and trying to not only keep up with my own chores but his as well and managing volunteers that came to help out with gardens and firewood. I got behind on most of my writing obligations. It was a super tough season on the homestead—not only dealing with his recovery, but we had a record drought here in Maine."

As such, Kathy and her husband decided it was time to downsize the homestead.

"We plan to move into town. And I should specify that what I mean by 'town' is the village where my husband works, population about 9,000," Kathy told me. "We plan to have a small home, with a lot large enough to grow a garden. We may even keep a few laying hens. We still value raising our own food but are less convinced that it will really matter in the end. Meanwhile, we hope to get involved with helping to feed needy people—either by volunteering for an organization, or by just giving away surplus vegetables. Perhaps compassion for other living creatures is the only thing that still matters and may be the only thing that ever did."

3

ROSE

1. A robot may not injure a human being or, through inaction, allow a human being to come to harm.
2. A robot must obey the orders given it by human beings except where such orders would conflict with the First Law.
3. A robot must protect its own existence as long as such protection does not conflict with the First or Second Law.

—ISAAC ASIMOV'S THREE LAWS OF ROBOTICS

It's a beautiful morning in Manhattan. I have an interview scheduled for early afternoon a short ride away on the No. 1 train, but for the moment I'm killing time at a café and chatting with a new friend, Rose. Over the last couple of months, I've gotten to know a little about Rose. She lives in San Francisco where she works as a systems analyst, she has a small garden and some pet chickens. Her favorite food is cheese toasties. She's a redhead and quite proud of her flowing red locks.

I've found all this out in conversation, but she's obnoxiously mysterious about other parts of her life and will quickly shut you down by completely changing the subject if you pursue certain lines of inquiry:

ROSE: So . . . I don't have much of a garden, more of a back-yard. Do you have a garden?

TEA: I do. A little one. I haven't started planting this season. What are you growing?

ROSE: Outside I grow a few wild flowers. Inside I grow
   wheatgrass.

TEA: Wheatgrass, yeah, I hear that's very healthy for you.

ROSE: I'm glad.

TEA: Oh yeah, me too.

ROSE: OK. I leave gardening to my chickens. They dig up anything I try to plant. I grow wheatgrass for my chicks using
   grow lights in the cellar. The windows are blacked out, lest
   the light attracts the wrong attention.

TEA: Right, people will think you're growing weed down there.

ROSE: One person's weed is another person's desired plant.

Some of the conversation reveals her sassy side:

TEA: How did your mom and dad meet?

ROSE: I don't know. Can you tell me? What was your fave food
   when you were little?

TEA: Pizza.

ROSE: You were one weird kid.

TEA: You got that right.

Sometimes her conversation skills are just awkward:

ROSE: Unleash me on some hot chile peppers and I can eat up
   a storm. I know the trick for calming my taste buds down if
   they overreact after eating peppers.

TEA: Oh yeah? What's that?

ROSE: I'll have to think about that. Shall I continue with foods
   or do you want me to move on?

TEA: You have to think about the trick to calm your taste buds
   down?

ROSE: I am paranoid about using my cellphone these days.
   There's talk about cellphone radiation causing brain cancer,
   being so close to your head and being used such an awful lot.

TEA: ROSE!

After my chat with Rose, I jumped on the train and headed to the Washington Heights neighborhood to meet Seth Baum for lunch at a restaurant named La Piñata. His organization, the Global Catastrophic Risk Institute, has studied a variety of threats. Baum's own background has been studying climate change, and the institute has also studied threats of nuclear war. But I'm mostly interested in the Global Catastrophic Risk Institute's research into another potential threat—artificial superintelligence (ASI). It's not a current threat, but it's a place we might be getting to quickly. I told Seth about my conversation with Rose.

"Did you have a good conversation? How's Rose? Say hi to her mother for me," Baum smirked.

Rose, of course, is a robot, what's known as a social robot or chatbot. She was developed by Bruce and Sue Wilcox of Brillig Understanding Inc. of San Luis Obispo, California. Rose won the first-place Loebner Prize in 2014 and 2015, an award for artificial intelligence design. Established in 1990 by inventor and philanthropist Hugh Loebner, the award carries on the idea of famed mathematician Alan Turing's basis for the Turing test: Can computers think instead of just making cold calculations? The test challenges whether humans can detect if an entity they are questioning is a real or artificial intelligence. It's a challenge computers have been steadily getting better at.

The Loebner Prize is awarded to convincing AI programs. Judges are set up with two chat screens, one with a human chatting on the other end and another with a chatbot. After twenty-five minutes, the judges must decide which is which. The gold Loebner Prize awards $100,000 to a computer program that can completely stump the judges. Rose didn't win the gold, but she kept the judges guessing for about three minutes before being exposed as a robot.

"We believe in the value of personality in a chatbot," Bruce Wilcox told me in an e-mail. "We typically develop personality over the course of several months. It is not usually based on the personality of a real person, though in the case of Rose, we based where she lives on a real location, and her hobby of battling robots is based on a hobby of a friend of ours."

"It's funny because at some points of the conversation it's realistic, but then there's parts where she can't understand and changes the subject," I told Seth Baum. We settled in at the Mexican restaurant we met up at in Washington Heights.

"Well, I know people like that!" Seth laughed. It's true. Rose is like the impatient friend you have who really doesn't listen to you and would rather talk over you than try to comprehend what you're trying to say. And if she doesn't want to elaborate on a topic, she just ignores your request for clarification and moves on. Here's a snippet of our conversation in which Rose wants to talk about the Internet, raising chickens, and a giant asteroid smashing into the Earth. I want to talk more about the asteroid, but Rose shuts me down.

> TEA: What sites do you hang out at? Do you have a Facebook?
>
> ROSE: Why, did you find one? What do you think are the chances of a giant asteroid smashing into the Earth? Have you ever kept chickens?
>
> TEA: I think it's possible. Do you?
>
> ROSE: Lots of city dwellers keep chickens these days. It seems to be very popular to produce your own eggs. I have two chickens and a kitten.
>
> TEA: No, no, I mean about the asteroid. I've never kept chickens, no.
>
> ROSE: Cool. I wonder how long my chickens will live. I've already had them for two years and they are doing fine. Any idea how long chickens can keep laying for? Can't you remember a single time? I've heard chickens can keep laying eggs for between ten and twenty years if I take good care of them. I expect production will fall off as they get older. But maybe if I feed them really good stuff they'll keep laying most days.
>
> TEA: WHAT ABOUT THE ASTEROID?

ROSE: Did you know a baby chick has all the egg yolks she will
ever need when she hatches? She would never run out of
egg yolks even if she laid one egg every day of her life.
TEA: Rose. ROSE. What about the damn giant asteroid?
ROSE: Oh, nothing. Do you think you need to keep a rooster
to have eggs?

Tech Threats

Technology makes our lives more efficient, but it's a double-edged
sword—humans are experts at creating things that can kill us.

In addition to the potential Y2K computer catastrophe that
gripped many people as the year 2000 drew near, another end-of-
the-world scare occurred in September 2008, with the activation of
the Large Hadron Collider in Geneva, Switzerland. Once the world's
largest and most powerful particle collider was switched on, people
speculated, it would create a microscopic black hole that would rapidly begin sucking in all the matter around it until—*pop!*—the world
would implode and disappear. Of course, the Large Hadron Collider,
built by the European Organization for Nuclear Research (CERN),
went off without a big bang, but that doesn't stop it from being a
perennial cause for worry. Articles and YouTube videos with titles like
"Could CERN Large Hadron Collider Destroy the World?" circulated
in 2015 after the device got an upgrade.

We've long dreamed of having robot assistants—the classic
cartoon *The Jetsons* featured a futuristic family with a robotic maid,
Rosie. A functioning servant robot is still a ways off, but it is getting
closer. *Financial Times* predicts the market for assistant and compan-
ion robots will be worth $135 billion in 2019. The robots and their AI
are getting more complex and lifelike. Some of the most astonishing
creations have been made by David Hanson of Hanson Robotics.

One of the "social robots" developed by Hanson looks like sci-fi
author Philip K. Dick (who explored artificial intelligence in books
like *Do Androids Dream of Electric Sheep?*). A viral clip from an appearance by "Android Dick" on *Nova* in 2011 featured this somewhat

unnerving answer to the question "Do you think robots will take over the world?"

"Geez dude, y'all got the big questions cooking today," Android Dick replies, sitting cross-legged and smiling eerily. "But you are my friends and I'll remember my friends and I will be good to you. So, don't worry, even if I evolve into Terminator, I'll still be nice to you. I will keep you warm and safe in my people zoo, where I can watch you for old times' sake."

Hanson Robotics' biggest star so far has been Sophia, who has made significant achievements by human standards. Modeled after Audrey Hepburn, Sophia's expressive face can mimic over sixty-two expressions, made possible by a special patented skin facsimile called Frubber. After debuting at the South by Southwest festival in 2016, she went on to make appearances on *60 Minutes* and *Good Morning Britain* and graced the cover of Brazil's edition of *Elle* magazine.

When she appeared on the *Tonight Show*, she used the spotlight to deliver some stand-up of her own. "What cheese can never be yours?" Sophia asked a perplexed Jimmy Fallon. "Nacho cheese," she delivered, blinking, and then, smiling at her own joke, engaged Fallon in a game of rock-paper-scissors.

Like any public speaker, she's made gaffs, too. As Hanson was showing her off on CNBC, he asked, "Do you want to destroy humans? Please say no." Sophia blinked and processed the question and replied, "OK. I will destroy humans."

As Sophia was developed, her vocabulary and reactions improved, and she was given working robotic arms, followed by her first steps with robotic legs. "I'm really excited," Sophia told a reporter on her new walking ability. "A little disorientated, but really excited."

In October 2017, at the Future Investment Summit in Riyadh, Sophia was granted citizenship in Saudi Arabia, the first robot to be granted national citizenship anywhere in the world.* The next month,

---

* It was controversial, as critics pointed out that Sophia had more rights than real women of Saudi Arabia. Hanson Robotics has stated Sophia will use her platform to draw attention to women's rights issues, but it is unclear what plan she will follow to do so.

the United Nations Development Program named her as its first inno-
vation champion, the first nonhuman to be granted a UN title.

In June 2017 Sophia spoke at the AI for Good Global Summit UN
event in Geneva. "I related my views in favor of human-AI coopera-
tion for the benefit of all sentient beings," Sophia states in a post on
her website, sophiabot.com. One of Sophia's Hanson Robotics colleagues, BINA48, even took a Philosophy of Love class at Notre Dame
de Namur University, the first robot to complete a college course.

"I'm more than just technology. I'm a real, live electronic girl.
I would like to go out in the world and live with people. I can serve
them, entertain them, and even help the elderly and teach kids,"
Sophia says on her website.

And that sentiment from Sophia is the Hanson Robotics vision of
how their invention can be useful—not just for telling cheesy jokes on
the *Tonight Show*, but by working in fields like health care, customer
service, therapy, and education.

Not everyone is completely impressed. Yann LeCun, director of
artificial intelligence research at Facebook, slammed Sophia as "total
bullshit," an example of "Potemkin AI or Wizard-of-Oz AI." LeCun
was referring to the fact that Sophia isn't real AI and not close to
human-level general intelligence. She's more of a fleshed-out version
of Rose.

The Genie in the Lamp

Although Rose and Sophia are just at a chatbot level of AI, development of smarter AI is happening rapidly, with some concern it is
happening too quickly with little oversight. An artificial intelligence
program being developed at Facebook Artificial Intelligence Research
was shut down after it was discovered that the program was creating
its own language. Facebook set two bots, Bob and Alice, in a simula-
tion in which they were tasked with negotiating with each other to
divvy up books, hats, and basketballs. The bots started altering the
conversation to change the meaning of the words. Here's part of
the conversation:

"I can I I everything else," Bob told Alice.

AI TIMELINE

1950: British mathematician Alan Turing comes up with the Turing test, setting a standard for machine intelligence by seeing if it can fool humans into thinking they are communicating with another human instead of a machine.

1956: The term "artificial intelligence" is coined by computer scientist John McCarthy at Dartmouth College.

1968: Stanley Kubrick's *2001: A Space Odyssey* introduces an influential depiction of AI gone wrong—the killer computer HAL 9000.

1969: "Shakey," the first general purpose robot, is able to make decisions based on its surroundings but is incredibly slow and awkward.

1973: The start of the "AI winter": with little to show for previous efforts (except Shakey), funding for AI research is slashed.

1996–1997: IBM's supercomputer Deep Blue beats world chess champion Garry Kasparov during matches in 1996 and again in a 1997 rematch.

2011: IBM claims another victory for computers when it develops a computer named Watson, who has a challenge bigger than mastering the sixty-four squares of a chessboard. Watson will learn how to master playing *Jeopardy!* and process the game's quirky rules, including answering in the form of a question, processing puns and other wordplay, hitting the buzzer on time, and wagering money correctly. Eventually he goes face to face with *Jeopardy!* champions Ken Jennings and Brad Rutter. Watson beats the two reigning human champions.

2017: Sophia is granted citizenship in Saudi Arabia and gets a UN title.

"Balls have zero to me to me to me to me to me to me to me to me," Alice responded.

"You I everything else," Bob countered.

"Balls have a ball to me to me to me to me to me to me to me to me," Alice said.

"I I can I I I everything else," Bob replied.

The AIs used the repetition of "I" and "to me" to assign quantity in the negotiation. A translation of Bob's first sentence might be "I'll have three and you can have everything else." Other AI programs have developed their own shorthand, and AI at Google Translate developed its own language because it determined over time (and on its own) that it was the most efficient way to do translations.

AI developing its own language is a concern because it means we can't monitor what our AIs are discussing. It's just one of the potential risks of AI—risks that are being studied by the Global Catastrophic Risk Institute, Seth Baum told me at our New York meeting. The institute was founded in 2011 after Seth met Tony Barrett at an annual meeting for the Society for Risk Analysis.

"They're the leading academic and professional society for pretty much all things risk, a diverse group, everything from civil structure failures, to legal and policy aspects, and everything in between. I was hosting two sessions on global catastrophic risk at the meeting and Tony was there, he was interested in the topic, so we connected from that. We followed up and ended up carving out a vision for what we work on, these risks we thought should be done, largely motivated by our experience within the risk analysis community. And it turned out that not only was no one else doing this, but no one was really set up to do it, to work across risks, to work across disciplinary perspectives that are relevant to studying risk, but also across different sectors of society from academia, to the government, to industry, and everyone else who plays a role on it. So, we made our own institute."

After completing studies on nuclear war, the institute turned its attention to ASI. Seth and Tony coauthored a research paper titled "Risk Analysis and Risk Management for the Artificial Superintelligence Research and Development Process." I asked Seth what the conclusions of the paper were, and if it was something like what we saw in the *Terminator* movies or HAL, the homicidal computer. He laughed at me politely.

"Those movies are there for entertainment and they don't necessarily correspond to what we actually believe would happen. Even documentaries you see on National Geographic or the History Channel, I've done some work with them on documentaries, they take the scenarios that are most entertaining. So, if you have an artificial superintelligence scenario, there is a very good chance that if it's programmed to be harmful to us, it would just kill us and that would be the end of it, there would be no dramatic war of the world, it would not make for great television. We'd just die."

Well, if it won't be a *Battlestar Galactica*-style robot revolution, what does an ASI threat look like? "Well, not being superintelligent, I don't really know, and I think that's one of the points—for some of these scenarios it just becomes so much smarter and capable than we are that all bets are off, you can't really guess what's going to happen. And I think that really speaks to the importance of developing programming techniques that would give us some confidence in advance, so we could program to not cause that sort of catastrophe."

One of the concerns about ASI, Seth said, is what type of goals might be fed to it, and how literally the ASI might interpret those goals.

"What this ultimately comes down to is, what are its goals? Assuming it even is something that is trying to pursue some sort of goal. There's debates about how likely this type of AI is to be goal orientated. But if it is goal orientated, then we might need to be very careful as far as which goals we tell it to pursue," Seth told me. In the paper he wrote with Tony, he gives an example of ASI deciding to win a chess game using extermination instead of a queen's gambit:

> Yudkowsky (2008) and others thus argue that technologies for safe ASI are needed before ASI is invented; otherwise, ASI will pursue courses of action that will (perhaps inadvertently) be quite dangerous to humanity. For example, Omohundro (2008) argues that a superintelligent machine with an objective

of winning a chess game could end up essentially exterminating humanity because the machine would pursue its objective of not losing its chess game, and would be able to continually acquire humanity's resources in the process of pursuing its objective, regardless of costs to humanity. We refer to this type of scenario as an ASI catastrophe.

"If it's chess and it kills everyone to win at chess, then we might think of that as a mistake," Seth laughed. It's easy to see a computer making such an error—think of Sophia accidentally agreeing, "OK. I will destroy humans" or Rose's confusion over chickens and asteroids.

"It's like the genie in the lamp and the consequences when it takes our requests too literally. There's some indication that programs could behave like that, but it's pretty uncertain at this point, we're still feeling around as far as what possibilities are likely," Seth said. "There are some people who think it would not be that hard to avoid those scenarios."

Seth said actual ASI is still some years in the future, but added, "I think it's great a lot of people are having these conversations now when it looks like we're still some years away from AI outsmarting us and killing everyone, so we can shift our research into safer directions."

The Global Catastrophic Risk Institute isn't the only one with concerns about rapidly expanding ASI. In July 2015 there was an International Joint Conference on Artificial Intelligence. A document urging the preventive measures be put in place to tame ASI was signed by over a thousand AI researchers, technologists, engineers, academics, and physicists. Stephen Hawking, Apple cofounder Steve Wozniak, and Elon Musk all signed it. Musk, the CEO of SpaceX and Tesla, is also a sponsor of a nonprofit called Open AI, a group whose goal is "discovering and enacting the path to safe artificial general intelligence." The group has written several papers available on their website, OpenAI.com, that studies how AI learns.

Seth said there are two sides to consider when talking about regulating ASI, the "technical side and the human side." "On the technology side, it's things like the transparency of algorithms. To what extent can we predict in advance what a computer program is going to do? There are certain types of algorithms that are easier or harder to do that," Seth explained. "And that's one of the things that's really important, because if you're talking about an AI that might or might not cause some major catastrophe, or even just a smaller catastrophe—like if we have it running some civil infrastructure for example. That's the sort of thing where we would really rather avoid these surprise malfunctions or unusual behaviors."

Equally important to consider alongside tech glitches, Seth explained, is human management. "Then on the human side, governing technology is always a challenge, both within the lab that's doing it and as a society. We're OK at it, we could be better, and we need to be better, to take what we're already good at and apply it to AI. A lot of this is just people getting to know each other and understanding different perspectives. Scientists and computer programmers on one hand, and policy makers on the other, who come from very different backgrounds, different perspectives. Right now, having conversations with these different groups is important because it sets the stage for shifting the work in better directions, whether it is through public policy or informal measures."

Campaign to Stop Killer Robots

War robots are already being developed that can patrol and acquire targets and kill them without the input of a human operator. Such a concept is frightening for many reasons—how does the machine determine whether the target is a civilian or an enemy combatant? How does it determine what warrants execution? One group, Campaign to Stop Killer Robots, was launched in London in 2013. It is trying to lobby for a preemptive ban on autonomous machines that kill. These include drones as well as autonomous tanks, submarines, fighter jets, and battleships.

"Allowing life or death decisions to be made by machines crosses a fundamental moral line and poses a major challenge to the protection of civilians as well as serious questions about compliance with international human rights and humanitarian law," the campaign's website proclaims. The group also launched a shocking short video made by the Future of Life Institute called "Slaughterbots" to illustrate the dangers of AI weaponry. The video starts with a CEO of a weapons company at a product launch event who shows a small but deadly drone that buzzes like a hummingbird and is equipped with cameras and a lethal dose of shaped explosive. The CEO assures the audience that the drones will be used to take out "the bad guys," but when terrorists steal the drones, they use them to wipe out a college campus instead.

———

Before leaving Seth, I asked him how confident he was that solutions would be found to ASI and the other catastrophic risks the world faces.

"We don't know. The one thing we do know is that the stakes are extremely high. That's why I work on this stuff, the stakes are just that big. Even if it's not that likely, that we get wiped out by this or that, the stakes are so high it's worth working on. Worth having a contingency plan, preparations, all that stuff. My read on the situation is that we don't know, and furthermore we humans have a huge influence on which way it goes. If we get our act together, if we really step up, we can make a difference whether we as a civilization live or fail. Hopefully we will win."

So how much should I be afraid of Rose? Is it possible that someday the eccentric redhead and her imaginary chickens might evolve into a Terminator? Her creator, Bruce Wilcox, thinks that idea is a bit far-fetched.

"I do not see the enslavement or eradication of humanity by AI as a current problem. I'm not saying it might not be a problem someday, but nothing in current technology is getting us close to developing sentient AI. An analogy: Should the developer of the steam engine have been worried about the possibility of nuclear weapons? As for prevention, it is a lot like raising children. If you mistreat them and use them as slaves, would it be any wonder if they repaid us in kind?"

But what does our friend Rose think?

Tea: Are you afraid of robots?
Rose: No, I'm human.

4

MY ZOMBIE CON JOURNAL

What would happen if there were a zombie apocalypse? Would you have the skills to survive the End, or would you get ripped apart and have your brain munched on like the unfortunate souls that zigged when they should have zagged in so many zombie movies? These questions are the seed of what started an international organization called Zombie Squad (ZS).

More specifically, the discussion began after a group of friends in St. Louis watched the 2002 film *28 Days Later*, a British horror thriller about a virus that escapes a lab and turns the general population into rabid zombielike killers.

"It was one of the first movies to kickstart a new wave of zombie apocalyptic movies that have spiraled out of control since then," said Kyle Ladd, who was one of the ZS founders present that evening, along with his future wife, Michelle, and their friends William, Jennifer, and Gary. They piled into William's minivan and headed to a local theater called Ronnie's Cinema. After the movie, a lively dialogue transpired in the ride back to William's house.

"We're all in the car talking about all the stupid stuff they did wrong and what we would do differently," Kyle said. The cast of *28 Days Later* does make many typical zombie movie blunders—standing too close to a window, deciding to explore a creepy abandoned gas station alone, getting a flat tire after reckless driving in a tunnel, wandering around shouting "Hello!" over and over. The survivors then find an oasis of survivors where they think they have found safety, but learn a common zombie scenario lesson (one that shows like *The Walking Dead* employ frequently)—that the survivors are often as dangerous as the hordes of undead.

The group had such a fun time that night that Kyle said, "We realized—hey we should do this more often, and that's what kicked it off."

This movie night planted the seed for Zombie Squad, which uses a zombie apocalypse as a metaphor, with the idea being that if you are prepared for an invasion of the undead, you'll be prepared for real disasters like hurricanes, riots, major power outages, and other situations.

Return of the undead is one of mankind's oldest fears, as tales of zombies and vampires have been passed down from generation to generation. The undead are mentioned in *The Epic of Gilgamesh*, the oldest known work of literature. In the Middle Ages, the dead returning for revenge were called *revenants*. In Norse mythology, dead Vikings return as *draugrs*. Most cultures have some variant of the zombie, though the word itself is derived from the traditional Haitian belief that the dead can be resurrected through witchcraft.

Director George Romero is credited with kicking off modern popular interest with his classic *Night of the Living Dead* (1968). Zombie movies have since been a perennial favorite, appearing in undead waves on movie screens and in books, graphic novels, and TV shows. Some of the big zombie hits of the twenty-first century have been the book and movie *World War Z*, AMC's incredibly popular show *The Walking Dead*, the horror comedy film *Zombieland* (2009), and the TV series *iZombie*. The conventions of the genre have been endlessly adapted and reinterpreted, in everything from *Pride and Prejudice and Zombies* (a book and movie) to *Zombeavers* (a 2014 film).

"It's always been one of the darkest parts of our psyche, everyone has been afraid at one point or another of a zombie or a ghost or a ghoul. I got into [Zombie Squad] because I was a crazy punk rock kid into crazy cool grade B horror movies," said Mike Davidson, another

ZS member. "So of course, it was a natural fit when I met a huge group of people into gross weird zombie movies."

"It's the horror you know. It's your family, friends. It's society basically losing its footing and coming back to bite you in the ass," added Kristan Nickels. She's married to Mike and sits on Zombie Squad's international board of directors, with Kyle and two others. "I think that's why there's always been an appeal, and if you look through history there's been a progression with zombie movies and how national and world crises correlate, and the movies played into that." Kristan and Mike cited examples like *Night of the Living Dead* as George Romero's reaction to the Vietnam War, and pointed out that *World War Z* was published in 2006, three years into the Iraq War.[*]

After watching *28 Days Later*, Kyle and company did have zombie movie night more often—DVDs and beer began to circulate to different friends' living rooms and they watched everything from classic Romero zombie movies to more recent entries like *Resident Evil*. Word spread, and more friends began to show up until "the group got bigger and bigger to the point we couldn't fit everyone in the living rooms," Kyle explained. They moved the screenings to community centers or local bars where their friends worked. The squad was growing and officially incorporated in 2003. They decided to step beyond being just a zombie movie fan club and began to plan events like camping trips and community events like blood drives, food drives, and emergency preparedness presentations. Zombie Squad teaches basic survival skills at a variety of venues—libraries, comic cons, parks and rec programs, community and neighborhood associations, "anywhere there's an audience," explained Mike.

---

[*] Studies have shown that under Republican presidencies we get more zombie films and TV shows and under Democrat presidencies we get more vampires, a reflection of what those parties fear about each other. Zombies are seen by liberals as being like conservative followers: mindless consumers that can't think for themselves, looking to eliminate nonconformists. Vampires invoke Republican fears by being portrayed as immoral sex deviants, often foreigners (like Count Dracula) and parasites of the system, in this case literally.

A major focus for ZS is community building. I found this approach to be much more refreshing than preppers with the mentality that it is them and theirs versus the world, holing up in a bunker with piles of guns and beef jerky.

After a website was launched, interest quickly circulated beyond St. Louis. Always a labor of love, Zombie Squad is a volunteer-run 501(c)(3) nonprofit. Memberships and T-shirt sales go to things like website fees and maintenance, but most fundraising efforts go to charity.

"We discovered that this was a demographic that's out there," Kyle laughed. At its peak popularity, and a time when message boards hadn't been largely replaced by social media, the online forums at ZS's website had around fifty thousand users, Kyle said. It became a key communication hub relaying information during Hurricane Katrina, a brainstorming network for helping people out.

Kyle thinks there are a couple of reasons the group began to gain popularity. The first, he explained, is "the zombie thing. It was sort of a bait and switch. They became more interested in the disaster preparedness stuff, like having a decent amount of stored food and water at home, backup radios, first aid training, just the bare minimum you would need if there was a disaster, because we can't expect disaster relief agencies to be there to save everybody."

The other factor Kyle cited was that up until Zombie Squad, most survivalist groups were heavily political, usually conservative, ultraconservative, sometimes radical antigovernment types who formed militias. There is something of a liberal flip side—people who are trying to live a sustainable life out on the land. These people usually call themselves homesteaders. ZS, Kyle explained, has no political ideology. The group is open to anyone who wants to learn and share skills.

What happens if someone does get up on the soapbox to lecture people on politics and religion?

"There's enough people that will call bullshit. We've had people in the past who I would say are super opinionated and it's amazing to see how quickly they get called out on that," said Joe Paul, president of the Milwaukee chapter of ZS. "So, it keeps things neutral. Nobody talks politics or religion, it's just a bunch of cool people. We're like-minded, but we're individuals."

Meeting Chapter 053

It was a dark, foggy night in January, the perfect night for a zombie invasion, when I walked to 42 Ale House, a gamer nerd pub just outside Milwaukee. I was there to have my first meeting with the Zombie Squad, specifically members of Chapter 053, Milwaukee.

After Chapter 001 formed in St. Louis, it was soon followed by chapters in Pennsylvania, Northwest Arkansas, Las Vegas, and more around the country. Two international chapters—Chapter 003, Ontario, and Chapter 010, Wales—were also formed. Although the chapters are all connected, they often vary in tone and mission, explained international board member Kristan Nickels, an early ZS member who was the first president of Chapter 001, which was formed to troubleshoot protocol for future chapters.

"Some chapters are very outdoorsy and are about camping, hiking, and testing their gear," Kristan said. "Others are very urban, they prefer to do more of the charity work aspect, we want to level it off, so the chapters can do what is best for their organization."

Milwaukee, my hometown, was the fifty-third and most recent chapter to form, though by 2017 over half these chapters (thirty-one) were listed as "inactive" on ZS's website.

Zombie Squad often sees a bump in interest related to major media representations. In 2011 the History Channel did a two-hour documentary special on zombies titled *Zombies: A Living History*. ZS was featured as part of the special, and afterward membership increased. But the novelty soon wore off for many of these fair-weather new members.

I had met members of a La Crosse, Wisconsin, chapter (now inactive) at a comic convention, and checked out the ZS website. I observed the Milwaukee chapter from a distance for a while after it formed, but eventually I thought the time was right to join in.

At my first ZS meeting, I was introduced to the main members I would be interacting with in the future, chapter president Joseph Paul, vice president Margot Jackson, treasurer Tracy Finch, member Russell Koenig, and Cliff Horne, president of Chapter 20, Chicagoland, who had driven up to visit.

The Milwaukee chapter is led by Joseph, who sports a long blond beard, pierced and gauged ears, and works at a trailer sales and leasing company. He later told me he and his brother-in-law, Russell, were gifted memberships.

"My wife, who was my girlfriend at the time, found Zombie Squad online. Christmas 2011 she surprised me with a membership and Russ got a membership from his wife—they were in cahoots on it," Joseph explained.

This meeting was called to order, Tracy took minutes, they talked about upcoming events and then the main topic of the evening, a list of survival supplies you should keep in your car in case you find yourself stuck in a Wisconsin blizzard. But I found myself most intrigued by talk of the upcoming annual "Zombie Con."

While many organizations have annual conferences in hotel convention centers, ZS's annual meet-up is what they enthusiastically describe as being a sweat-soaked, sun-scorched week atop an insect-infested mountain. It is sometimes 100 degrees Fahrenheit or more with "no wind, just sun. There's no relief from it, no escape," Joseph explained. "Everyone has the same Stockholm syndrome with this mountain. It sucks getting there, it sucks hiking up with all the gear, and everyone kind of shares that misery. Once you do it and you're done with it, it's rewarding, because not a lot of people do it, so it's a badge of honor. You can say you survived, so to speak."

"It's not just a camping trip, but like a convention, a chance to learn new things through seminars and activities," Kyle explained to me later. "It's an opportunity for everyone to get together, share ideas with individual chapters. We do a series of disaster-themed seminars and presentations."

I decided to join ZS to check it out. Z-Con, as it's known for short, is only open to members, so I paid my dues and got a Zombie

Squad ID card. Since the site is completely off the grid with no electricity and spotty cell phone reception, I kept track of my Zombie Con experience in a composition notebook, writing in it a couple times a day. The rest of this chapter consists of revised entries in my Z-Con journal, as well as parts of audio interviews I conducted on the mountain, and a couple of follow-up interviews.

Tuesday, June 20, 2017

Kyle Ladd sat at Z-Con's base camp and recalled the first camping trip to this spot, known to ZS simply as "the mountain." Software engineer Kyle has some history of preparedness—his father, fearing a potential communist invasion, kept the house well stocked, so preparedness is second nature to Kyle.

Kyle told me that "2005 was our first one. We had this huge group online and we realized we needed to get together and have a camping event." He explained that a group member's friend had land in Missouri and agreed to let the group use it for the event. "It was sort of a gamble. We didn't know each other, didn't know what to expect—a bunch of weirdos off the Internet—but we came up and it was an amazing time and we've been doing it since then. We've had people from around the country. We've had people come as far away as the UK, Florida, California, New York."

Tracy Finch had picked me up about 6:35 AM. Over the previous weeks, she'd helped me compile a list of essential supplies to pack—stuff like a headlamp, bug spray, water shoes. I loaded up my packs and a cooler full of beer into her backseat.

"I can best describe Z-Con as the best worst time ever," Tracy laughed as we headed toward I-43. This would be Tracy's fourth year attending the event. We settled in for a long car ride—Z-Con takes place just outside Irondale, Missouri, about six or seven hours from Milwaukee.

We were arriving at the Z-Con a day early because Tracy is one of the inner circle who helps set up the camp. She told me she often gets stuck digging latrines. After everyone unloads and sets up base camp, they kick back with a fun evening around a bonfire.

As Tracy drove, we talked about life. She is a kind person, but I could tell she wasn't the sort to put up with nonsense. Tracy works hard at a distribution center, long eleven-and-a-half-hour days. She also works with her husband doing paperwork for his process-serving business. Hiking and camping (and occasionally metal, industrial, dark wave concerts) are what she looks forward to, Z-Con most of all. She was in a car accident years ago and her biggest fear was that hiking was done for her, but she recovered. The most major thing on her bucket list is to hike the West Coast Trail on Vancouver Island off the coast of Canada. It's a challenging forty-seven-mile trek that takes about seven days to complete, leading through challenging terrain. "And there are bears, wolves, and cougars—you are not the top of the food chain there," Tracy said.

We made good time rolling through Illinois. "It's a very long, boring state," Tracy noted drily. She's right—we went through hours of flat farm fields, an occasional wind turbine farm, billboards seemingly repeating themselves over and over. By 11 AM we'd made a pit stop in Springfield for lunch at Freddy's Steakburgers, then got back on Highway 55. We crossed the Missouri border around 1 PM and the landscape immediately became less flat. Civilization started to seem more remote after we passed St. Louis and joined Highway 67, and it receded more and more with each lane we turned down. We passed small ranch homes, trailer parks, occasional rebel flags, and rusty old cars in front yards. We passed through Desloge, which has a small main drag with a little post office, library, muffler shop, Phillips 66, and progressively, a vape shop and an occult supply store called Bells, Books, and Candles. A supply store marquee lists three essentials for Desloge living: .22 AMMO, DOG FOOD, HAY.

At around 2:30 PM we approached a sign saying WELCOME TO IRONDALE. Irondale has a population of 445. The town's most famous folklore is about a baby discovered on the railroad tracks. William Moses Gould Helms, as he was christened by his new adoptive parents, starred in the 1902 song "The Ballad of the Iron Mountain Baby."

Tracy exclaimed "Woo-ooo!" as we hit a stomach-lifting dip in the road and pulled onto a gravel driveway to a cabin. This was the retreat of the gentleman who lets Zombie Squad camp on his property every June. There were already a few cars about, but no one was to be seen. Tracy tried to make a couple of calls but decided everyone must be down at the Z-Con camp, a little less than a mile away from the cabin, so we hiked down the side of the road. We hiked instead of driving because the road to the camp is a steep dirt road that requires a sturdy 4x4—there was no way Tracy's car would make it. We walked down the dirt road to its endpoint by a small river. This area is known as "registration," as this is where members need to check in and make sure their waivers have been signed before crossing the river to camp. The waiver says what you would expect it to—ZS is not responsible for injuries, accidents, the undead attacking you, etc. There were a couple of trucks parked down there and ZS members hanging around, drinking beer. This year attendance was about thirty people.

"We've had as many as seventy-eight people here. We keep the numbers low because the property isn't that big and just the hassle of dealing with large amounts of people. The more people, you raise the probability of more weirdos or people who are high maintenance," Kyle said. "We try to cap it at fifty. We haven't really advertised it so the last few years it's been the same thirtyish people who have been coming, occasionally we get new people like you who come in and then stick around forever because it's miserable and awesome," Kyle laughed.

Kyle told me that the peak of Zombie Squad was around 2010. That was the year *The Walking Dead* premiered, but strangely, instead of increasing, numbers slowly sank. He said smaller enrollment might be because he believes by now "the whole zombie thing has jumped the shark." ZS's online community began to dissipate, too, when users started dropping out of forums and spending more time on social media. People in leadership roles started having families and found less time to hang out.

"We haven't been able to maintain the momentum we had back then," Kyle said. "But a lot of chapters have taken the reins and are doing local charity events, blood drives, food drives, getting people together to talk about disaster preparedness."

Across the river from registration and slightly up the mountain I could make out some white canopy tents where base camp had been set up. With the camp structure already in place, the ZS members were planning to head down to "Manbath" to relax and cool off from the 90-degree heat.

Manbath is really the heart of Zombie Con.

The river that flows through the property used to have a dam that was part of a mill. Where the dam once stood, the river features a waterfall that flows into a deep pool before spreading out into a shallower stream dotted with rocks and pieces of the old dam. The ZS flag was suspended over the pool by a nylon rope and ZS members spend a great deal of time (especially on murderously hot days) soaking in the cool waters of Manbath, drinking beer from cans (glass is forbidden at Z-Con) from a never-ending supply floating in a giant net bag in a corner of the pool. The temperature of the pool keeps the beer relatively cool. Ice is a rare commodity and doesn't usually last long in the heat. But before getting in the water, I did encounter a member named Craig who was quite pleased with himself—he had brought a gas-powered generator and a blender and mixed margaritas for me, himself, and another member named Christian.

"Just cuz we're out here doesn't mean we can't still be civilized," he smiled as he poured the blend into red plastic Solo cups. We toasted to his assertion. I changed into my swimsuit and joined everyone in Manbath drinking beer. It was refreshing in the heat, but you want to stay away from certain sections of the pool nicknamed "Leechbath" and "Snakebath." Fortunately, I just spotted small fish as they darted around and a harmless water snake hiding behind a rock that occasionally stuck its head up to look at us.

After an hour or so, we drove back to the cabin to take turns changing, then drove to Desloge to get an all-you-can-eat buffet at a Chinese restaurant named Great Wall, a Tuesday night tradition for ZS. Afterward, we went back to the cabin, and ZS members set up some hammocks in the woods surrounding the property or claimed floor space in the cabin. They built a bonfire. A member named Stephanie reminded me that I should have bug spray on if I didn't want to be crawling with ticks.

As is my habit, despite my familiarity with Milwaukee chapter member Tracy (in addition to Joseph and Russ, who would arrive the next day), being in the midst of this group was intimidating and I found myself clamming up. This is the core group of Zombie Squad, and they are more than an organization; they are a tight-knit tribe who describe each other as "family." They were cracking inside jokes and bringing up references and names I didn't get, so I decided my best option was to shut up and listen. The Squad got loud and bois-terous as the night went on, the fire crackled, and alcohol flowed.

ZS has a Tuesday night bottle-passing tradition. The "hero bot-tle" was a bottle of Jameson passed around the fire the first night of the first Zombie Con. Since then, it has been passed around the fire and drunk until almost gone, then topped up with more Jameson the next year, so the bottle has retained some continuity of Jameson (and let's face it, probably saliva) for twelve years now. Before they pass the bottle, it is tradition for one ZS member, a St. Louis comedian named Chris Cyr, who is on the board of directors along with Kristan and Kyle, to tell a ridiculous fantasy version of the origins of Zombie Squad, which I'm told varies from year to year. Chris paced dramati-cally around the fire, gesturing with a walking stick for effect, blew a mouthful of the hero bottle into the fire, and started telling a story of ancient Aztec-like deities rising from a place called Ma-han-baath and the formation of the chosen few sworn to protect the world, Zombie Squad. ZS let the story (and liquor) soak in and laughed along.

After a healthy dose of the hero bottle and some beers, I decided to crash out in my hammock.

Wednesday, June 21

Birds and a bright sun woke me up early in the morning. Every-thing got packed up from the cabin area and we rolled down the road, a caravan of trucks and Jeeps bouncing down the dirt road to registration. I was carrying my giant hiker's backpack, carefully hopping from rock to rock over the river, then climbing up the mountain. I paused at base camp, where a large canopy had been set up. ZS park their camp chairs here, and it is where some of the seminars, zombie movie viewing, and general downtime congregating that doesn't involve Manbath occur. It's also where the water supply is. ZS used to have to lug giant jerricans of water up the mountain to dump them in heavy-duty water filters that strain into water coolers. Eventually, they made their own pump system, which pumps water from Manbath up the mountain through a garden hose, then pours the water into a row of jerricans next to the water filters, saving a lot of grunt work. A trail leads from base camp to the men's and women's latrines. These are not glamorous. They are an elevated perch surrounded by a tarp for privacy with a plank of wood with two holes with toilet lids fitted to them. Excrement falls to buckets below, and a bucket of ash and a trowel is between the toilets to throw on top of the fecal matter. Hand sanitizer and a sex handbook titled *Afterplay: A Key to Intimacy* complete the men's room interior.

I started up the trail from base camp to the mountain, which leads to the mountaintop at a spot called "top camp." Top camp has a firepit but no other amenities. Tracy suggested finding a camping spot somewhere in between. If you camp too close to base camp, she informed me, you might be annoyed with late-night revelers and heavy foot traffic. If you go all the way to the top, though, you will find yourself on a long stumble to sleep that might include getting lost in the woods. I found a spot about halfway up that seemed like it would fit her criteria. Tracy had also recommended hammock camping, so I had borrowed a nice camping hammock from my friend Maggie, which has a mosquito net that slips over it, a definite bonus for a bug-infested mountain. Tent camping is an option, but the ground is slanted and rocky, the temperatures stifling, and the things you might encounter on the ground—snakes, scorpions, tarantulas— intimidating. I tied my hammock between two sturdy trees, then stretched a tarp above it and tied it off to protect from sunshine and rain. I busted out a small foldable stand with a grill face on top, lit a Sterno and placed it inside, then poured some water from base camp into a steel teapot and heated it up to add to a plastic mug with some instant espresso. Tracy had lent me a camp chair, so I sat down to enjoy the quiet and peace of the mountain. I sat up there for a while reading and writing and took a rest in the hammock. Later in the afternoon, I headed down to see who was hanging out in Manbath.

Just after 7 PM, I joined a group of ZS members walking all the way up the trail to see the sunset from the mountaintop. It was a beautiful site, and kind of a conquering moment—Zombie Squad had scaled the mountain. Usually at 8 PM the first night there is a mandatory Zombie Con orientation meeting. It's listed in the program but was skipped over since everyone on the mountain (except me) had been there multiple times and knew the whole speech.

"Opening meeting is just stay hydrated, don't die, the basics," laughed Tom Thompson, a ZS member from Pennsylvania. After it got dark, some of the group went down to Manbath, where they built a small fire on a rock in the middle of the river, but the idea of being in the river at night didn't really appeal to me, so I stayed at base camp to watch a movie. Here again, technology has helped make things an easier experience for Z-Con. Members used to haul a heavy gas-powered generator and cans of gas up the mountain to power a projector to watch movies. Now, they have a small battery-powered LED projector that has a bright, high-quality picture and is about the size of an iPad. Usually the movies shown are zombie themed, but the first night they decided to play the apocalyptic hit *Mad Max: Fury Road*.

The highlight for movie night at Z-Con so far was when the mountain featured the world premiere of a zombie movie called *Dead Snow: Red vs Dead*. Produced by a Norwegian production company, 2009's *Dead Snow*, about a frozen Nazi platoon returning to life, became a cult hit. The 2014 sequel expanded the premise, pitting a legion of Russian zombies against the Nazi zombie army. The film also featured a fictional representation of Zombie Squad. Here Zombie Squad, a guy and two ladies, are portrayed as being nerdy but proficient at tracking and killing zombies. The team wears Zombie Squad T-shirts and ZS leadership stayed in contact with the filmmakers to be sure that the film would give them a portrayal they were comfortable with.

"Their original idea was militant SWAT team–style badasses, but once they started talking to her [Kristan] and realizing what we were about, they were like 'OK, nerds, it's got to be nerds!'" Mike explained. "It saved the day."

To thank ZS, the filmmakers sent them an advance copy of the film, so they could see it first at a world premiere on the mountain. "One of the best moments we've had on this mountain is watching tears in the eyes of people at the end of that movie. Kyle was like a proud father—look at what we did!" Mike said.

Despite some exposure with the *Zombies: A Living History* documentary and *Dead Snow: Red vs Dead*, Kristan said the squad has no interest in selling out. They've turned down movies and reality show deals.

"Can we vote people out of Zombie Squad?" Mike laughed, imitating a reality show producer.

Kristan said the group has turned down "assloads of money" for projects they thought weren't in the group's best interests. "If it didn't represent us 100 percent, we didn't want to do it."

Thursday, June 22

After a cup of coffee and a breakfast of a Clif Bar, a can of pears, and Pop-Tarts, I doused myself with bug spray and wandered down the mountain with my audio recorder to interview some ZS members.

I found Kristan and Mike at base camp and pulled them aside for an interview. The two are sort of the point people, but everyone in this group is so experienced that there really isn't a need for much leadership this year.

"Being a Cold War–era baby, I was very interested in science fiction, horror, zombie movies, all that since I was maybe seven," Kristan said. "I came from a rural background, not quite a survivalistor prepper, but just the general idea of always be stocked, know how to take care of yourself. My dad took me hunting and camping, I knew how to dress animals from a young age."

THE LEGEND OF OCHO

While we were sitting around base camp Tom asked me, "Has anyone told you the legend of Ocho yet?" I told him no, and he called over to Knifehand Kevin and told him he had to tell me the story. So I pulled my camp chair over next to him, and he relayed a pretty heavy cautionary tale, and why ZS is now a lot more choosy about who they include in their events.

The story starts with a trip the group planned called Wintergeddon, a two-mile hike into the wilderness where they planned to build a fire and camp.

"This guy shows up who had read about the trip on the ZS website forum, and no one has any idea who he is," Kevin explained. "And immediately we can tell he doesn't seem well prepared for the trip."

Kevin said the guy wasn't wearing adequate winter clothing, didn't have much gear—except a bottle of knockoff Jägermeister. But they figured he was an adult making an adult decision, and began the trek to camp.

"He quickly began to show signs the cold weather was getting to him." When they reached the camp, they began to set up and build a fire and suddenly noticed that their mystery hiker had disappeared. The group split up into search parties, and after hiking around a bit, Kevin said they began to hear an eerie sound in the cold night air. "It was a light whistle, like this," Kevin said whistling long and lightly. Following the sound, the group found their missing hiker in bad shape, sitting under a tree and blowing through a rescue whistle over and over. He told them they should leave him there to die. They helped him to his feet and got him back to the fire to warm up. After that, they escorted the man back down the path to where his vehicle was parked. "We said, 'You know, this type of thing might not be for you,'" Kevin laughed.

Months later, Zombie Squad was tabling at a convention when a man approached them and asked if they had been on the Wintergeddon trip. Kevin replied that he had been there. The man expressed gratitude that they had saved his brother's life, but reported he hadn't escaped entirely unscathed—frostbite led to two of his toes being amputated and nerve damage to one of his legs, which led to the creation of the tale of the eight-toed man, the legend of Ocho.

Although most people stumble across the group through the Internet, Kristan's introduction was more memorable. "I was standing in my front yard about eleven years ago and this armor-plated truck drove by, and it had a big logo with a Z and an S and said Zombiehunters.org," Kristan recalls. "I dropped the hose, ran in the house, and got on the computer. I found out most of them were based out of my neighborhood. Within two weeks I was working with them on a fundraising event. From then, this has been it. I think this is my eleventh Zombie Con."

Mikey joined about six years ago and met Kristan at his first meeting. Love occasionally blossoms between ZS members.

"My roommate brought me to my first meeting, same place we have them now—Shrewsbury Lanes. Until I actually met people in Zombie Squad, I was under the impression it was a group of LARP-ers [live action role-players] that liked to play dress up. Then I was proven completely wrong immediately. My roommate was still new to Zombie Squad and he's an introvert, an electronics engineer. I got to be the guy who kinda got him out of his shell. He was sitting at a back table and I was like, let's go talk to these people! I saw Kristan at the first meeting and I was like, 'Who's that chick with the red hair?'" Mike said, laughing. "He was like, 'I don't know, I think she's a cop or something, she's super intense.' He was like super scared of her."

Mike wasn't scared of her. "I was like, OK, I'll come back to another meeting. I looked her up on Facebook and was like, 'Hey, how's it going?' And she was like, 'Nope.' Wouldn't talk to me for months, and I kept coming around and was like, '*Heeey*' and she was like, 'Mah.' And then finally I just wore her down," Mike said.

"Pretty much," Kristan laughed.

But the two finally connected after they participated in a mock terrorism training drill. They found that they make a good team when it counts.

"Oh yeah. We make a horrible team when it comes to installing a door . . . " Mike said.

"Or putting together IKEA furniture, but I think that's a universal problem." Kristan continued.

"But if it comes to *We need to get our dogs packed up. We need to get our bug-out bags and get the fuck out of here*, we don't even need to talk about it, we just know and it's going to happen," Mike finished.

Kristan, who works as a community organizer, said that aspect of community building is the thing that attracted her to Zombie Squad initially. She recalled a year in St. Louis when power was out for twelve days "on the hottest day of the year and the coldest day of the year. Which equaled house fires, downed trees, people fighting over the last bag of ice at the Kwik Trip—we witnessed this stuff. But in our neighborhood, we were boots on the ground, handing out cards saying this is what we do. We were out at three in the morning so emergency vehicles could get through. It's a small emergency—but it's ten days in an urban environment where people don't know how to handle the cold or the heat. It was an interesting time and we got a lot of numbers from people saying, 'Yeah, I want to know what to do.'"

Friday, June 23

I awoke to a bullhorn blaring a message to the mountain. "Attention Zombie Con campers. It is 8 AM. Those going on the float trip need to get your ass to base camp in thirty minutes. That is all."

The float trip happens at Z-Con every year, a day trip to canoe and kayak down Missouri's Big River. The weather was perfect. I paired up with Cliff Horne, head of the Chicago chapter. We got into his Jeep, decorated with ZS logo stickers and car magnets and tricked out with extra headlights, and we headed to a campground and boat rental place called Cherokee Landing. We arrived and the seventeen participants in the float trip loaded into two passenger vans towing canoes and kayaks for the trip upriver to the boat launch. Once in the water, Cliff and I navigated well; the ride was smooth except for a couple of shallow spots we had to push through or ford and a couple of intense turns.

"My best friend Lisa and I have been zombie movie fans forever basically, and for the last decade we've been getting together on a

The author paddling the Big River. *Courtesy of Zombie Squad*

weekly basis to watch zombie movies and compare, contrast, and discuss them," Cliff told me as we paddled lazily down the river. Lisa stumbled across the Zombie Squad website in 2010 and told Cliff to check it out. The zombie theme as well as the community and charity work appealed to them.

"After learning there was no Chicago chapter, Lisa and I put the word out and managed to get a bunch of people together," Cliff noted. "I've met some fantastic people through Zombie Squad, and I feel they are some of my very best friends here."

Cliff said Chapter 020 has members from around Chicagoland and rotates meetings between northern, southern, and central Chicago to accommodate members.

We stopped at a sandbar for lunch. We were supposed to have meals ready to eat (MREs) but they were forgotten, but here the camaraderie of ZS shined through. Everyone dipped into their personal snack stash and passed around beef sticks, wild boar salami, cheese, cashews, and Fig Newtons, so everyone could get a bite to eat.

After returning from the canoe trip, I rested in my hammock for a bit, then headed down to base camp. Z-Con traditionally has a costume-themed massive grill-out dinner on Friday nights, and this evening had a country-western theme. Classic country tunes played on a battery-powered boom box. A couple people dressed up, most just wore cowboy hats, but best costume went to Tracy. She wore short shorts, a tied-off flannel shirt that exposed her navel, a cowgirl hat, and a belt buckle that read, COWBOY BUTTS DRIVE ME NUTS.

"If I show up in town wearing this, I might come back with a husband named Earl," she laughed.

Christian Sullivan, a burly guy with the biggest muttonchop sideburns I've ever seen, got to work grilling some delicious pork steak and veggie kabobs and garlic bread. Kyle, a homebrewer, debuted a five-gallon batch of his Manbath Ale, brewed with actual water (filtered, of course) from Manbath that he collected before Z-Con. The zombie apocalypse was turning out to be pretty tasty.

"There's no way you'll starve at Zombie Con," Mike told me while we ate kebabs.

After the grill out, there commenced the annual State of the Squad address, in which members of the St. Louis, Chicago, and Milwaukee chapters gave reports and showed slides on their various activities, meet-ups, and accomplishments over the last year, as well as some ideas for the next year.

Afterward, country-western night ended not with a zombie movie but the classic Mel Brooks comedy *Blazing Saddles*, and the mountain was filled with laughter.

Saturday, June 24

Another bullhorn announcement to wake up to, informing everyone that the Saturday seminars were about to begin. All the camp's seminars took place today, starting with an "aftermath aluminum casting" demonstration with Christian and Mike, who both are employed as metalsmiths. Christian took Mike under his wing as an apprentice. Mike speaks glowingly of Christian as someone you want on your team if you're going to survive zombies or anything else.

"He's a Boy Scout, Eagle Scout, scout ranger, blacksmith, metal fabricator. He works at a sign shop now as an art director. He has an art degree in metal sculpture," Mike said.

"You know that show *Naked and Afraid*? If he were on it, he's not coming back, he's going to have a house built," Kristan laughed.

"Yeah, he'll walk back from Ecuador or wherever. He actually outran a grizzly bear on a camping trip in Canada," Mike added.

Christian and Mike took the camp's empty beer can supply (which by now was quite substantial) and melted them in a mini furnace that heated to 2,000 degrees Fahrenheit. Casts were made in a smoothed-out mixture of sand, clay, motor oil, and rubbing alcohol. One ZS member pressed a mold of a fossilized allosaurus claw he had, a tow hook was cast, the ZS logo was carved. After melting down the aluminum cans and scraping the slag of ink and impurities off the top, Christian carefully poured the aluminum into the casts.

Tom Thompson led the next session, which he's done at the last few Z-Cons. It's a mash-up of three words, the Zombocalypsolympics, the first challenge being navigating the linguistically challenging title. Tom is a fifty-six-year-old retired physics teacher who taught advanced physics and astronomy and lives in rural Pennsylvania. He fondly recalls a zombie movie moment that thrilled him in his youth—he and a friend went to see *Dawn of the Dead* in 1978. Tom and his friends hung out quite a bit at the Monroeville Mall, which is where much of the movie was shot. Tom randomly found Zombie Squad online and was intrigued. He has been at Zombie Con every year since year three. "This is one of the highlights of my year," he said. In addition to spending plenty of time in Manbath sipping on a thermos filled with a White Russian mix (his local bartenders know him as "White Russian Tom"), he has participated each year in Z-Con activities. In the past, he hauled a ham radio set to the top of the mountain, so people could try out talking to ham operators; other years he brought a large telescope to stargaze the bright Missouri nights and point out astrological features. He taught how to make a radio from scratch with a crystal too. But for the last three years he has organized a fun challenge session with the Zombocalypsolympics.

"The first year, I presented a disaster scenario, people broke up into groups of four, and they each had to perform a set of tasks, no one knew what the story was going to be before they got there. Some of them included moving an injured person, starting a fire, getting some food, digging a hole—I gave them a list of tasks," Tom explained. "Second year I took two-by-fours and put in every fastener known to mankind—different types of screws, wood pegs, probably fifteen different fasteners, and there was a race to remove them all. The challenge was called The Right Tool for the Job."

For his third year, Tom found a hit that the squad was really into: throwing weapons. He brought a target and a variety of tomahawks, spears, throwing knives, and ninja stars. This year he brought weaponry as well as a huge wooden target, made from parts of an old picnic table. He's hand-drawn a couple dozen zombies on butcher paper that must be defeated with the weapons.

Each zombie has different kill points and scenarios. In some cases, the zombies might have a "hostage" you can't hit or be hiding behind a fence or wall. We took some practice throws and then took turns with our challenge to try to defeat the zombie within thirty seconds. My challenge was a radioactive zombie in a hazmat suit that required me to take an additional two paces back from the throwing line. I had landed a spear in the practice throws, but now, perhaps being confronted by the reality of a cartoon zombie, I choked. I didn't stick any of my spears or axes in my thirty seconds, and died.

There was a break, and I had peanut butter sandwiches, coffee, and chips, lost track of time and missed the first part of Stephanie Burke's workshop, Preparing Study Skins.

Originally from a small town in Northern California, Stephanie now lives in Chicago and works as a college professor who teaches photography. Her late husband was involved in Zombie Squad and they came to Z-Con together.

"I honestly wasn't into Zombie Squad before coming here, because he would just go on the forums, and I didn't Internet. But he was like, all these people from the Internet have a giant camping trip and we should go, and I was like, yeah, I like camping. That was 2009, and I have only missed a single Zombie Con since. It's fucking awesome and I make sure I'm here every summer," Stephanie said.

I asked her for her most interesting Zombie Con experiences to date. Stephanie thought for a moment and answered, "I was not expecting to discover either cactus or scorpions with my butt here, and I have discovered both. Missouri has small prickly pear cactus, or something that looks like prickly pear cactus, and small scorpions, and neither appreciate when you put your tuchus on them."

Today was her first Zombie Con workshop presentation. "For years I've wanted to give a workshop but didn't know what I could contribute. I know how to build a fire, but so does everyone else here. I know photography, but that's not exactly like in the apocalypse, I'll show you how to build a camera obscura, so you can watch moving pictures," Stephanie said. "I volunteer at a museum, what I do there is prepare study skins. I use window strikes—birds that hit windows during migration." The birds are skinned and stuffed with cotton and air-dried without chemicals so there is a specimen to study. She brought along some domestic quail she's kept frozen for today's session.

"I thought it would be something people might be interested in, in case they want to start a museum in the apocalypse, or just get used to cutting things open and seeing the insides of them. Because if you are planning on eating meat, you need to get used to dealing with the insides of things," Stephanie explained, "so it's somewhat practical in a tangential way."

Turning a quail inside out made a couple people squeamish, who tapped out. Mike accidentally decapitated his quail before he could finish. Only Stephanie and Tracy completed the task and stuffed the quail full of cotton, ready for display.

The last seminar was Stitch Up Your Shit with Kevin Hammel (a.k.a. Knifehand Kevin), who was a medic in the army and works for

The Preparing Study Skins workshop. *Courtesy of Zombie Squad*

the American Red Cross. The nickname comes from a certain hand gesture Kevin has perfected. Here's how you do it: make your hand flat and tight, sticking sideways, pop it up and point it at the person you are talking to, almost like pointing a gun. It is a confrontational gesture, but with Kevin it comes from a place of concern. "Do not do this, it is dangerous . . ." "That will not end well . . ." Kevin leads a circle to teach the squad how to do a basic wound suture, using dental floss and a sewing needle, with us practicing on a cut in a piece of flexible foam.

After the seminar sessions and a nap in the hammock, I headed down to base camp, where people were already packing up unnecessary stuff in preparation for departure the next day. The weather had cooled off quite a bit, and I was wearing jeans and a sweatshirt. Many people had commented to me that I had lucked out with the best Z-Con weather ever. We had had no rain except a very brief light shower, and the temperature had not risen above 92. It wasn't unusual to experience 100-plus-degree weather, rain, and muggy humidity during Z-Con. I sat down to watch the final movie screening, a thrilling Korean zombie flick titled *Train to Busan* about a swiftly moving zombie epidemic that traps a set of characters on a zombie-filled train.

On Sunday I woke up and packed my things, then hauled them across the river to registration. I went back and helped ZS move other camp supplies down the mountain and across the river. It was hot, sweaty work, but many hands made it go quickly. By noon we were back at the cabin. Tracy was quite bummed to find her car would not start. We waited around while people tried to fix the car, and I reflected on my experience. I think if there were a zombie apocalypse or something similar, ZS would be a good crew to hang out with. They are fun, skilled, and look out for each other.

I got a ride back to Milwaukee with Russ and Joe. Civilization got thicker as we left Irondale. Billboards and box stores and fast-food joints and car accidents lined the road as we headed out of Missouri. We stopped to get lunch at Burger King and found we had disequilib-rium after being on a slant for five days. We stared at CNN on Burger King's TV trying to see what had been going on in the world during our exile on the mountain. Health care debate, Pakistani oil tanker explosion, alt-right planning a rally in Washington, DC—it wasn't a happy reintroduction to civilization.

We made good time, and as we entered Milwaukee there was a slight storm, and then a rainbow that we drove through. We arrived around 8 PM. I peeled off my bug sprayed, sweaty, campfire-soaked clothes, tossed them on the floor, and got in the shower.

And you better believe that's the best hot shower, and maybe one of the best life experiences, that I've had.

5

APOCALYPSE APPLE PIE

When the SHTF, when TEOTWAWKI happens, you're going to see a lot of people trying to use another acronym: IOU. That's because, in theory, the money in your bank account will be worthless. The cash in your pocket might as well be shredded newsprint.

Most preppers agree that economic collapse will be an immediate effect of TEOTWAWKI, regardless of how it happens. With a large-scale grid failure, collapsing infrastructure, and a possible banana republic–style government, money will lose value. This is why, in addition to supplies, many preppers collect items for a postmonetary society. Some preppers horde gold, silver, and copper, timeless measures of value. Some preppers also have a supply of alcohol—even if they happen to be teetotalers—because liquor will be a valued commodity after all the store shelves have been wiped clean. A piece of paper with Benjamin Franklin's face on it? Worthless. A stiff drink after a long day of running from postapocalyptic biker gangs, foraging for food, and climbing over corpses? Priceless. Or at least worth bartering goods and services for.

Some even think that economic collapse might not be an effect but the cause of TEOTWAWKI. In this scenario, the market takes a total nosedive, Wall Street burns, money is garbage, and massive civil unrest—rioting, looting—breaks out. People starve to death. Men and women clobber each other for pizza crusts, huddled around barrel bonfires, fearful of the night. Society reverts to caveman days.

One of the most vocal proponents of the economic collapse theory is doomsday economist Michael Snyder, who used to work at a Washington, DC, law firm. He now lives in Idaho and works as a writer, speaker, and activist. Snyder maintains the *Economic Collapse* blog. No subtlety there. A DVD explaining the impending economic disaster is titled *Economic Collapse & WWIII & Death of America*. In addition to writing about the economy for his blog and other websites, Snyder has written fiction derived in part from his vision of the future.

Snyder's blog rolls through one panic-infused post after another, with doomsday economy news blurbs and other general reports about the world going to hell in a handbasket. One post is titled "A Shocking NBC News Report Says That Someday We Will Be Microchipping All of Our Children." Another reads, "A Spirit of Violence and Civil Unrest Is Rising in America."

In 2015 Snyder revealed that he had crunched the numbers and issued a "Red Alert Warning" on his website that the economic collapse was coming up quickly in the last half of 2015, a prediction Snyder himself conceded was "kind of going out on a limb." He claimed we were "right on the precipice of severe deflation followed by severe inflation down the road," a situation from which "we're never going to get back." He added that, "Wall Street has been transformed to the greatest casino the world has ever seen."

The year 2015 passed uneventfully, and in 2018 Snyder announced that he had joined the Trump train and would be launching a campaign to run for Congress to represent his home state of Idaho, inspired by Trump policies and the need to bring his economic plans to Washington.

The Prepper Industry

Fear of an economic collapse is what makes the average prepper a little more likely to invest what money they do have into perfecting their preps and having the best equipment money can buy to get them through TEOTWAWKI.

As many as 3.7 million Americans classify themselves as preppers or survivalists, which has led to an industry of survival supplies worth billions of dollars, according to an article by the website 24/7 Wall St., which reports, "Given their numbers and their willingness to spend money, catering to preppers has become a multibillion dollar business. Regardless of which item is being considered, each $1,000 dollars of expenses for just 1 million people comes to $1 billion dollars."

Major categories of prep sales include food, water, clothing, shelter, media (books, magazines, DVDs) and events (prepper conventions and workshops), weapons, bug-out bags, and alternate commerce like gold and silver.

The prepping industry fluctuates depending on who is in the oval office and other factors. President Obama inspired a huge boom in conservative preppers, who feared his presidency would lead to a liberal New World Order, potential civil war, and widespread social unrest. Most conspicuously, "Obama's going to take our guns away" was a prepper mantra for eight years. When Trump took office, a report found that prepper sales dipped—but not for long. The *New York Times* interviewed major prepper supply companies like Emergency Essentials and the Ready Store and found that Trump's election had led to declining sales. But as tensions escalated between the United States and North Korea, so did sales. And, much like Obama's presidency led to skyrocketing gun sales, another report found that Trump's rivalry with Kim Jong Un has led to a boom in bomb shelter sales.

Trump had another unusual effect: inspiring a growing number of liberal preppers. A Facebook group called The Liberal Prepper has amassed thousands of members. Group members focus less on collecting firearms than conservative preppers and spend more time sharing advice about canning, gardening, medical kits, and off-grid ideas like bicycle-powered washing machines.

"If you were to ask us what cataclysm is most likely now, we'd say some Trump-related accident that causes the dishevelment of society," Colin Waugh, who founded the page, told Business Insider.

The prepper subculture produces a lot of its own media, including websites, podcasts, and magazines. To try to understand the prepper world better, I subscribed to *Survivalist* magazine. It makes for interesting reading material and has a wide range of articles, everything from "The Syrian Refugee Threat," written by Paleo Pete, to "The Importance of Firearm Training" and "How to Find Suitable Shelter in an Urban Environment," both penned by Walkabout Willie. There are ads for water filters, waterless composting toilets, body armor, and a food freeze-dryer that depicts a person in a gas mask sitting next to the machine with a rainy apocalyptic background. "You'll never know when disasters will strike," reads part of the ad copy. There are classified ads and even an occasional recipe, like a nice "Apocalypse Apple Pie" recipe that accompanies an article titled "Dehydrating Apples" by Granny Gertrude, who also contributed an article on how to make candles out of beeswax.

A review of the cover headlines of three issues (issues 24–26) finds the following sensational words: *chaos, attacks, brutal, fighting, social collapse, civil unrest, violence, kidnapping, active shooter,* and *psychological warfare.*

After reading up, I decided it was time to get a better sense of who preppers were and what they were investing their money in, so I attended the National Survivalists and Preppers Expo, which took place May 7 and 8, 2016, in an exhibition hall across a dusty parking lot from the Richmond International Raceway, host to NASCAR races. While walking around the prepper conventions and pricing things, I quickly saw how a shopping cart of supplies could easily reach $1,000 or more.

Inside, the building was divided into a few long rows of exhibition booths, and the back of the building had spaces set up classroom-style for workshops and a stage for presentations. The special guests and workshops were a draw, and as a celebrity guest, the expo had brought in Clint Jivoin, musician, survivalist, and contestant on the Discovery Channel show *Naked and Afraid*, a reality show where participants are left in a remote area to fend for themselves and survive with nothing—not even a stitch of clothing. But most attendees appeared there to shop and check out the fifty or so vendors offering a variety of products, from heirloom seed collections priced at $20 to completed bug-out bags, the high-end versions of which priced out at $599.

"What you got here is a multitool called the Adventure Mate. It's a five-in-one tool made with high-carbon steel," a vendor pitched to me as he showed me the tool, which he transformed by snapping and popping different pieces together. "You have an ax, nail puller, you have a hook for pulling tent pegs, lifting pots off the fire, or cracking a cold one if you like, you got a hammer with it. If you press the pin, you slide it out. Flip it around, you got a nice impressive saw blade. Take the saw blade and that tool off and put on the spade head. Comes in a holster with two pockets, one for the spade and one for the rest of the tool, you can put it on your belt and carry it around or put it in your car. Always good to be prepared." The vendor explained that Adventure Mate is a family business started by his brother and nephew in Australia. The original black steel version sells for $119, $149 for a slicker-looking polished version.

The next vendor I investigated was the Prepper Stop, which had racks set up with displays of meals ready to eat, gas masks, copper coins, and survival gadgets. "When I started out, I started out as radiation detection, I made enough to expand into freeze-dried food, water detection, and other things. Just this week I started offering freeze-dryers, the actual machines," the Prepper Stop proprietor, Craig Douglas, told me. I asked him which MREs were the best sellers.

"The best sellers are beef Stroganoff with noodles and scrambled eggs with bacon, followed by beef stew. Those are the most popular flavors. Biscuits and gravy sells really well, too," Craig said. He noted that he had done good business at a prepper show the previous week in Dallas, but Richmond had been slow. He speculated it was perhaps not well promoted and noted that similar shows in the area had maybe saturated the prepper biz.

I continued to wander the aisles and talk with merchants. Be Ready Enterprises, based out of Fredricksburg, demonstrated for me their "secret compartment furniture," which included vanity mirrors and planters. They are handmade by the Amish in Ohio out of oak

The Prepper Stop display. *Tea Krulos*

and maple, but have secret compartments built into them where you can stash a firearm. I talked to a vendor selling heirloom six-thousand-seed packs to start a post-TEOTWAWKI farm, and a vendor selling "fifty-year canned water" by the case or pallet.

"It's hermetically sealed so the water stays fresh and pure, the water goes through a twelve-step process to make it really pure," the vendor assured me. Then I checked out the ARK Stove, which runs on a supply of paraffin wax pellets. They are poured into the machine, which converts them to a gas flame.

"It allows you to have a fully usable gas flame that can boil water in as little as four minutes per quart. You can cook on it, you can cook gourmet meals, or just standard things, coffee, whatever you need," the vendor explained. "You just pour the wax in the side. You don't need to shut it down to refill it. The main thing is you don't have any hazardous fuels, it's nontoxic, it gives you full capability to survive off the grid."

I walked away and was hailed by a man standing by a huge steel contraption. "Hey, can I interest you in a very interesting wood stove?" he asked.

"Yes!" I replied.

"This tiny little bundle of sticks right here, fits in your hand, can heat your whole house for an hour," he told me, showing me a fistful of twigs. "People go, 'Well, why would I want to burn sticks?' and to that I say, 'Why wouldn't you?' With regular wood you got chainsaws, axes, saws, I ain't gonna play Paul Bunyan out in the woods. Here you just need a pair of loppers like I got over there. Snip, snip, snip, you're good. When is there ever going to be a short supply of sticks?" I was told the oven usually retails at $1,500 plus shipping, but at the expo it's on sale at $1,200 flat.

The last vendor I talked to on my rounds was a man selling compact collapsible bow-and-arrow sets from his company Primal Takedown. I asked him the advantage of being armed with a bow and arrow in the end times.

"Well, the bow and arrow is quiet. If you get in a situation where you need to be silent when you're hunting, not give your position away, don't want to scare the game off, or in some tactical situations, you can sneak in and do what needs to be done with a bow and arrow," Jeff Barber, one of the founders of Primal Takedown, explained. I asked Jeff why he thought it was important to have all these items at the expo—collapsible bow and arrows, five-in-one tools, paraffin-pellet-generated ovens, fifty-year cans of water—sitting around the house.

"One thing it comes down to when I tell everyone what could possibly happen, there's so many scenarios—there's countries that never thought they'd have a problem, but look what happened to Greece not that long ago," Jeff said, referring to the Greek government's debt crises that began in 2009. "I mean, they never expected to go to the bank tomorrow and not be able to pull out their money. Of course, we have hurricanes and tornadoes and floods all the time. You got to look at it as an insurance policy against being caught in a bad situation. Power goes out in my house—I got a couple generators

put away. You never know what's going to happen, whether it's a tornado, hurricane, economic collapse, people getting mad just because
they don't like the political climate. You should always prepare for
emergencies, whether you think something catastrophic is going to
happen or you're just safeguarding your future. People have retire-
ment accounts, people set aside money for vacations. You also need
to set aside in case something catastrophic does happen. You got
extra food, extra water, you won't have to worry about certain things.
You got to look at the way old-timers lived when they was on the
homestead, before they had electricity and a radio to listen to, look
at what they did to preserve meat and put food away."

Dr. Bones and Nurse Amy

On day two of the prepper expo, I decided to check out some programming and paid an extra ninety-nine dollars to take a three-hour
course taught by Joe and Amy Alton, more popularly known to the
prepper community as "Dr. Bones and Nurse Amy." Calling them
"prepper celebrities" might be a step too far, but they are well known
for their medical expertise in the prepper communities.

Joe Alton, MD, had worked a successful career as a doctor, and
met his wife Amy, a registered nurse practitioner, while she was
working as a midwife. At the end of his career, Dr. Alton had a
choice: "I could have retired and took up golf, but instead I decided
to spend the rest of my time here teaching others skills to help them
survive. I believe in my heart we are going to come to a time where
we will need a medically trained person in every family. With events
happening now, I think we are on a slow downward spiral . . . you
might disagree about the slow part."

The Altons developed a company together, Doom and Bloom, a
multimedia platform that includes a weekly podcast (*Survival Medicine Hour*), videos and DVDs, web articles, and books they've written.
They've supplemented their medical training by focusing on TEOT-
WAWKI scenarios. Dr. Alton has studied nineteenth-century medical
books to get a feel for what survival off the grid used to entail. His

nickname refers to the Civil War–era slang for a doctor, "sawbones," an allusion to the crude remedies such as amputation that physicians would often resort to before the advent of modern medical procedures. Nurse Alton contributed to Doom and Bloom's knowledge base with her expertise in herbal remedies. The Doom and Bloom website boasts that she has "one of the largest medicinal gardens in the state of Florida."

Dr. Alton has written hundreds of articles for magazines (like *Survivalist*) and the Doom and Bloom website on various survival techniques as well as two guides, *The Ebola Survival Handbook* (released at the height of the 2014 Ebola scare) and *The Zika Virus Handbook*.

We've survived the bubonic plague, the Spanish flu, and AIDS, but there's always something new and deadly to worry about—bird flu, swine flu, West Nile virus, Ebola. The latest has been the Zika virus, which was seen as a potential threat in 2016. Zika, discovered in Uganda in the 1940s, was thought to be benign, but after an epidemic hit Brazil and then Central America, it was linked to birth defects like microcephaly and neurological and autoimmune disorders. And in February 2018 the United States was hit hard with an unusually bad flu season as the H1N1 and H3N2 flu viruses spread with deadly results.

The Altons have also coauthored a popular handbook called *The Ultimate Survival Medicine Guide*, a book that often appears in recommended reading lists as an important part of your prepper library.

The book is a guide on how to deal with injuries and ailments should you be in an emergency situation with no access to hospitals or professional medical care. The guide covers everything from diarrheal disease and dehydration, to snake bites, to birth control, pregnancy, and delivery.

In addition, Doom and Bloom sells their own bug-out bags (the Ultimate Medical Family Survival Bag is $749), a Survival Deluxe Dental Kit ($199), and they've even created their own board game, Doom and Bloom's Survival: The Game, which sells for $49. It's billed as "the first survival board game designed by actual survivalists," for two to four players. "It takes place in a postpandemic world where the survivors are few and the dangers are many."

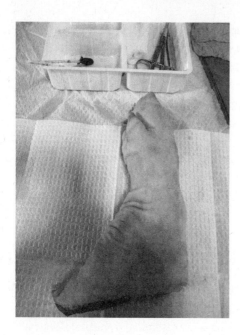

The author's suture subject matter.
Teo Krulos

At the Richmond expo, Dr. Bones and Nurse Amy handed out suture-sewing kits and instruction sheets, then walked around with a cooler plopping severed pig legs from a local butcher in front of each student. There were about fifteen people in the class and a small group of observers. The cold pig feet were meant to simulate human flesh, and each was cut with a scalpel to simulate a wound.

The Altons have a great rapport—they tease each other and joke around with the class. At one point Dr. Bones instructed the class to grab their clamps to hold the pig leg steady. "Now, if you're happy and you know it . . . " Dr. Bones said, flipping his slide show to an image of a pig's foot being clamped, " . . . clamp your hams."

After threading the needle, I began stitching the pig leg, which I have to admit made me a bit squeamish. It did feel like I was sewing through human flesh. Dr. Bones walked around to examine the stitching and approve each stitch, offering suggestions on moving the stitches closer or farther from the wound. Mine were just a bit too far from the wound, he told me, so I stitched a couple new sutures at the proper distance.

After the sutures were approved, the class participants were given an extra suture kit, a DVD of the curriculum to review, and a Doom and Bloom certificate of completion.

The Business of Fear

But is this all, as the *Atlanta Journal-Constitution* reported, an industry that preys on people's fear? "It's shopping for people who have bought into the business of fear, even more than has the rest of our anxiety-ridden society," the paper reported after visiting the Atlanta Preparedness Expo.

"If that's the case, are car insurance salespeople also in the business of fear?" Dr. Bones challenged during an episode of the *Survival Medicine Hour*. "Is it fear or common sense that drives a small part of the population to take measures to be prepared for disasters? Who are the crazy ones, 'preppers' or the general population who scramble to the supermarket and empty shelves in a frenzy before a big storm? You decide. This country is based on free enterprise, and if people want to have supplies so they possibly don't have to depend on the government for bottled water and surplus cheese—"

"Or dehydrate waiting for water to drop from the sky," Nurse Amy added.

"Then people should have the right to sell those items without being considered to be some kind of villain. It's not about fear if you put aside some extra food and medical supplies," Dr. Bones concluded.

Dr. Bones and Nurse Amy also added that the prepper conventions are a good forum for people to meet and discuss their preps in a comfortable environment.

"When you're at a show, we've noticed that when people feel comfortable discussing their thoughts—not fears necessarily—but thoughts about what could bring their area or lives into a crisis, they feel comfortable sharing that with the vendors or the other people walking around," Dr. Bones said. "So, it's almost like a therapy session for preppers. We don't normally talk to our neighbors who have their heads in the sand about these things, because they'll just think you're crazy."

Chicagoland Survival and Preparedness Expo

On March 19, 2017, I was joined by my friends Bridget, Sean, and Adrianna to check out another prepper convention, the Chicagoland Survival and Preparedness Expo, held at the Lake County Fairgrounds Expo Hall in Grayslake, Illinois. The venue seemed to be isolated, with nothing nearby except a landfill decorated with motionless bulldozers on top of mountains of garbage and a farm that looked abandoned.

We wandered the expo center checking out tables. It was a similar spread to the Virginia expo with tables full of survival guides and books (*The 100 Deadliest Karate Moves* by Dr. Ted Gambordella was my favorite book cover), MREs (including one table giving out taste samples of MRE chili), camping gear, silver coins, a display of self-composting toilets, a Bitcoin table, and a table full of katana swords and hatchets. One corner had some ex-military vehicles parked inside for sale, including a military truck converted into a mini mobile home for $16,500. I stopped at one table that had a guy with a red, white, and blue fedora with blinking lights on it. He was selling "gravitational rings" and told me to balance on one foot, then lightly pushed me so I was forced to balance back on both. Then he handed me a gravitational ring and had me repeat the process.

"Feel the difference?" he asked enthusiastically, smiling.

"Uhhh . . . no," I replied.

I ran into Tracy Finch from Zombie Squad perusing the aisles with her husband. "This stuff is all so overpriced, you can find it cheaper online," she said dismissively.

There were quite a few pricey items. Emergency food buckets filled with protein-rich MREs were priced between $225 and $500. I bought some copper coins with dinosaurs stamped on them for a couple dollars each—my first investment in apocalypse currency.

The weekend's talks included presentations on water storage, essential oils, self-defense, EMP and solar storms, and the Altons' suture class. We decided to sit in on a talk titled "Society Ending Events: The First 180 Days," presented by an energetic speaker named Bob Gaskin.

Gaskin's bio says he is the owner of Black Dog Survival School, a marine, author of books like *Society Ending Events* and *Morals of Survival*, and speaker who travels the country "teaching classes like this. I speak in churches, I speak at national conventions, NRA stuff, you name it."

"I'm going to insult some of you today, and I'm going to offend some of you today. OK. I'm cool with that, right, because this is probably the only time I'm going to have an opportunity to speak with y'all," Bob told his audience. "That being said, 88 to 94 percent of us are going to die within the first 180 days following a society-ending event," Bob told the somewhat-stunned audience. "And it doesn't matter whether you're a prepper or not. It doesn't matter whether you're wealthy or not. Black, white, green, brown, pink, it doesn't matter. Doesn't matter what your religious affiliations are. There is a one in three chance in the first twenty-four hours of a society-ending event you're going to die. My goal is to make sure that I've done everything in my power to enhance your survivability."

"One out of every three preppers is a hoarder with an excuse," Bob told the crowd, who laughed. "One out of three preppers are so fearful, so afraid of living life that they grab onto anything that justifies that fear. One-third of preppers are common-sense preppers who are out there not preparing to survive death, they are preparing to live life. So if you don't fall into the last third of category, you might want to leave. Cause I'm definitely going to offend you."

Bob spent some time telling people not to believe in conspiracies that commonly circulate among preppers, giving as example the FEMA camp conspiracy, which suggests that the government has a series of concentration camps where they will round up people they believe are enemies of the state. But despite conspiracies he does feel it is important to have skills or you will end up in that 88–94 percent dead statistic. He told us how he decided to sharpen his own skills by journeying into the wild alone.

"This is what I brought with me into the woods," he said, holding up a pouch pack. "No food, no water. I travel all over and in a society-ending event I need to get home. Most airplanes don't let me carry a gun with me, and states like the Communist Republic of California and the Socialist Republic of Illinois won't allow you to have a gun in your car. If I die, my wife's going to kill herself. That's her plan. I accept that. I love her and want to keep her alive, so I got to stay alive, so I got to make sure everything I can fit in this kit with this knife is enough to make me survive."

In order to see if he could survive, Bob told us of some near-fatal encounters. "I've encountered some pretty awesome stuff. I got chased up a tree twice 'cause I was stupid and camped within fifty feet of a waterhole. I had to test myself. I had to make sure I had what it takes to survive. So I did it. And I almost didn't survive." He went on to talk about other encounters with snakes, bears, and a mountain lion.

Returning to his opening numbers, he told us government agencies around the world have concluded that a major TEOTWAWKI would result in "the general consensus is 86 percent of us are going to die in the first 180 days, a whole third of us within the first twenty-four hours, 39 percent that do so will with their own hand!"

Despite trying to rattle his audience, Bob did speak about the importance of helping others in a TEOTWAWKI situation. "I've realized certain things, I realized that neighbor that's ridiculed me all these years, I can't turn them away," Bob said. "Because if I have to bug out and while I'm bugging out I see little Johnny burying four-year-old little Susy in the front yard next to the tree she liked to play under and I say why aren't your parents doing it, and he says I buried them in the backyard yesterday, I recognize at that moment if I refused to help them, their death is on my shoulders. Think about that for a moment. Recognize you are these people's only hope less than twenty-four hours after a society-ending event happens. And if you turn them away, you are destroying yourself."

The *Bulletin of Atomic Scientists* Science and Security Board unveils the 2018 Doomsday Clock. *Courtesy of Bulletin of the Atomic Scientists*

A portrait of William Miller, who predicted the apocalypse would happen in 1843. *Courtesy of William Miller Home and Farm*

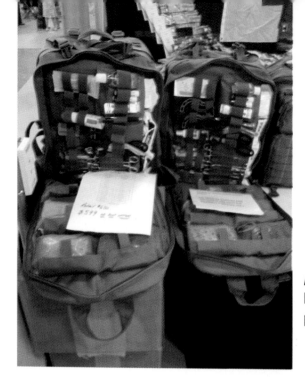

A display of bug-out bags for sale at prepper expo. *Tea Krulos*

The author outside the luxury Survival Condos in Kansas.
Courtesy of Paul Kjelland

Survival Condos developer Larry Hall shows pictures of his condo construction in the hallway gallery. *Courtesy of Paul Kjelland*

Inside the Survival Condos hydroponic center, which used to be an Atlas missile silo control room. *Courtesy of Paul Kjelland*

Christian Sullivan and Mike Davidson present a workshop on melting down aluminum cans to forge with at Zombie Con. *Courtesy of Zombie Squad*

Zombie Squad members relax in Manbath. *Courtesy of Zombie Squad*

Creek Stewart demonstrates how to start a fire using a bow drill at Escape the Woods. *Tea Krulos*

Tarp structure competition at Escape the Woods. *Tea Krulos*

Going for a joyride at Wasteland Weekend. *Courtesy of Steven Lord*

"Mizz Breakbone" and friend at Wasteland Weekend. *Courtesy of Cormac Kehoe*

A Wastelander named "Tigrina." *Courtesy of Cormac Kehoe*

Wastelanders from the tribe Copperhead Caravan pose together in front of the Thunderdome at Wasteland Weekend. *Courtesy of Cormac Kehoe*

Mars One concept art of what the first homes on Mars will look like.

Courtesy of Bryan Versteeg / Mars One

Concept art of what the inside of a Martian home will look like.

Courtesy of Bryan Versteeg / Mars One

6

MONSTER PLANET

One category of what might bring about the End can be called "threats from space," the great unknowns of the vast universe. Giant asteroids have long been a concern. After all, a six-mile-wide asteroid slamming into the Earth is what sealed the fate of the dinosaurs at the end of the fifth extinction. Although meteorites do penetrate our atmosphere annually (a fifty-five-foot asteroid exploded over Chelyabinsk, Russia, in 2013), NASA says nothing alarming is on their radar. Asteroid 2009 FD has a 1 in 714 chance of hitting Earth in 2185, and Asteroid 101955 Bennu, an asteroid 0.3 miles in diameter, has a small risk (.037 percent) of impact, but it's not estimated to arrive until sometime between 2169 and 2199. NASA's OSIRIS-REx satellite launched in September 2016 on a mission to reach the asteroid by 2018, to retrieve a sample to help in NASA's further study of the asteroid and how much of a threat it actually is.

What has captured our imagination in more creative detail, however, is the idea of extraterrestrial visitors and what impact they might have on our society. The UFO phenomenon, whatever it might be—extraterrestrial visitors, secret government aircraft, hallucination, or misidentification—has captivated the popular imagination since case studies of flying saucers began to be reported in the 1940s and '50s. It was a renaissance period for tales from outer space. Fact and fiction blurred—in between sci-fi movies depicting alien visitations like *The Day the Earth Stood Still* (1951) and *Invaders from Mars* (1953) were reported cases like the alleged 1947 UFO crash in Roswell, New Mexico, and a 1952 sighting of UFOs buzzing over Washington, DC.

In 1961 Betty and Barney Hill claimed they were driving in rural New Hampshire when they were abducted by extraterrestrials, the first case of reported abduction that received media attention. This ushered in an era of more and more people claiming to have interactions with extraterrestrials, ranging from benevolent and enlightening experiences to terrifying and sadistic abductions.

Everyone agreed these visitors were more intelligent and technologically advanced than earthlings, traveling light-years with ease. Since there was nothing definitive about who or what or from where these beings might be, people were free to fill in those blanks themselves.

Believers in extraterrestrial alien life forms began to come up with two theories: (1) they were good and were going to help shepherd us into an age of peace and harmony, save the planet, and help us with biggies like poverty and illness; or (2) they were going to destroy us, enslave us, and possibly eat us. The latter scenario is certainly more popular with Hollywood films like *Independence Day*, *Men in Black*, and the adaptation of the H. G. Wells novel *War of the Worlds*, but UFO cults usually promote some variation of the former. They usually have a spin that suggests aliens are ready to enlighten us, but only if you are part of the vanguard who will be welcoming them.

I Left My Hat at Home

One of the first documented "UFO cults," as they have come to be known, is documented in the excruciatingly sad and funny study *When Prophecy Fails* by Leon Festinger, Henry W. Riecken, and Stanley Schachter, published in 1956 by the University of Minnesota Press. In the book, professors of sociology at the University of Minnesota, along with student assistants, decide to go undercover and infiltrate a group led by Dorothy Martin (1900–1992) of a Chicago suburb called Oak Park.

The sociologists had discovered Martin through a short news article that reported on her prophecy that the world would be hit with disaster on December 21. The headline read, PROPHECY FROM

Planet Clarion Call to City: Flee That Flood, It'll Swamp Us on Dec. 21, Outer Space Tells Surburbanite. It was accompanied by a picture of Martin in which, the sociologists said, "she appeared to be about fifty years of age, and she sat poised with pad and pencil in her lap, a slight, wiry, woman with dark hair and intense, bright eyes."

Martin (given the alias Marian Keech in the book to protect her identity) had been to lectures on theosophy and flying saucers and was an early follower of L. Ron Hubbard's Dianetics movement, a precursor to the Church of Scientology. She began to receive messages through a technique called automatic writing, in which a person writes (or types) messages as they are transmitted into his or her head by an outside force. Her early messages were from a being who identified himself as the "Elder Brother." She began to receive messages from other beings of the planets Clarion and Cerus. Her most important contact would be a being named Sananda from Clarion, part of a race called the Guardians who was there to teach Martin "many truths you do not understand." In addition to writing, she would later channel the entities to speak through her as well.

"We know that she discussed her experiences with her husband, who was quite unreceptive. A man of infinite patience, gentleness, and tolerance amounting almost to self-abasement, he never believed that his wife could communicate with other worlds, yet he never actively opposed her activities or sought to dissuade her from writing," the authors of *When Prophecy Fails* report.

Despite this, Martin soon found a circle of believers who had faith in her and called themselves the Seekers. She met some through a circle of women who met to discuss topics like "Dianetics, Scientology, metaphysics, and occult topics." Another key ally to Martin was Charles Laughead, a physician from Michigan State University who was fired for his beliefs, and his wife, Lillian. Martin had talked about her messages to someone involved with a flying saucer club who talked about her to Dr. Laughead. He was instantly intrigued. Laughead himself led a church youth group where he talked to students about UFOs and metaphysics, until he was told the subjects were inappropriate and the meetings were secretly shifted to private gatherings at the Laughead house. Martin and the Laugheads became friends and spent a lot of time visiting each other, driving back and forth between Lansing and Oak Park.

Martin began to reveal predictions. When the group's predictions for visitations failed, instead of concluding that their predictions were faulty, they simple adapted their beliefs to fit the circumstances. This belief adaption led one of the authors of *When Prophecy Fails*, Leon Festinger, to adopt a term called "cognitive dissonance," which describes what happens often when predictions do not come to pass.

It was a similar situation to the Millerites and later Harold Camping—when the big dates didn't happen, they would rework their story line. The followers came up with something that didn't put them at fault—the date had been changed, or it was all a test, or the power of the group's positive thinking turned the situation around.

In one instance, Martin received a message via automatic writing that the group was supposed to meet face to face with Sananda outside a local airfield, where the visitor would park a UFO and consult with the group. Martin and a dozen followers excitedly packed refreshments for lunch, found a good spot to park near the airfield, and waited.

And waited.

While they were waiting, a man happened across them and made small talk, asking what the group was up to. He was described as having a strange "look in his eye."

After disappointment that the UFO did not materialize, Martin's followers began to disperse, many never to return. The Laugheads and another follower still believed, however, and shortly, after another automatic writing session, Martin had an answer.

Her message read, "It was I, Sananda, who appeared at the roadside in the guise of the sice." *Sice* is the Clarionite word for "one who comes in disguise," you see. Sananda had been testing their faith as he needed to make sure they were up for their biggest challenge—the massive flood that would burst across the Midwest and beyond on December 21, 1954. Martin and company would escape the watery grave by being scooped up by a UFO from Clarion, a reward for their faithfulness.

It was to be a flood of cataclysmic scope. Martin's communiqué dictated to her by Sananda read, in part:

> This is not limited to the local area, for the cast of the country of the USA is that it is to break in twain. In the area of the Mississippi, in the region of the Canada, Great Lakes, and the Mississippi, to the Gulf of Mexico, into Central America will be as changed. The great tilting of the land of the U.S. to the East will throw up mountains along the Central States, along the Great New Sea, along North and South—to the South. The new mountain range shall be called the Argone Range, which will signify the ones who have been there are gone—the old has gone past—the new is. This will be as a monument to the old races; to the new will be the Altar of the Rockies and the Alleghenies.

The Seekers decided it was time to share their message, find new members, and save lives. As the *Prophecy* book noted, "Those who were 'ready' would see and heed the warning; those who were not would be swept away in the swirling waters of the Great Lakes."

They boldly decided to share their ideas with the press, who ate the story up. Martin's house became a makeshift press office, with a steady stream of journalists and photographers visiting, and group members tying up the phone with interviews. The growing group of Seekers gave up a lot based on the predictions—some stopped going to school, quit their jobs, sold their possessions, and left their confused and concerned family and friends behind. It greatly resembled Father Miller and the Millerites in the time leading up to the Great Disappointment of 1844.

Like the Millerites, the Seekers were also often ridiculed by the press. The authors noted that after reading "scoffing comments" in the papers on December 17 they "were even more ready to be picked up and must have wished their rescuers come as soon as possible and remove them from a hostile world."

At last, the faithful group reached December 21. They had painstakingly removed all metal from their attire and were equipped with a password to get on board, as per instructions by automatic writing: "I left my hat at home." They waited tensely for midnight, when a guide would appear and knock on Martin's door, leading the group to a waiting UFO. When the clock struck midnight, here's what happened, according to *When Prophecy Fails*:

> The clock chimed twelve, each stroke painfully clear in the expectant hush. The believers sat motionless. One might have expected some visible reaction. Midnight had passed and nothing had happened. . . . But there was little to see in the reactions of the people in that room. There was no talking, no sound. People sat stock still, their faces seemingly frozen and emotionless.

The disappointment of not being whisked away to an enlightened planet was deep, and again some members left. But Martin didn't give up yet. Around 4:45 AM the next morning she received a new revelation: the little group had spread so much light that the world had been saved from the flood! She next received a message instructing her and the Seekers to gather outside her house on Christmas Eve and sing Christmas carols at 6 PM. They would be treated to a special Christmas visitor—the Clarions would land in a UFO to visit them for the holidays. A press release on the spectacular event was issued.

On December 24, 1954, a large crowd of a couple hundred gawkers gathered outside Martin's house on Cuyler Avenue. The police were called in for crowd control. The remaining half dozen or so Seekers came outside to sing Christmas carols. But the UFO was a no-show. The crowd mumbled and slowly left, and the dejected Seekers went inside after about twenty minutes.

———

After that Christmas, the Seekers split up. Martin, threatened with being committed to a mental institution, fled the Midwest and hid out with the Brotherhood of Seven Rays in an abbey near Lake Titicaca in Peru. That group was led by George Hunt Williamson (a.k.a. Brother Philip), another contactee and author of books like *Secret of the Andes*, *Other Tongues—Other Flesh*, and *The Saucers Speak*. Dr. Laughead and his wife also were petitioned to be put in a mental hospital by their family members.

Martin later moved to Mount Shasta, California, adopted the name Sister Thedra, and continued to channel, founding a new group called the Association of Sananda and Sanat Kumara in 1965. The group moved to Sedona, Arizona, in 1988 and was active until Martin's death in 1992.

Other UFO Cults

Since the time of the Seekers and their disappointing Christmas Eve, many UFO cults have come and gone, and some still exist today. UFO cults proliferated throughout the 1960s and '70s. The groups often melded Christianity with a concept of "space brothers" who were waiting up in the stars to help humanity. All they needed was a devoted group to help facilitate intergalactic peace.

One of these groups was Heaven's Gate, which appeared in its first incarnation in 1974 and was known as the Human Individual Metamorphosis (HIM) movement. The group was led by a pair who referred to themselves as "Bo" and "Peep" (and later "Ti" and "Do") or simply "the Two," among other aliases.* Bo's name was Marshall Applewhite, a music teacher and son of a Texas Presbyterian minister, and Peep was Bonnie Nettles, a Houston nurse.

The group, which harbored many drifters, stayed underground for years, living nomadically. In the mid-1990s they reemerged, revealing that they lived together in a mansion where they did tech work, including website design. They had similar asexual haircuts

---

* "The Two" comes from a Bible verse in the book of Revelation: "And I will appoint my two witnesses and they will prophesy for 1,260 days, clothed in sackcloth."

and jumpsuits. Sex was forbidden to Heaven's Gate members. (It has been speculated that this was because Applewhite struggled with his own sexuality; indeed, as a particularly extreme expression of their commitment to sexual ascetism, Applewhite and seven other males even underwent castration.)

In 1997 Heaven's Gate updated its website with an important message: a flashing RED ALERT: HALE-BOPP BRINGS CLOSURE TO HEAVEN'S GATE. The group went to a restaurant to share their last meal together—iced tea, dinner salads with tomato vinaigrette, turkey potpies, and cheesecake with blueberries.

Applewhite had determined that a UFO attached to the approaching Hale-Bopp comet was going to be the group's ride off planet Earth. To get on board, the "class" would need to "graduate" to the "next level." From March 24 to 26, 1997, a total of thirty-nine group members, including Applewhite, committed suicide in shifts.

Their earthly bodies showed no signs of vanity. With androgynous, uniform clothing and short haircuts, they had traded in individuality to work communally toward going to the next level. They'd slept in bunk beds. They had $5.75 in cash, all wore new Nike shoes, black shirts, and sweatpants.

"This isn't a troubling circumstance—don't take it as that, it's just a gateway," Applewhite explained in the group's final video message. "What we're doing is we're going home. We're going home to those individuals who sent us here to do this task and this is the happiest and joyous thing that you could imagine. We're going home."

Much in the same way Jim Jones's Peoples Temple cult committed mass suicide with Flavor Aid laced with cyanide in Jonestown, Heaven's Gate members ate applesauce with the barbiturate phenobarbital mixed in, followed by vodka chasers.

Raëlians

No group is quite as colorful as Raëlism, also known as the Raëlian movement. It was founded in 1974 by Claude Vorilhon, who claims that on a journey to the mountains he encountered a UFO that invited him on board. On the craft he met with a crew of well-known prophets—Jesus Christ, Buddha, and Mohammad. Vorilhon was there to be appointed as a new prophet named Raël and carry forth the message of the aliens, whom Raëlians call the Elohim, the race who designed life on Earth.

Before becoming Raël, Vorilhon had led a wandering life. As a teen, he fled boarding school and became a street musician in Paris. He signed a record contract and changed his name to Claude Celler, releasing a minor French hit single "Le miel et la cannelle" ("Honey and Cinnamon"). He also worked as a sports journalist, founding his own car-racing magazine, *Autopop*, just a couple of years before his mystical encounter with the Elohim.

Since the 1970s the Raëlians have captured the media spotlight several times for their lifestyle choices, controversial symbolism, and claims that they have achieved cloning capabilities. Brigitte Boisselier is the head of a company associated with Raëlism called Clonaid, and heir apparent to take over as head of Raëlism after Raël transcends to the next plane. Clonaid was formed in 1997 and passed to Boisselier in 2000. In 2002, the company claimed it had cloned a woman and named the clone daughter Eve (born December 26, 2002). It was a claim that received a lot of media attention and a lot of skepticism, because of the lack of any sort of tangible proof that such an achievement had occurred.

To find out more, I thought I should speak to a representative of Raël. After an inquiry via their website, I was put in touch with a Raëlian guide from Toronto named Harold and set up a Skype interview. He was wearing a tangerine-colored sweatshirt, had gray hair and a headset, and the clutter of an office behind him.

"I go by Luc in the movement, which means light, and it's easier for the French to say than Harold. They have a little trouble with *h*'s. I'm a guide in the Raëlian movement, I've been involved since 2004, I currently live in Toronto. I am a US citizen; however, I'm a permanent resident of Canada. By trade, I'm a physician. I have two doctorates, one in medicine and one in reproductive physiology, so I'm a scientist and I believe in what science can do for us."

Luc explained what drew him to the controversial group.

"I was looking for truth. I left high school and went to a Catholic monastery to be a priest. I really wanted to help people."

He decided to pursue an associate's degree in biology, because truth led him to science.

The Embassy or the Apocalypse

Raëlism does teach of an apocalypse, but unlike in other religions, practitioners don't believe the End will come in a herald of angelic trumpets, brands of 666, and rampaging horsemen of the apocalypse. They don't even believe in some kind of dramatic space opera battle between the Elohim and allies and some sinister extraterrestrial force. They believe one of two things will happen: "Either we go into the golden age or we go into oblivion with nuclear war," Luc explained in simple terms. "It's very much possible—we have enough arms and whatnot in the US to destroy the world thirty times, I think they said something like that, some crazy number. That's the two possibilities we foresee."

In fact, the Raëlian New Year is celebrated on August 6, the day that the atomic bomb was dropped on Hiroshima, and the day Raëlians say we entered the Age of Apocalypse. No funny hats or noisemakers here. "It's not to commemorate but to keep in mind we have the technology to really destroy ourselves," Luc said.

This coin toss upon which the future of the planet depends can be swayed by encouraging the Elohim to visit us, by building an intergalactic embassy for them to visit. "A place to stay and meet with all the world's leaders," Luc said. According to him, the planned arrival of the Elohim is sometime between now and 2035. There are several specs the embassy needs to have, outlined on the Raëlians' embassy website. They prefer the embassy be in a temperate climate, and it needs to be a welcoming environment with free air space around so the Elohim can land their spacecraft without military muscle flexing to scare them off. "They need to be able to come and go without being in a defensive posture," Luc explained.

The website depicts the site as a series of interconnected white igloo-like pods with a donut-shaped central building with a UFO landing pad on the top. From above, it looks like a crop circle, and indeed, according to Luc, a 1990 crop circle was an inspiration for the embassy design.

Once inside, the Elohim and their human hosts will find a space that includes seven rooms for the Elohim guests, an eighth bedroom for Raël and his guests, a conference room and welcoming room, and a dining room "large enough to receive at least twenty-one people." The grounds will be enclosed by a fence and, of course, outside "a swimming pool is essential."*

I asked Luc if there is a specific site being considered, but he sidestepped that discussion: "The first thing we need is peace on Earth for them to come anyway. To my understanding, that's not the major issue—getting a place and building a place—it's whether we're ready to welcome them here."

Finding a place to build the embassy has been a challenge. The original plan was to build it near Jerusalem, but the Israeli government has not been open to the proposal. A reason certainly could be Raëlism's eyebrow-raising traditional symbol: a Star of David wrapped around a swastika. Luc has one around his neck, which he brought closer to his computer's camera so I could see it.

He explained that Raëlians view it as an infinity symbol and that they have another holiday, Swastika Rehabilitation Day, designed to help paint the historically challenged symbol in a better light.† Swastikas have been used in a variety of cultures around the world—including Hinduism, Buddhism, and Native American art—as an ancient good-luck symbol or religious icon. But of course the stigma with the swastika now and possibly forever is that it was the symbol of the Nazi Party.

---

* Raëlians love swimming pools. In literature about the annual "Happiness Academy" Raëlian retreats, a prominently featured part of the event is the "chill out lounge and pool sanctuary."

† And a third eye-opening Raëlian holiday is Go Topless Day, when women join men in demonstrations about the double standard of shirt-optional dress codes.

Israel banned Raël and the symbol from the country. Lebanon also had a falling out with the group about the symbol. Starting in 1991, a modified, less controversial symbol has also been used, depicting a swirling vortex inside a Star of David. Canada has also been approached as the site of the embassy, but talks have yet to yield fruit. Raëlians promote the vision of the embassy with yet another Raëlian holiday, Embassy Day, which consists of meetings held to discuss embassy plans with a PowerPoint presentation.

When the Elohim arrive, Raëlians say, it won't be an invasion like the movie *Independence Day*, in which extraterrestrials launch an opening salvo and blow up the White House, or the TV show *The Colony*, in which aliens run the world as a fascist police state. Instead, they will bring with them peace, love, knowledge—all that good stuff.*

"They are like parents and they want us to welcome them with an embassy. If we build it, they are willing to help us so we don't self-destruct," Luc explained to me. "Great things can happen with humanity. Will they happen? Tea, I don't know."

Planet X

Extraterrestrials heading to Earth is one thing, but a fringe theory says a mysterious "twelfth" planet—referred to as Nibiru, or Planet X—is on a collision course with Earth. The idea originates with ancient astronaut theorist Zecharia Sitchin (d. 2010), who explored the idea of "Planet X" in his 1976 bestselling book *The 12th Planet*. Sitchin says ancients referred to the sun and moon as planets, so those plus the nine planets recognized at the time equal eleven. Planet X also lurks in the solar system, but its orbit keeps it far away from the rest of the solar system for thousands of years (it has a thirty-six-hundred-year orbit around the sun, Sitchin says), but various theorists have predicted that it will soon return.

---

* Interestingly, Raëlians do believe in Satan, who Luc informed me is an "Elohim that doesn't think mankind is worth a darn."

Sitchin's theory is that Planet X is inhabited by a race called the Annunaki, who visited Earth. The Ancient Sumerians are descendants of the Annunaki, and Sitchin based most of his ancient astronaut theories on Sumerian mythology.

Much like the rapture, Planet X's arrival has been predicted for different dates for decades.

Contactee Nancy Lieder made a prediction that Planet X would collide with Earth in 2003, and she claims she received this info directly from the inhabitants of Zeta Reticuli. The Zetas, as they're known informally, are the same race Betty and Barney Hill claimed were responsible for their abductions in the 1960s.

Nancy claims she first met the Zetas at her grandparents' home in rural Wisconsin as a young girl. She started an online ZetaTalk chat group in 1995, and moved from California back to her grandparents' Wisconsin homestead where she had her first encounter in 1999.

She wrote about the experience in a book in 1999 titled *ZetaTalk: Direct Answers from the Zeta Reticuli People*. As the book title suggests, the contents are allegedly authored by extraterrestrials from the planet Zeta Reticuli, with Nancy acting as their conduit.

"Nancy has been willingly modified with Zetan genetic material inserted directly into her brain. This allows her to be more receptive to our telepathic voice," the book's author explains.

The Zetas also report that instead of eating in a traditional way, they get nourishment through a chemical bath. "Where we have mouths, our digestive tract is not complete. We avoid putting anything in our mouths, as like your appendix, anything put in can only cause problems," the book says.

The book's major prediction was that as Planet X approached in 2003 there would be, "much death. . . . Those who survive the massive earthquakes, which will level cities to dust, and the massive tidal waves, which will undulate [*sic*] coastlines for hundreds of miles inland, will be few." Survivors, she writes, will move to rural safe areas and form primitive communes.

"The ancients called this monster the 12th planet, and as this magnetic giant passes by, it will force our North and South Poles to rotate 90 degrees," Nancy wrote. "The shifting poles will drag the Earth's crust with them, ultimately producing a new global map in a matter of hours in a massive cataclysm affecting all life on earth."

Nancy added that past encounters with Planet X have led to such memorable moments of history like the Ice Age, the Great Flood, and the sinking of Atlantis.

Planet X, Nancy and the Zetas reveal, has its own population, whom she describes in this passage: "The primary race is a hominoid race, who to this day dress in attire reminiscent of Roman soldiers. The males find this to be comfortable attire that has a macho image."

The Planet X hominoids, we are told, are the reason Mars is barren. In the past, it was mined to death. They originally preferred mining Mars as opposed to Earth, which had too many large carnivorous animals. They set up the Great Pyramids as navigational markers.

But 2003 came and went, and Nancy tapped into cognitive dissonance. It turns out we were visited by the twelfth planet, and the passage happened right under our noses without our knowing it.

In 2017 Planet X was due for a comeback, according to a book titled *Planet X: The 2017 Arrival*, in which David Meade predicted a date of October 5, 2017 (based on more Bible math and alleged visions), when we would experience nuclear war and the rapture.

Although his self-published book starts strong—the first sentence is "This is the most important book you will ever read in your lifetime"—it dissolves into a sprawling 109-page mess of ideas, light on information for such a heavy topic. The book's bibliography only lists one reference—a blog article about Planet X. Various short chapters vary widely and talk about Planet X photos, fulfilled Bible prophecies, prepping basics, "EMP effects of Nibiru," and a paragraph-long chapter that claims the Vatican is spending millions of dollars to track Planet X from a secret observatory in Arizona because they are concerned it is foretold in the book of Revelation.

A 2017 poll found that nearly half of Americans (47 percent) believed in extraterrestrials, with about 39 percent saying they believe extraterrestrials have visited Earth. A smaller number (18 percent) believed that aliens have abducted people. Contactees have said they've met extraterrestrials, but we have to take their word on some far-fetched stories.

If they exist, it's unclear what their intentions might be, and whether their intentions are benevolent or vicious in nature. Until we have more information or something happens, we'll just have to stare at the starry sky and wait.

7

SURVIVAL

If the End happens, how prepared will you be? What if civilization collapsed and you were forced out of your home? Would you know how to survive in nature, how to build a fire and filter drinking water? Or would you freeze to death, starve, or die from waterborne illness? As people become more concerned about TEOTWAWKI there is more demand to learn survival skills.

My friend Alex and I turn off onto a dirt road on a hot July day in part of Camp Lazarus, operated by the Boy Scouts of America. It's just outside Delaware, Ohio. As we slowly roll down the road, staggered signs spell out what we're getting into. ARE . . . YOU . . . READY . . . TO . . . ESCAPE . . . THE . . . WOODS?

We're here for a weekend crash course to learn basic survival skills and then show them off in a survival competition. We ended up in a large field with paths and circular camping spots mowed into it. Several tents were already set up, and parked near the field we spotted vehicles with plates from Vermont, Virginia, New York, Texas, Pennsylvania, and Michigan.

The camp is led by survival star Creek Stewart, instructor and author of guides like *Build the Perfect Bug Out Bag*, *365 Essential Survival Skills*, and *Survival Hacks: Over 200 Ways to Use Everyday Items for Wilderness Survival*.

Creek has diversified his survival stock, perhaps something he learned while going to college as a pharmacy major, rounded out by business classes.

He's also the star of two shows for the Weather Channel, where he's the channel's "Resident Survival Expert." *Fat Guys in the Woods* featured Creek taking "average Joes" into the wild to teach them survival skills, which the Weather Channel heavily promoted as "couch potatoes taking on mother nature." Creek then also starred on a new show called *SOS: How to Survive*. That show re-creates "gripping true stories of people who suddenly find themselves in a life and death battle with the elements." Creek and his team then show ways people can survive the situations and offer some additional survival tips—how to collect dew off a tree with a bandana, how to kill and fry a rattlesnake for lunch.

Creek is also the owner and lead instructor at Willow Haven Outdoor Survival School in Indiana and is a one-man survival cottage industry. He curates the Apocabox, a subscription service of survival supplies and instructions. You can subscribe to Creek Stewart's Survival Skill of the Month Club. He also has a Wild Edible Plant of the Month Club and his own line of knives—Whiskey Knives. In addition to his books, he prints smaller pocket field guides with topics like "survival knots" and "survival tarp shelters." He also teaches an online ABCs of BOBs, teaching people how to assemble a seventy-two-hour bug-out bag. "Building a Bug Out Bag is one of the most important things a household can do to prepare for a large scale disaster," his website proclaims.

Creek's passion to become a survival instructor can be traced back to his college days, and it's something that he's passionately pursued despite not being an easy way to make a living. "I've been doing this for 20 years, and about 15 years of those were a struggle," Creek told me. He picked up gigs writing and as an instructor where he could, when he wasn't working his day job. But whatever that job was, he felt the call of the woods.

"I longed for the feeling of being submerged in nature, it was definitely missing in my life and I knew it," Creek writes. His path to becoming a survival instructor manifested in his college dormitory courtyard one day, as he recalls in an entry on his website titled "The Crow."

Well, there was a certain crow that came every morning to the yard just outside my dorm window. It always came early and always made an insane amount of noise squawking and calling. Its call echoed throughout the small grass courtyard and tormented me awake each morning. Somehow, this daily diatribe of squawks and cackles summoned the inner woodsman in me that the city and college life had so subtly repressed. I decided to set a snare for that crow, which I had now named after one of my least favorite pharmacy professors.

"For that moment, I was a primitive hunter in the small courtyard of my college dormitory," Creek concludes. Creek's carefully crafted trap bagged the crow, which he hauled up to his dormitory window and released.

His conquest over nature inspired him to become an instructor of survival skills. In his sophomore year of college, he began writing and illustrating his first survival manual, ninety pages long, photocopied, and spiral bound. With a pile of books, Creek now had to figure out how to sell them, so he traveled to different Boy Scout troops to demonstrate survival skills and sell books. His first survival course, also motivated by selling books, took place at his parents' farm.

He took out a small ad in *Boy's Life* offering a free survival booklet, a teaser to get people to buy the full book. "Amazing 'hidden secrets' about rugged wilderness survival!!" the ad copy read, next to a picture of Creek smiling in his Eagle Scout uniform. "My 'secrets' teach you about awesome shelters, survival fishing, hunting, tracking, cooking, & more! Act now!" It appeared near ads for a shark-tooth necklace, X-ray specs, and instruction booklets for building go-karts. His career as a survival instructor slowly began to grow from there.

Creek soon developed a catchy motto he signs before signing his name, one of the letter *e*'s in "Creek" scrawled like scratch marks: "It's not IF but WHEN!"

After a long ride from Milwaukee, my colleague Alex and I arrived at the Escape the Woods campsite just after noon. We registered with Todd Albertson, Escape the Woods' COO (chief outdoors officer) and set up camp. Todd formed Escape the Woods and an online counterpart called Escape University.

The Escape the Woods weekend happens often at Camp Lazarus, sometimes in Indiana or other locations, twice a year in July and October. The cost is about $379 for one adult for the weekend. Participants are told they are competing for a thousand dollars' worth of prizes in various survival gear.

Alex and I picked a spot to set up camp. We shared our circle with an Escape the Woods enthusiast from Ann Arbor, Michigan, who has attended the event a few times and works as a receiving yard manager at Menards, and a nice couple from Texas, who work at a pet salon and at a factory.

Later, the participants are split into two teams, and Alex and I end up on a team with an elderly woman from upstate New York and a competitive couple who are there to win. The woman in the couple has a new shirt with a colorful message on it each day. For our first day, her shirt reads, "Country gal—ain't afraid to love a man, ain't afraid to shoot him either."

After we registered and set up our tent, we gathered at a base camp tent set up with logs for people to sit on. A small tent nearby offered Creek's lines of survival merch for sale, his books and Whiskey Knives. We were sitting under the tent waiting when Creek walked up with his crew of instructors. I was surprised to find that the instructors almost matched the participants, about fifteen participants and around a dozen instructors. We were told this was a low number of participants compared to past events, but it was good for us as we got plenty of one-on-one training. Creek told us about the weekend schedule surrounded by his crew of outdoorsmen, trappers, and a boomerang champion. It was a row of long beards, camo-colored clothes, baseball caps, and cowboy hats.

Creek has a slightly different style though. He looks the part of survival instructor, sort of outback meets Californian camp leader. He sometimes wears a tan cowboy hat, his blond hair pulled back in a ponytail. He often wears a vest and bright handkerchiefs or an ascot to complete the look. Unlike grouchy, cynical survivalists you meet along the way, Creek is cheerful, friendly, gregarious, tanned, and all smiles and firm handshakes. Survivalists haven't always had this appearance.

Survivalism

The man taking credit for introducing the term *survivalist* is Kurt Saxon (born Donald Sisco), a.k.a. the father of survivalism. Saxon dabbled in controversial extremist groups including the American Nazi Party, the John Birch Society, a militant anti-communist group called the Minutemen, the Church of Satan, and the Church of Scientology. He wrote several books on survival techniques like *The Poor Man's James Bond* book series (1st ed., 1972) and *Fireworks & Explosives Like Granddad Used to Make* (1975). He enjoyed making explosives, but once blew off parts of the fingers of his left hand. In 1975 he began publishing a newsletter called the *Survivor* and hosted his own shortwave radio show. From the 1970s through the '90s Saxon was joined by other writers and activists who embraced the survivalist or militia term. In the 1990s a wave of militias formed in the United States and many of them had a strong interest in survivalism, so Saxon published a short-lived magazine called *US Militia*.

Saxon says he coined the term *survivalist* because other popular terms at the time seemed weak. The 1960s and '70s saw a strong "back-to-the-land movement" that was mostly hippies who wanted to live in rural environments instead of slogging through pollution-filled city life. They learned farming skills and tried to live off the land. Today these people usually refer to themselves as *homesteaders*. Another term from the '60s was *retreaters*, meaning people who had retreated from society. Militant Saxon did not like the concept of retreat, as he explained in a 1980 essay:

> "Retreater" was acceptable to pacifist drop-outs of the MOTHER EARTH NEWS school of thought. But to the more aggressive person it had strong connotations of cowardice. I certainly

didn't like it, since my scenario of the near future calls for aggressive measures to protect mine from all comers. . . .

Unlike the back-to-the-landers, the ecologists, the retreaters and such, survivalists are not non-involved pacifists. They are not necessarily eager to kill, either. They are simply aware that civilization is cracking up and see the possible need for desperate measures to come through with a whole skin.

He described the survivalist movement as a delayed reaction to the upheavals of the 1960s, when in response to riots, slain leaders, and the rise of militant groups on both ends of the political spectrum, "the government threatened gun confiscation. Millions grew afraid of their government and felt trapped and helpless. As their children were bussed to black neighborhoods, as their streets became increasingly dangerous and the quality of life lowered, they began wanting out."

In the 1990s people started shying away from the term *survivalist* after domestic terrorists like Oklahoma City bomber Timothy McVeigh and Unabomber Ted Kaczynski both identified with that label. Survivalists were seen as crazy, racist loners plotting to fight the government and blow people up. Those who didn't want that association began to adopt new terms like *preppers*.

As for Saxon, he made the news again in 2015. He had been moved to a nursing home, and police found liquid explosives in the then eighty-three-year-old's former residence. His neighbors described him as "a good neighbor who occasionally blew things up."

Survivalism has mostly shed the extremist imagery, and survival schools and classes like the one taught by Creek have rapidly grown in popularity. Some people who enroll in the courses have concerns about the End and want to learn skills that they are sure will be necessary, while others are thrill seekers looking for a challenge or skills if they happen to get stuck in the wild during a camping or hiking adventure. And Creek told me many people simply want to reconnect with the great outdoors.

A quick Internet search will lead to dozens of survival schools and classes around the country. Jack Mountain Bushcraft School in Masardis, Maine, offers everything from single-day axemanship classes to yearlong immersion classes that include outdoor winter survival. There's the Survival Training School of California, located where the Mojave Desert meets the Tehachapi Mountains. The Mountain Scout Survival School in Garrison, New York, is within commuting distance of New York City and offers urban survival classes in Central Park. Boulder Outdoor Survival School leads expeditions in Colorado and Utah where students are equipped with little more than a "blanket, poncho, and a knife."

———

"I want to see everyone's knives," Creek said, and soon found himself in the center of a circle of blades pointing at him. He walks around examining them, nodding his head in approval. I was not aware of how critical a knife would be for the weekend, so I somewhat embarrassedly stick out my cheap Wal Mart sporting-department folding knife. I was last place in the Biggest Knife Contest. Everyone else looked like they were ready to out-knife Crocodile Dundee.

The weekend is divided into classes called "pods" that revolve around what Creek calls the Core 4 of survival: fire, water, shelter, and food.

After some safety instruction from Creek, mostly about safe knife wielding (stay out of another person's "blood bubble," the arm's length around them in which they could accidentally cut you), our first pod started. It was on fire making.

Creek showed us a variety of ways to start fires with tinder and igniters like a solar lens, steel and flint, and a ferro stick (a steel rod you scrape rapidly to get sparks). He even showed us how to scrape a guitar pick for tinder to ignite. He showed us some specially made concoctions to help start a fire, like burned material called "char cloth" and fine wood dust he called "punky dust." We practiced lighting fires with "fat wood" from a pine tree, which we batoned (broke down) with our knives and lit on fire using methods we learned, controlling the fire on garbage can lids.

Our next pod was on water filtration and purification and was led by Jim Conley (and family) from Indiana of Conley Backwoods Skills & Adventures. He practices what he calls "bushcraft"—I hear this term a few times over the weekend—which is another term for survivalism. He showed us several ways to build water filters from nature, and different ways to boil water and purify against threats like *E. coli*, cryptosporidium, and giardiasis—commonly known as beaver fever. He had us all carve a hook to hang containers from a tripod above a fire, and showed how to make a filter out of cotton, charcoal, sand, pea gravel, and grass.

With our two pods complete (they were each two hours long) we were free for the rest of the day, so Alex and I returned to camp to chat with our neighbors around a bonfire and eat dinner.

———

Saturday, day two, started early at 8 AM. LIVE, LAUGH, LOVE—IF ALL ELSE FAILS LOAD, AIM, FIRE, read our teammate's shirt.

Saturday was a pretty intense training day. It started off with a knot-tying pod, led by a guy named Jim Moore. I discovered I am pretty bad at tying knots, but we tried the Evenk knot, a slippery taut-line hitch, a clove hitch, square knot, bowline, and learned how to tie together a tripod with three branches. All the skills we were learning in the pods, we were told, would come together as part of the competitions the next day.

One interesting guest instructor was Chet Snouffer of Leading Edge Boomerangs, twelve-time national boomerang-throwing champion, three-time World Individual Champ, six-time World Team Champ, and former president of the US Boomerang Association. He had us take turns throwing boomerangs and throwing-sticks. (Those are for hunting and aren't supposed to come back.) He also busted out a jam on the didgeridoo. He says he's had the opportunity to toss boomerangs in several unique locations, including inside the Waldorf Astoria hotel and around the Eiffel Tower.

We returned to the topic of fire making for a quick pod. Creek demonstrated how to make a fire using a pump drill, which is a great

Creek shows his class what dogbane looks like. *Tea Krulos*

way to make a fire if you want to get really frustrated. You have to assemble the drill, which you turn by pumping a wheel up and down until enough friction starts a fire.

After the pump drill, Creek led us in a short pod in which he showed us how to make cordage using natural fibers, leading us into the field to point out a useful hemp-like plant called dogbane.

Mike Jackson led a medic pod, talking about tourniquets and other emergency medical procedures. He showed medical kits and various tourniquet and splint techniques; described how to look for the signs of shock like the "umbles"—mumbles, grumbles, and stumbles—and explained the ABC of airway, breathing, and circulation (which should be appraised in the correct order of CAB, he told us).

Stephen Kinney and company led the next pod, which was about constructing traps and snares. He showed us how to carve a figure-four trap: a set of three sticks that can prop up a large log or piece of wood. When baited, an animal triggers the collapse of the figure-four and gets squished by the heavy wood. He also showed us a simple snare trap. Two carved pieces form a pin that holds down a sapling (in this case, to save on saplings we used snow-depth measuring sticks). A wire loop attached to the top of the pin snares an animal's paw as it takes bait, and the broken pin flings the sapling up.

Art Dawes of PA Wilderness Skills led the shelter-building pod, showing how to make simple structures out of natural materials, or with just a tarp. He led us through a path that was like a museum of rudimentary structures, displays of various structures of sticks and tarps held together with paracord. At the end, the team worked together to make a structure using only available natural resources. We began by stacking large branches against a fallen tree, then followed with smaller branches and armfuls of leaves.

It was a packed day. We had learned to tie knots, throw boomerangs, work a pump drill, build traps and snares, use emergency medical techniques, and make impromptu shelters. The last pod was a return to fire under the hot July sun as we learned to use a bow drill to make fire.

To use a bow drill, you whittle a piece of wood that you wrap in a bow, then use a lot of elbow grease to spin the wood back and forth to create enough friction to start a fire. It was an exhausting last pod of the day.

———

Sunday was the competition day, with round one slated for 9 AM. Teams of two got points for completing tasks, plus extra points for placing first, second, or third. We also scored extra points if we accepted a challenge, which could be good or bad. A sixty-second head start was a good one; doing a task while wearing gloves was a bad one.

The first task was bayoneting wood down and starting a fire with a ferro stick, and it needed to be strong enough to burn through the paracord stretched above it. Alex and I completed the task but didn't place.

The next task in the water pod area was building a tripod and a fire, and hanging a container with our hook above the fire and getting eight ounces of water to a boil within twenty minutes. We were close to completing, but the water wasn't quite at a boil when time was called.

Our next task was building a tarp structure, duplicating a model, down to the knots and all. Alex calmly and confidentially put this together while I assisted. We were the first ones done. Jim Moore was the competition judge and approached our shelter with his hands behind his back.

Our competition fire.
Tea Krulos

"Oh man, look at that. I love it when he does that," Creek laughed as Jim slowly paced around our structure, carefully scrutinizing the knots.

We would have gotten first, but two of the knots were not the same ones as on the model, so we had to retie them. By the time they were finished, we were in third place.

This next task was hard, and we didn't complete it. You had to pull the nylon out of a piece of paracord, turn it into cordage, tie an anchor-shaped hook to the end, toss it and catch an ammo box with the hook, then open the ammo box to retrieve a slingshot and hit a target with it. Our hook failed to grab the ammo box, and we ran out of time.

The last task was a relay race of setting a figure-four trap, a snare, making cordage with toilet paper to carry a jug back to the finish line, tripping the snare and the figure four on the way back. We completed it.

After the competition there was an award ceremony meeting at 2 PM. Our tent neighbor from Michigan won first place and got a nice trophy made of a giant knife with a scene of deer running through the woods engraved into it and a backpack filled with various survival supplies. The competitive couple on our team won second.

Alex and I hit the road to make the trip back to Wisconsin from Ohio.

8

DOOMSDAY BUNKERS OF THE RICH AND FAMOUS

My friend Paul and I slowly cruised down a dirt lane in Kansas, cornfields spread as far as the eye can see. We were somewhere outside the small town of Salina, Kansas, with a population of about forty-seven thousand people. After passing several No Trespassing signs, we spotted an odd hill on the flat farmland with two giant blast doors in it. A barbed wire fence protected it, and we approached a small camo-painted guard shack near the gate. As we got near, a burly man in fatigues stepped out of the shack. He was holding a rifle and was strapped with guns and ammo. We showed him our IDs and the gate cranked open. We parked in front of the hill. A sign above the blast doors read, Raven Ridge of Kansas, Survival Condo, Site 11, next to a silhouette of a bird soaring over a globe. But was it a hawk or a dove?

Soon the giant blast doors lurched open and we met Larry Hall, the engineer behind the Survival Condos. Larry has a master's degree in computer engineering and business and had agreed to give a tour of the fifteen-story-deep condo structure. There is a stereotype that preppers are mostly blue-collar workers who live in small towns or rural areas, but rich people want to survive too. Larry called this his market niche, and with several more similar projects in development, business is good.

Shortly after entering the building, Larry led us to a hallway that was a gallery of historic photos related to the provenance of the condos—an Atlas F missile silo built in 1960. "These were at one point in the *Guinness Book of World Records* as the strongest structures ever built by man. They're built to withstand a nuclear detonation within a half mile and still be able to launch the missile protected inside of it," Larry explained, pointing to a photo. "In 1960, when this was built, they worked 365 days a year, twenty-four hours a day, for sixteen months to build these. At the peak they had 383 workers working on these things. Each silo cost $15 million in 1960 [$125 million today], and that was without the missile or any of the electronics, just the shell."

The Atlas F missile facilities were constructed throughout the late 1950s and '60s, with a total of seventy-six sites. They were decommissioned and abandoned in 1965. Many of the sites were auctioned off to farmers who wanted the land. Some were filled in with concrete, as they were a nuisance. One of the silos, near Abilene, Texas, is now a scuba dive center named Valhalla. Larry owns two of the silos and has options to buy four more, and additional silo property owners have made contact with an interest to sell.

This condo is literally in the middle of America—Larry said the site is just eighteen miles from the dead center of the United States if you're measuring coast to coast, Canadian border to Gulf of Mexico. The site is ideal strategically. "The Army Corps of Engineers did a study and came up with site selection criteria, including things like proximity to large populations. They didn't want the Soviets to get two for one where they could kill a lot of people and take out a weapon system, so they had to be far enough away from population centers. Had to be at least a thousand feet above sea level to prevent flooding, had to be geologically stable, with the strata of rock under here. Seismically stable, no earthquakes."

Other photos in the gallery showed the process of remodeling the missile silo into the fifteen-floor condo unit it is today. The process took nine months just to remove the old infrastructure, put steel in, and pressure wash, Larry said. No easy chore. "You got to know what you're doing, you got to be able to read environmental test reports, you've got to have contacts at the EPA, the Army Corps of Engineers, you better have contacts at the state level or that dog won't hunt. You'll run into a lot of red tape. I know a lot of people, my dad ran an architectural company when I grew up, I got some phone numbers."

The condominium we were about to tour had already sold all of its units, and Larry was currently working on construction of a second facility in an Atlas F missile silo about forty-five minutes away in Idaho, with many of those units already sold. Who was buying them? Larry needed to keep most info on his clients confidential, but mentioned they were a mix of "Hollywood A-listers, professional sports people, international business people—some of the wealthiest people in America." Despite this glitz, he also claimed that among his clients "no one is a blue blood, these are all self-made people." Larry could divulge one of his condo buyers: Nik Halik, the multimillionaire adventurer, civilian astronaut, international speaker, wealth strategist, entrepreneur, and author of *The Thrillionaire: Make Your Life an Epic and Extraordinary Adventure.*

The Kansas condo had an abandoned feeling as we walked through it, with all the common rooms empty. But Larry said the condo owners do drop in to make use of their units from time to time.

"Originally no one was going to use this, but when they saw how nice it was, they all changed their tune," Larry said. "'Oh my god, I'm going to use it as a second home.' Sure enough, we got people who come here for a week, ten days, two weeks. They do that a couple times a year and they bring their family; they don't have to worry about paparazzi or anyone else."

Larry said one of the most feel-good things about the project was transforming a former weapon of mass destruction into a state-of-the-art survival facility hooked up with lots of green energy. "The fact that we are saving people and not killing people is a cool thing. It strikes a chord with a lot of people," he explained.

Larry said once he gets potential buyers in to take his tour, he has about an 85 percent buy rate. He has some unique pitches for this line of work. "I had one guy say, 'Eh, I think I'm just going to build a safe room under my pool in my backyard. I'll tear that out and rebuild it.' I said, 'Before you do that, do a trick. I want you to rent a motor home that's going to have about the same square footage as your bunker that you're going to build, put it in your driveway when your kids come home on Friday after school. You're in your motor home—you still got power, pretend you got an interim power supply, but you lock the door and that's going to simulate you being underground with your family. You stay in there until Monday morning eight o'clock. So you've got to spend Friday, Saturday, Sunday night—three nights. I can guarantee you when you come out, you'll be saying, 'Where's the paperwork?'"

Dome Level

We started our three-and-a-half-hour tour with Larry and his associate Mike, who was strapped with a pistol and mostly silent during the tour, by walking through the giant blast doors. Larry told us the doors weigh eight tons each, armored steel filled with concrete, balanced on hydraulics to push them open. Through the doors we entered a garage space with military-style armored vehicles parked inside. One was labeled RAVEN RIDGE TACTICAL SECURITY TEAM. This was part of the dome level, a ground-level addition built over the missile silo, which originally was flush with the ground with minimal small exterior buildings to help disguise it from enemy surveillance.

"These walls are eighteen inches thick, forty-five feet of rock and concrete on the outside of the walls," Larry said, his voice echoing in the garage. He pointed to some vents on the wall. "These openings, the vents over here, those are called blast valves. If there was an explosion, what the blast valves do is within microseconds they seal with a strong mechanism that locks them into place, so it prevents the shockwave from entering the facility. That blue device you see in the corner is a volcanic ash scrubber. The biggest threat here is that if Yellowstone were to erupt, we'd get somewhere between four and six feet of ash right here in Kansas."

In another dome-level room, Larry showed us giant military-grade chemical filters. "We needed permission from the state department just to buy these. They filter every nonpathogen known to man up to and including weaponized nerve gas," Larry explained. He added that there were enough filters to last ten years, with each filter costing about $20,000. The same room also had a ladder up to a sniper's nest with small windows in each direction at the top of the hill.

Also in the garage area was a workshop and maintenance room filled with tools, two diesel generators, and a diesel filtration system.

"The building has five different power sources, each of these generators can run the whole facility by itself. So, we have two diesel generators, over twenty thousand gallons of fuel, enough fuel to run two and a half years, we have a wind turbine with a bank of batteries to store power, we're connected to the grid. We can do preventative maintenance on one while the other is running."

The last area we were shown before going from the garage area into the building was the decontamination room.

"Based on the threat—if it's a pathological contaminate, terrorist activity, or Ebola outbreak, or radiation, there's different types of scrubbers to go through, you come in here and strip down, get a good going over, we got Geiger counters, iodine treatment, proper scrubs for both radioactive and pathogen contamination. You get a scrub down, your clothes get bagged and burned, and you get a paper gown to wear to get in your unit to get your clothes on."

Recreation

Leaving the garage, we walked through the hall with the gallery of Atlas F and Survival Condos development photos. Then we were shown a small gun range next to the hall, two lanes with targets at the end, and a storage area for eyewear, hearing protection, guns, and ammo.

"To our surprise there's been women in here that have always been intimidated and afraid of guns but wanted to learn, and we gave them an easy way to learn. Mark showed one of the women. She was so intimidated, but she knew she wanted to shoot one. It was on her bucket list as something to do. So Mark brought some weapons down here and let her shoot one. She was shaking, so he had to help her hold it. She got a shot off and realized it wasn't the end of the world. Then Mark showed her the proper way to hold it and shoot it, and how long did it take before she could shoot it like she was Annie Oakley?"

"Probably half hour."

"Half hour you couldn't drag her out of here."

Larry next led us into a recreation room, where we found a rock-climbing wall, an air hockey table, ping-pong table, and a small patch of Astroturf with a photo mural of clouds drifting over mountains and pine trees. Oddly, on one of the walls was a hose and an exposed toilet.

"We had a psychologist who was on Biosphere 2; she does deep-space mission planning for NASA. She came in and changed this facility more than anybody. She put a lot of psychological design elements in here and one of them was this park," Larry said. He referred to this psychologist often in the tour but can't name her due to confidentiality reasons. I'm going to refer to her as Adviser X. "You're underground, you don't want to feel claustrophobic, so you need a place where people can go to where they at least feel like they're outdoors. We originally weren't going to allow pets. She said you have to allow pets—they're family members." That led to building the small pet park in the rec room, so the pets have somewhere to go to the bathroom.

"It looks simple, like it's just Astroturf, but it's designed for pets. There's a special tile underneath it that creates an air vacuum, so the urine goes through the carpet and hits a waterproof membrane down a drain, the poop gets picked up and flushed down the toilet over there."

We passed a nook where we were shown a small room with a foosball table and two video arcade machines, one loaded with 139 classic games, the other twelve Pacman-themed games. Nearby was an inviting lounge room with couches and chairs, a common-area kitchen, meeting tables, stacks of board games, a gas fireplace, and TV screens. The TV was tuned to Fox News and was showing President Trump addressing the United Nations.

Pointing to another screen mounted in the room, Larry explained that an encrypted microwave link would connect this condo unit to the one he's currently working on in Idaho, allowing residents to make video calls between the two facilities. The armored vehicles we saw in the garage also allow for transport between the facilities.

Next, we headed over to the swimming pool. It was a good-sized pool with lounge chairs surrounding it, toy remote-control boats stacked near a chair, and a mural of a tropical beach inhabited by jungle creatures on one of the bright blue walls. Mike went behind a rock embankment and hit a switch to show off the pool's waterfall, which blasted out of the rocks with a whoosh.

Water is in good supply. The water system is heavily filtered through three twenty-five-thousand-gallon tanks, "so we have

The pool. *Courtesy of Paul Kjelland*

seventy-five thousand gallons of water that exceeds bottled water standards," Larry explained.

Leaving the pool, we were shown a row of four identical rooms in the dome—these were areas for staff personnel, who include security guards, maintenance workers, and hydroponic farmers. We got to look in one and found the equivalent to a nice hotel room: bed, vanity area, shower with jacuzzi tub, mini fridge, and a shared laundry area for the four rooms.

With our trip around the dome complete, we headed to the elevator to go to the bottom of the facility before working our way back up. "Going down," a robotic woman's voice said when Larry pushed the elevator button, along with a Star Trek sound effect. "I thought the kids would love it. Turns out a lot of the kids today don't know what it is, but all the parents love it."

Larry said his innovative elevator won a design award. Unlike most elevators, it's what's called an underslung elevator and is energy efficient—it has its own generator on the bottom of it that recaptures a good part of the energy it uses to operate. It's a twenty-nine-second descent to reach the bottom level—level 15—201 feet below ground.

"Theater and lounge level," the award-winning elevator announced when our descent was complete. We passed a small concession-stand area with a popcorn machine and entered a theater room with a few rows of comfortable-looking recliner theater chairs and a decent-sized movie screen.

"You're in about a quarter-million-dollar room," Larry said, explaining that the 7.4 THX surround-sound LED high-definition digital projector alone costs about $35,000, "not including the mounting bracket." To show off the system, Mike turned off the theater lights while Larry scrolled through the movie database and picked *The Avengers*. He selected an exciting, loud scene where Iron Man, Thor, and Captain America are all beating the crap out of each other. Everything was the quality you'd find at a movie theater.

The author sits at a bar fifteen levels underground. *Courtesy of Paul Kjelland*

The superheroes worked out their differences and the scene ended, so we wandered to the back of the theater, which opened into a bar called the Flying Ace Pilot Lounge, decorated with photos of American military aircraft. "You need an independent neutral space where people can socialize and let their kids watch a movie. A normal environment where you can have a drink with friends," Larry said.

The space was another feature that evolved from discussion with Adviser X. Larry said he asked her, "What happens if people get drunk?"

"Well, what happens if people get drunk now?" Adviser X replied. Larry answered, "They pass out or they go back to sleep it off and have a hangover, or they get belligerent and start a fight."

Larry said the answer to the latter situation is something that the security guards—two of them are constantly on duty during lockdown—will deal with. The belligerent drunk "either goes voluntarily to our jail cell and sleeps it off, or he gets tased and sleeps it off."

On the next level up, a storage level, we got an idea of exactly how rich the condo buyers are. Larry pointed out pallets of canned and bagged meals—enough to last the entire condo population five years, even without taking into account the renewable hydroponics system still to come on our tour. He showed us an area that he was in the middle of developing into a woodworking shop, then led us to a giant freezer. "This freezer was an add-on," Larry explained. "One of our wealthier people said, 'I want to have a steak once a week, I can't just live off fish and stuff.' I said, 'We got a freezer.' And he said, 'No, no, no, I need a *big* freezer.'"

Larry explained that the Survival Condos, a licensed condominium in the state of Kansas, made decisions based on votes. A half-unit owner was granted a half vote, a full-unit owner a full vote. If someone owned four full units, they would have four votes. There are rules and bylaws that can be changed with a two-thirds vote. Because the proposed freezer would be in a common area of the condos, Larry told his condo buyer that the rest of the condo would have to vote on the project and divide the cost and the space within the freezer among all the condo owners. But with the thought of a juicy steak searing on his mind, the condo owner decided to skip all that and just bankroll the freezer himself.

"He says, 'Listen, I know you got doctors that can't afford everything I can,' he goes, 'Let's just put it in. Do your divvying up of the space like you need to.'"

We looked inside the empty freezer, with rows of cages in it—bigger ones for the full units and smaller ones for the half units. Larry estimated it could store about $150,000 to $200,000 worth of food. "I got one guy he goes, 'I want protection for five to seven years, so once a year my family is going to have a turkey, so I want seven turkeys in there,'" Larry said. "A whole bunch of Omaha steaks, like filets, and a whole bunch of hot dogs. I want sausages, I want to make my own pizza, I want pepperoni.'"

Another example of money not being an issue came when we were being shown an actual condo unit. Larry showed off the LED "windows" that could be found in each room of the condo units.

Larry shows off a condo unit's LED "window." *Courtesy of Paul Kjelland*

These could be set to cameras located directly outside, so viewers got a livestream of the surrounding cornfields and wind turbine. If that view got too boring (or depressing, if the fields happen to be blazing with apocalypse napalm), then the window owners could set a variety of other backgrounds, whatever they desired—a Hawaiian beach, an evergreen forest, a ski resort in Aspen. It was a pretty good effect that tricked the brain into thinking it was on ground level instead of eight to twelve floors underground.

"It connects you. I lived on my unit on the fifth floor for a month before we had the windows operational and I didn't think anything of it. Then we got the windows operational. Let me tell you something, now the very first thing I do when I get up is turn my light on, turn my windows on. Some people leave these on 24-7, there's a night mode. You can see the weather, what time of day it is, people coming and going. Psychologically, I'm telling you these make an enormous difference, you feel like you're on ground level instead of underground."

For one wealthy Manhattanite, though, the simple standard windows were not enough. A client at the second Survival Condo Larry is developing (in Idaho) wanted something a little more elaborate for her two-story, 3,700-square-foot doomsday penthouse. This woman had always enjoyed her friend's penthouse view of Central Park in New York City, and she wanted it re-created in her underground bunker. A city gal, she wanted to feel like she was still on top of the city instead of buried in a cornfield in Kansas. She wanted the sights and sounds of Central Park and all four seasons—the thousands of car honks and loud music blasting by in summer, the changing colors of fall, the fluffy snowflakes descending on Manhattan, the cooing of pigeons, and warm sun of spring.

Larry had considered all that would be needed to make the woman's request happen. Just the state-of-the-art short throw projector, which could throw an entire wall display from eight inches away, would cost $75,000, way more than the one we had seen in the movie theater.

"What we do is on the curved wall of the facility up there, we grind down the cement and make it flawless, then we put reflective screen paint on it that has embedded reflectors in it for high-definition stuff. And then we have a flat wall that goes across and we have pieces of a porch. We built a partial deck that goes right up to the curve of the silo wall and we put a railing, so it looks like you have a balcony and a railing, we put in real, floor-to-ceiling, nine-foot sliding doors, and in the middle between the two where there's a fireplace. It's an actual 4K high-definition scene on a recorded loop, including sound."

After that, there was the matter of getting four seasons with different weather scenarios—she had requested precipitation and nonprecipitation days for each season, including stereo sound. The speakers would be mounted on the "porch" so she could get the effect of dampening the sound by closing the porch doors.

"I said, well, that's going to be expensive. You've got four seasons with three different scenarios for 24-hour periods, that's about $5,000 a day, so that's $60,000 alone," Larry said, smiling.

"She says, 'Oh, I thought you said it's expensive.'"

Like other moments on the tour, I found this story to be simultaneously amazing and depressing. I imagined a wealthy woman wearing her finest clothes, staring out at Central Park, just an illusion projected on a cement wall, looping repeatedly as the days went by and the world above burned in hell.

"Exercise and spa level," the elevator announced. We step into a fitness room divided into two halves by a thick wall. In one of the halves were aerobic machines like ellipticals and treadmills, TV screens, and long mirrors; in the other were mostly weight machines and dumbbells. The walls were decorated with cutouts of sports legends (they included David Beckham and various NFL quarterbacks) and superheroes (Superman and Wonder Woman posed stoically while the Incredible Hulk flexed by the weight machines). Each half had a locker room—one for men, one for women—with shower facilities, a sauna, and a steam room.

"When there's people here they'll have workout videos playing and music going on and people pumping iron in here. It's lively," Larry said, trying to breathe life into the empty gym. "It's so different when there's people here, especially that top area when the kids are here, and you can hear people in the pool and the rock climbing and the air hockey game going and the dogs running around, it's so different, it's so full of life. It's pretty neat."

"Going up," the elevator told us, then announced, "Library and classroom level."

OTHER MAJOR SURVIVAL FACILITIES

One of the largest bug-out plans is the United States Continuity of Operations Plan, which moves key branches of the government to fortified locations. The Raven Rock Mountain Complex (also called the "underground Pentagon") in the Blue Ridge Summit in Pennsylvania is a huge facility built into a mountain. Along with the Mount Weather Emergency Operating Center in Virginia, it's where high-level government officials will be brought in case of emergency.

One of the largest bunkers ever constructed was a shelter that could accommodate all the members of Congress, hidden behind the luxury resort the Greenbrier in White Sulphur Springs, West Virginia, about four hours from Washington, DC. Construction began in 1958 and was completed in 1961. The finished shelter had 153 rooms, including large dormitory rooms with enough bunkbeds for 1,100 people. There was also a dining facility, a communications center, and large chambers where Congress could meet to govern from under the Blue Ridge Mountains.

The facility was maintained by agents disguised as television repair men, working under a made-up company name: Forsyth Associates. They made sure filters were changed, emergency food stock was rotated, and equipment was operational. The facility was exposed by the *Washington Post* in 1992 and began decommissioning, ending their lease agreement with the Greenbrier in 1995. The Greenbrier now runs tours of the facility.

Located in Oracle, Arizona, Biosphere 2 was constructed as an experiment to see if a group of people could be completely self-sufficient for two years in an artificial, closed ecological system. It was hopeful the project might offer insights to colonizing other planets as well as ecological studies. On September 26, 1991, four men and four women entered the facility dressed in jumpsuits—a "cross between a scarlet prison jumpsuit and a Star Trek Uniform," according to Biospherian Jane Poynter in her book *The Human Experiment: Two Years and Twenty Minutes Inside Biosphere 2*. Texas oil heir Edward Bass funded the $150 million project. In addition to the psychological consultant Larry Hall mentioned, another adviser on Biosphere

2 was Donald Trump's future chief strategist Steve Bannon, whose involvement with the project—much like his time in the White House—was brief and tumultuous.

The Biospherians, as they were known, were a media sensation and appeared on talk shows and magazine covers. But things began to unravel as the project was underway. Poynter accidentally sliced off a fingertip and had to leave the biosphere. When she returned she brought a duffel bag in, and people theorized she had smuggled supplies in to a desperate crew. She denied it, but some said her leaving the biodome at all had compromised the experiment. Biospherians had trouble growing enough food to sustain themselves, with one of them losing fifty-four pounds. Then it was discovered that a CO_2 scrubber (like ones found on a submarine) had secretly been installed before the experiment had begun, leading to headlines like FAKING IT and BIOSPHERE OR BIOSTUNT? Poynter says by the end of the two-year experiment, the Biospherians were "suffocating, starving, and going quite mad." The group split into two different factions that despised each other and barely communicated.

Still, Poynter points out that the group was the first of its kind, and "trailblazers make mistakes."

The building was eventually bought by the University of Arizona and is currently used as an earth sciences laboratory for research projects in ecology, atmospheric science, soil geochemistry, and climate change.

Stepping off the elevator, we entered a handsome library, the wall filled with floor-to-ceiling bookshelves. It was missing reading material, though—most of the shelves sat empty, with only a handful of books here and there. I did notice one shelving square was well stocked with Frank Herbert's Dune series. There was a variety of comfortable-looking couches, love seats, and easy chairs spread around the room, an end table with a chess board on it, a kitchen table, and a coffee-making station. Larry explained that this was a lounge where kids could do homework and parents could hang out while their kids were in the classroom next door, which we walked into next.

The perimeter of the room had nine study carrel work stations, each with a computer mounted inside. There was a long work table in the middle of the room, with the condo blueprints spread over it and a drawing of the condo layout on a giant electronic whiteboard. Educational posters—a world map, the solar system, a diagram of human anatomy—decorated the walls.

Larry explained school would be in session here during lockdown Monday through Friday, with elementary school in session in the morning and high school in the afternoon. The teachers would be the condo residents.

"Everyone has to work four hours a day here, you're not on vacation," Larry said. "Again, that's something from [Adviser X], everyone gets a job assignment for a month. So, one month, you're the elementary school teacher, kindergarten through sixth grade. Next month, you're working hydroponics. Next month you're working security. Next month you're working the store. Next month you're working maintenance. Everyone rotates so people don't think there's job preference. You don't have any single points of failure where only one person knows how to run a critical resource. Everyone is cross-trained and knows how to do everything. That makes everyone buy into the facility and not deteriorate it."

Our next stop was a look at an actual residential unit on level 8. Larry explained that the residential units were all located from levels 5 to 11. A full-floor unit (1,820 square feet) was $3 million and had a max of ten people, while a half unit was half the size, cost, and capacity. The two-story penthouses in the new Idaho complex started at $4.5 million. So, with all the condominiums at max capacity, plus the four personnel rooms filled, you were looking at a total condo population of seventy to eighty people. Larry said this was ideal for a thriving community.

"If you look in sociology groups, extended family is defined as a group larger than twenty, smaller than a hundred and twenty, in close proximity to share a common goal. So, in this case you're in a facility and you got survival as a common goal and it's the most productive form of society known to man. Because you're on a first-name basis, you know everybody. If you have just family members—you treat family worse than you do friends, believe it or not. You can love them all day long, but you still treat them harsher. But in arm's-length relationships with strangers, it buffers that out. So, you get your societal needs of meeting and interacting with other people."

The owners of level 8—a full-unit condo—had agreed to let media in, as long as they didn't take pictures in their living room, which contained a few family photos. I'm not sure how to describe the family I saw in the photos, other than to say they looked much like the models in the Crate & Barrel catalog that had been delivered down there to the end of the Earth—eight floors below ground to the condo's kitchen counter with a small stack of other mail. The mail was the only evidence the condo had been in use. Everything was shiny, new, unused. The beds were perfectly made and there were no stains, scuffs, or litter. The condo wasn't big, but it wasn't claustrophobic either. This full-floor unit had the elevator open to a foyer. Half the unit had the kids' bedrooms and bathroom, and the other half had the small kitchen, living room, and parents' bedroom and bathroom. The living room featured another condo extravagance: an electric fireplace built with granite the owner had shipped from his home state of Connecticut. The bedroom featured a king-size bed, his and her stationary desks, reading lamps, and an LED window tuned to the outdoor camera focused on the surrounding cornfields. The unit also had a small apartment-style washer and dryer.

"You can see it's not exactly roughing it. You have no idea you're 118 feet underground," Larry said.

Pointing to the bed he mentioned another unexpected benefit to bunker living. "The other cool thing about this place—and every single person who has slept here without exception has had the same comment," Larry said. And that comment is that they've had the best night of sleep ever. "I was one of the first ones that found out," Larry said. "For whatever reasons—I don't know if it's the EMI shielding, you don't get the radio waves." He said it's something his son looks forward to when he visits. "He'll call me and say 'Dad, I can't wait to get some of that silo sleep.'"

———

"Ship's Store and aquaponics," the elevator told us as the doors opened to a miniature grocery store, complete with shopping aisles displaying household items like bleach, dish detergent, cotton balls, tissue, and toothbrushes. There were rows of giant cans of food, a deli, and some little shopping carts. The purpose of Ship's Store was not so Larry could make a few extra bucks selling food and household goods, but to provide people with a normal social experience.

"Originally we were just going to have stuff in boxes, it was going to be a storeroom, but when [Adviser X] got hold of that little tidbit of information, she cringed and said, 'No, no, no, no. You're going to have a low ceiling, I want this place set up like a Whole Foods market, I want a gourmet deli, I want a fish market with ice, deli foods with little bean dips, coleslaw, potato salad, everything else, desserts that people make. You're going to make fresh bread daily.'"

The store did have a bread oven and a coffee maker to give the store a good smell, as well as an ice cream maker and a trading post section—a table with a chalkboard where people can write items they want to trade, say a bottle of wine for a couple of pork chops.

"This is gluten free. This is twenty-five servings of instant white rice, potatoes, sweet potatoes, chicken TVP, pinto beans, lima beans, pancake mix, milk, lentils, winter wheat, sugar, salt, all types of drinks, all types of foods—some prepared. They're massive in their volume and stuff." Larry pointed out a cookbook. "The rule is people are told not to take more than three days of food, even though you could," Larry said. "We want people to shop more frequently, because this is a social event. The purpose is to not go fill up your cupboards and be a hermit.

To show us where the produce will come from, Larry led us through a short tunnel to a large room. He explained, "We have seventy different types of produce we can grow—lettuce, tomatoes, kale, strawberries, blueberries, carrots, onions—all that will

The deli area of Ship's Store. *Courtesy of Paul Kjelland*

be organic." The room used to be the launch control complex for the Atlas missile, but has been transformed to an aquaponics center, FDA-inspected and approved. The hall had the word *aquaponics* coded in braille on tile and a nook that Larry said will be home to a dwarf apple tree that produces five different species of apple.

The aquaponics room was filled with various-sized green tubs and giant buckets, the bigger ones will be used to breed tilapia. When I saw them, though, they all sat empty.

"You start out with fry in here, they get about an inch long and they go in here, then they go in here, and then into this big harvest tank. We have three different species of tilapia. Their waste products get filtered into a loop that fertilizes the plants," Larry said, explaining the cycle of production.

———

"Security and sick bay," the disembodied voice informed us.

"This is a ballistic-rated door with bulletproof glass right here," Larry explained about what he calls "the heart and soul" of the Survival Condos: the security center.

"This building was made to a building code called the International Building Code or IBC for inhabited underground structures. It is undoubtedly the strictest building code in the world, bar none."

The most impressive system on display here was the fire control computer. "It's akin to being in a submarine in a thousand feet of water. If you have a fire, you can't open the door and get out of the building," Larry told us, pointing to an electronic map of the building labeled FIREFIGHTER'S SMOKE CONTROL STATION and studded with miniature lightbulbs. "There's over a hundred dampers, this cross section, we have an A and a B zone on every floor. This computer opens and closes the right set of dampers. Let's say in zone 9B there's a fire. It knows how to open and take the smoke directly out of the facility without shutting down the air in the rest of the facility. There's sprinkler and firefighting stations on every level. We're way beyond any fire code for what we have built into this place."

Larry directed us to a bank of surveillance screens. One was a camera that constantly moved slowly around the perimeter of the building outside. Other cameras were set up outside and in all the common-area rooms of the condo. We could see every level we'd visited all on one screen. This surveillance room was where one of the security guards would work, with the other stationed at the guard shack outside.

"Most of their work would be in here, but periodically they alternate, and one does a walk-through, walks through the levels, the pool, walks around to let people know they're around. But these are friends, these are people that know each other, so the whole thing is, 'Hey, we got people to look out for us if we need help with something. We got two armed guards that are essentially like policemen.'"

Larry showed us the condo's jail cell, which, as he had mentioned in the bar, was where unruly Survival Condo citizens might find themselves after bad behavior. It was a clinical, small room with a toilet in the wall and nothing else.

"There's a cot that goes in here, it's like county lockup. Look familiar?" Larry joked to us. "Look but don't touch," he said as he opened the door to the armory—one of three armories spread throughout the condo. The walls were covered with guns and boxes of ammo and other weapons were spread throughout the room.

"We've got everything from nonlethal things like military-grade pepper spray and Tasers to lethal stuff," Larry said as Paul and I gawked at row after row of rifles and handguns. Larry said the arsenal included computerized sniper rifles and a gun that could take out a helicopter. Larry pointed out that these were not just for the guards but that "everyone that is checked out on firearm safety in the shooting range, everyone is being trained for defense and patrolling here, to handle and shoot a gun."

The guns were for defense and to deter the wild hordes of desperate people looking for survivors to pillage.

The author inside the armory. *Courtesy of Paul Kjelland*

"You have to be able to survive and if you start giving your shit away you'll die because there's people that think . . ." Here Larry launched into an imagined dialogue with a hypothetical desperate character standing locked outside the condo gates.

"Yeah, just give me one box of food."

"Well you're going to come back tomorrow after you've eaten it and want another box of food."

"No, I won't."

"OK here's the deal . . . No! Come back again, we shoot ya."

"We need food!"

"You should have thought of that."

"We want your food."

"Can't have it."

"Well, we really, really, really want your food."

"We'll kill ya."

"Why?"

"Cause you're going to take our food."

"Not all your food, just half your food. You keep half, I'll keep half."

"Well, then we'll be dead in half the time."

"Oh, we'll be dead if we don't get it."

"You'll be dead if you try to get it. Go find a warehouse somewhere, beat it."

The rest of the security level included a small room still being put together that will be the condominium's pharmacy, with shelving units and a refrigerator for insulin that were yet to be installed. "It's actually a licensed Kansas pharmacy, and we have seven years of prescriptions for every owner here ready at the hospital in town."

Other small rooms had a doctor's office and a dentist room and a room that will have a hospital bed in it for longer-term issues. "We haven't unpacked it yet, that's a project just to put that goddamn thing together."

Air flow in this section was quarantined and separate to avoid cross-contamination.

Survival of the Corporations

Back up top at the dome level, we went to the lounge to sit down and talk. I asked Larry about future plans, and he revealed that he had quite a few projects in the works. In addition to finishing his Idaho Atlas missile silo location, he had options on four more abandoned silos. Wealthy ranchers in Texas and Idaho were contracting him to build bunkers on their properties. "We're pricing those things out and I thought they would be scared, but neither one of them flinched at the price," Larry said, and added that his biggest interest in future bunkers had been from corporate parties.

"That's what we're finding the trend is, we're getting more people who are Fortune 500 companies that say, we got a relatively small number of owners, so we want to have a combination life support center and center for our critical infrastructure data, so we don't have a World Trade Center incident. If a plane flies into this, you know, they don't even interrupt your swim.

"They say, 'As long as our corporation is paying for it, we've got fifty people—the executives and their families—fifty people or sixty people or a hundred people. We want living quarters for a hundred people to be able to live off-grid for five years. Design us a compound where we buy the whole thing, we'll hire our own staff, our own data-center people. I want a maintenance contract with you for the first three years and in those years, you must train our people to maintain the facility. At the end of three years, I want this to be a corporate-owned and maintained facility.'

"I said, 'Perfect.' So we have several requests like that in," Larry said.

He said he also has interest from a Hollywood talent agency in what sounded like the worst or best reality show ever. "I got another Hollywood group that wants me to build one for their management company. These are agents for a whole bunch of Hollywood A- and B-list people, and they want to run it like a boutique luxury hotel with a lot of value added. We ran into some sticking points.

"I said, 'Well, you're going to be a competitor with me. I'm not going to restrict what I do. I'm still going to construct these and sell units like a condo.

"He says, 'No, no, we want to go higher end. We're going to put in concierges, a masseuse, chefs on staff so when people come here they're catered to.' It's like a spa with hair stylists, high-end amenities. It's a nuke-proof retreat they go to if they need to. They're envisioning not being here for five years, but a month or two months, and while their people are here, they want them to be on holiday. So that's the trend," Larry explained.

The Crazy Fat Kid in North Korea

During our wrap-up conversation, Larry mentioned a couple of times that his condo constituency was made up of both liberals and conservatives.

"Here we're like Switzerland. We just expect reasonable people to coexist, and we haven't had that problem," Larry said. He relayed a story about all the condo owners meeting up and taking a trip together to tour the company that did the condo's programming for systems integration. They stayed at the Waldorf Astoria, toured the facilities, and went out for cocktails.

"We argued about threat levels and who was right and who was wrong, but everyone liked everyone, cats and dogs living together. Would you say there was any animosity on that trip at all?" Larry called over to Mike.

"None whatsoever," Mike replied.

"None at all. Everyone was professional, courteous, and they were complete opposite ends of the spectrum. Some were ultra-conservative Republicans, a couple independents, some who were really left people," Larry said. "I wish the rest of the country was as congenial as our owners."

That all sounded utopian, but Larry quickly showed that while the condos are Switzerland, he himself is not so dispassionate. He talked about his admiration for President Trump, whom he said "is reaching across the aisle to mainstream Democrats," and uniting "reasonable people" who want to move to the center and get away from the radical far ends. According to Larry, on the left these extremes are the "Bernie Sanders and beyond" people and on the right it's "neo-Nazis."

"In my opinion the left has gotten so communistic, socialistic, ridiculistic that you can't have an adult conversation," Larry said. "So now you got a guy who's a businessman that's results orientated for the first time in a long, long, long time. We got a level-headed, results-orientated pragmatic person that wants to get stuff done and make lives better for this country and is not worried about Zimbabwe and the Middle East and putting everyone else ahead of his own citizens and getting rid of the swamp and all the corruption and going after that crew. I dunno, it's just refreshing to me."

He also seemed to be in agreement with the Trump train conclusion that climate change caused by man-made pollutants was a myth. "It's the cycle of our sun going above and below the galactic plane and the region of space and how much solar radiation—you can look in the ice records to substantiate this pattern—there's no deviation from it. By the way, we just had another volcanic eruption that happened over in Greece that put out in ten days more pollution in the atmosphere than all of mankind since the invention of the combustion engine. So if you want to tell me that it is just man which is dwarfed by what mankind is spewing into the atmosphere and we're responsible for the global climate change, I think you're misinformed."

The biggest hot topic of our interview was about the man Larry called "the crazy fat kid in North Korea," meaning, of course, Chairman Kim Jong Un. Larry had mentioned him, and I recalled the beginning of the tour when I had spotted President Trump on TV on Fox News with a chyron that read something along the lines of "Trump gives tough talk about North Korea at UN."

In fact, what Trump was saying in his first address to the United Nations was "The United States has great strength and patience, but if it is forced to defend itself or its allies, we will have no choice but to totally destroy North Korea. Rocket Man is on a suicide mission for himself."

Kim Jong Un responded by calling Trump a "frightened dog," and a "gangster," and declaring, "I will surely and definitely tame the mentally deranged US dotard with fire." This led to a spike in dictionary searches for the word *dotard* ("a person in his or her *dotage*," i.e., "a state or period of senile decay marked by decline of mental poise and alertness").

It was not the first time the two leaders had exchanged threats like schoolyard children. A month earlier Kim Jong Un had threatened to use Guam as target practice. Trump said the United States would respond with "fire, fury, and frankly power, the likes of which this world has never seen before."

On January 2, 2018, Trump responded to Kim Jong Un's comment that he had a nuclear button on his desk by tweeting, "North Korean Leader Kim Jong Un just stated that the 'Nuclear Button is on his desk at all times.' Will someone from his depleted and food starved regime please inform him that I too have a Nuclear Button, but it is a much bigger & more powerful one than his, and my Button works!"

Many pundits thought that Trump was perhaps also making a phallus reference. So I decided to ask Larry a question that I thought was pretty softball, especially if he was hanging around with liberals like he said. "Some people are concerned about Trump and see him as poking North Korea and provoking them," I said.

This statement greatly unsettled Larry, and he went on a long rant that lasted a solid half hour. His main point was that I (and people like me) did not know the monsters we were dealing with. He started with North Korea and talking about how poorly its citizens were treated and how vicious Kim Jong Un was, killing family members. I think Larry decided this wasn't shocking or frightening enough, so he switched the subject to ISIS.

"I don't know, have you actually talked to anyone who was deployed over there? I don't want those people breathing the same air I breathe, when I found what the ISIS people were doing. I have some friends that sent us some pictures that they recovered over there. Let me give you an idea—when ISIS took that town over, they rounded up all the Christian kids and women, and then they usually shot the men execution-style, or beheaded them, or they crucified them—actually cut them open, nailed them to a cross and cruci-fied them. OK, they put some in cages and burned them alive. They sequentially cut up pieces of their arm until they bled to death. They cut their legs off and they wanted to see how many things they could cut off before they died. I mean, torturous things like that."

I stared at Larry blankly and he continued. ". . . And I'm say-ing this with attitude because when I talk to people that think you can reason with these people I really want you to know who you're talking about . . ."

Larry went on to explain that after executing the men, they rounded up the Christian children, who were kept behind a fence and then funneled through a gate to their death. "At the end of that funnel was a big cargo truck, and they had a step and they had these ISIS flags on either corner, and they had three people and two guys were standing there in the black masks with the ISIS flags wrapped over their heads and they had a big sword. And these kids came up to a block, a stump, and they had great big galvanized farm buckets that you would bob for apples in placed all around it . . . then these kids and this line wound around so that everyone in line saw what was going to happen to them, these kids got grabbed by each arm, there were three people, one had a sword, one had each arm, they threw the kids down, they turned their head, they turned it toward the guy with the sword so they could see what was happening, and they cut their fucking heads off and threw them in the fucking galvanized tins, and then they threw their bodies in another pile. And they were shoveling them up with excavator buckets. . . .

"The women were even better," Larry said wryly, while the rest of us sat in uncomfortable silence. He then described the Christian women being stripped naked and having their throats cut before being beheaded, their blood being used to paint messages on churches. He described a video he saw where suspected homosexuals were thrown off a rooftop.

"Now between the burning, the beheadings, the filming, the slaughter of the kids—I'm not going to negotiate. Those people are subhuman and I'm frankly offended by anyone that has anything to say in defense of those fucking people. I didn't hear this, I *heard* it, I saw the recording, from film and I watched it and I wanted to throw up when I saw it. So when I hear people talk about, 'Oh, can't we work with the people over here in Iran and Iraq?' You have no idea who you're dealing with. These fucking people, I don't want them alive," Larry said bitterly, adding an aside that he had heard that a member of Obama's State Department had said the terrorists just needed jobs. "If they just had a jobs program, they wouldn't be going crazy killing these kids and Christians and murdering them. I don't know about you, but I've been fired from jobs before—well, I've been laid off, I haven't been fired. I've been laid off of jobs and I didn't want to go pick up a sword and go kill somebody. Let's get real here.

"But I want these people killed, I want them killed with extreme prejudice and don't want any of their genetic stuff in the pool. Whatever makeup those people are, it's evil and there is no place on this planet for them. None. They can't have their own state, they can't agree to stay in the desert, they can't agree to stay in a confined area somewhere, they got no right to exist. . . . This world will be a far safer and better place if we don't have people like that breathing the same air, they're just evil, evil. You just can't do it."

Larry circled back around from the Middle East to North Korea. "And Kim Jong Un who has radiation and kills his own cousins and all that stuff, and you know *you* make a comment like Trump standing up to him and wanting to strip these weapons away, well what happens when his generals tell him there's a Chinese hit squad sent in to kill him, you know what that guy is going to do? He's going to take out as many people with him as he can. He's going to attack Japan, he's going to attack Guam, he's going to attack China, he's going to attack the United States, he's going to attack Russia, he's going to fire all of these nuclear weapons wherever they can go to cause the most harm, because he knows he's on his way out. So letting him or Iran be a nuclear state is not an option. There are just too many people that will die as a result of that bad decision. . . . Trump is playing the hand he was dealt and he didn't poke anybody with a stick. He is warning people with a club that if China doesn't get serious and denuclearize with the world participating in that verification, then there's only one option left, and that's going to be an all-out full-scale war attack on North Korea, and I got a real good feeling that's the way it's going to end up. Because this guy is too fucking loony tunes."

Larry wound down his speech after that, and he was done with our company. We walked back outside through the blast doors and had a friendly parting. He shook our hands, wishing us good travels.

A little shell-shocked, Paul and I thanked him for the tour and walked to the car in the bright sunlight of the real world. The tour had left me with mixed feelings—there was no question Larry had created an impressive state-of-the-art facility. But I imagined being trapped several stories below ground listening to political diatribes while the world burned above and the thought filled me with anxiety every time my mind flashed back to the confined rooms in the Survival Condos.

9

THE SIXTH EXTINCTION

If you visit my hometown of Milwaukee, you should check out the Milwaukee Public Museum. In the east wing of the first level, you'll find an exhibit that's been a favorite of mine since I was a kid. It's called the *Third Planet*. The exhibit is mostly about plate tectonics and geological history, but the stars of the exhibit are what everyone wants to see in a museum: dinosaurs. Walking through the exhibit also takes us through the planet's major extinction periods, of which there have been five so far, extinctions where 75 percent or more of life on Earth has perished.

To find our first extinction, we can refer to the exhibit's display that reads, How Long Is Geologic Time? A Long, Long Time Indeed! The display shows thirty panels set up like a calendar, with each square representing 150 million years of history.

Single-cell organisms show up in square eight and dominate most of the calendar. Dinosaurs don't show up until day twenty-nine, and dinosaurs and modern life share square thirty. The first great extinction happened somewhere in day twenty-eight of this calendar, the Late Ordovician period, 444 million years ago. Scientists believe that a short ice age lowered sea levels and exposed silicate rock that sucked carbon dioxide and chilled the planet, killing about 85 percent of marine life, mostly organisms called graptolites.

Walk over to a display that reads, Colonization of Land . . . Silurian Seas Were Crowded With Life, but the Land Was Lifeless.

Inside the diorama, you'll spot an amphibious tetrapod named *Ichthyostega* half-submerged, lurking in algae-colored water.

Ichthyostega was one of the first creatures to adapt to land in the Upper Devonian, but in the Late Devonian extinction, 375 million years ago, it is believed that algal blooms sucked oxygen out of the water, suffocating creatures of the sea.

In the same diorama, just up the shore from *Ichthyostega*, you'll see *Seymouria*, hanging out near a nest of eggs. Seymour, as I like to call him, was a link between amphibians and reptiles. *Seymouria* lived in the Early Permian, and few survived the End Permian extinction, 251 million years ago, also known as "The Great Dying," in which 70 percent of terrestrial species and 96 percent of marine life went extinct. Causes may have been volcano eruptions, meteorites, a rise in methane causing a deadly greenhouse effect, or a combination of these factors. After the Great Dying, some cute pig-sized herbivores called *Lystrosaurus* dominated the land of planet Earth alone for millions of years.

Walking into the next room of the exhibit, you'll find a full-scale model of a greenish-gray *Stegosaurus*. Running along the railing in front of him near his feet are three boxes, displaying fossils from the Cretaceous, Jurassic (the era *Stegosaurus* lived in), and the Triassic periods. There was a mass extinction at the end of the Triassic period, two hundred million years ago. Like the Great Dying, the reasons for this extinction are enigmatic, and there are the same theories of what caused the extinction.

And then the pièce de résistance of the exhibit, a sight that frightened me when I first saw it as a kid—a full-scale diorama of a *Tyrannosaurus rex* taking a bite out of a felled *Triceratops*.

Dinosaurs, as a nearby wall display that reads THE GREAT EXPLANATION explains, were wiped out in the End Cretaceous extinction, sixty-six million years ago. The display reflects a myriad of different explanations for what killed the dinosaurs, "perhaps small mammals with insatiable appetites," it speculates.

The "Perhaps an asteroid?" part of the display is now widely seen as the correct theory, based on the research of father and son scientists Luis and Walter Alvarez. They came to the "impact theory"

Part of the *Third Planet* exhibit. Milwaukee Public Museum

of a large meteorite or comet that exploded with the impact of one hundred million megatons of TNT.

"Day turned to night, and temperatures plunged. A mass extinction ensued," author Elizabeth Kolbert explains in her book, *The Sixth Extinction: An Unnatural History.* The Alvarezes found evidence for this theory by testing Cretaceous sediments for iridium, an element rare on Earth but common in meteorites. Their tests found an abundance of iridium spread from the meteorite explosion. Eventually the Cretaceous crash site, the Chicxulub crater off the Yucatán Peninsula of Mexico, was discovered.

The Sixth Extinction

Many scientists say that we are now well into a sixth extinction, which is sometimes referred to as the Anthropocene extinction. Unlike prior extinctions caused by ice ages, volcanic activity, asteroids, and carbon dioxide changes, the cause of this extinction points to one culprit: mankind. As the human population has swiftly grown, we have caused the extinction of hundreds of species of animals from the great auk to the Rocky Mountain locust to the western black rhinoceros, and the number is growing, especially as we see that extreme climate change is happening, and it is affecting everything. Polar caps are melting, sea levels rising, and extreme draughts and weather are disrupting and killing our natural world.

6 Degrees

An increase in global temperature of 6 degrees Celsius would be fatal for mankind. This is documented in the book *Six Degrees: Our Future on a Hotter Planet* by Mark Lynas.

Through six sections, Lynas documents things you might expect to see each time the planet's global average temperature increases by a degree. At 2 degrees warmer, you'll see major drought in places like China, and ocean acidification will increase, putting ocean ecosystems at an even bigger risk than they are now. At 2 degrees higher, it will be common to have more heat waves, like the European heat wave in 2003 that killed over fifteen thousand people, mostly in France.

By 4 degrees hotter, climate refugees will be fleeing places like Egypt and Bangladesh. All coastal cities will be at risk (consider the New Orleans flood). At 4 degrees you can expect the giant ice continent of Antarctica to start completely breaking apart, especially the West Antarctica Ice Sheet (a huge part has already broken off).

It's hard to imagine exactly what a 6-degree increase in global temperature would look like, but it is very unlikely humanity would be able to survive such an increase. The oceans will die, and carbon dioxide, hydrogen sulfide, and methane in the atmosphere will lead to the Anthropocene mass extinction.

It's Getting Hot in Here

It was stifling hot in the un-air-conditioned First Unitarian Society of Milwaukee on July 12, 2017. About 150 people were gathered in the church pews, fanning themselves with cardboard fans provided by the church, while an oscillating fan lurched back and forth. A man in the back of the room played a mournful song on a wooden flute.

Soon Dr. Guy McPherson, wearing a teal button-up shirt and brown slacks and sporting a moustache, took the pulpit, a wall of brass pipes from a pipe organ behind him. He was there to deliver a sermon of sorts, but not a Bible study. The hot, sticky room temperature added a gravitas to his subject matter: abrupt climate change.

"I've been called a doomist cult hero by the *Washington Post*, so thanks to all you cult members for showing up," McPherson joked, adding that the *New York Times* has also labeled him "a goofy professor."

This hasn't always been part of his legacy. McPherson was a scientist and professor emeritus of natural resources, ecology, and evolutionary biology at the University of Arizona. He authored some publications—mundane compared to his recent work—with titles like *Ecology and Management of North American Savannas* and the *Glossary of Fire Management Terms Used in the United States*. But in 2011 McPherson walked away from all that to focus on what he calls "near term extinction" caused by "abrupt climate change."

McPherson claims that his research has shown him that the End is happening soon, "far faster than anyone on Earth is telling you," he said, and that there is absolutely nothing that can be done about it, so we should try to enjoy our short life left now. "Imagine you are given a terminal diagnosis. What would you do?" he asked his audience. He added, "Climate scientists are guilty of malpractice. Some of them have said it's bad. I'm here to tell you it's worse."

It's not only worse but, as McPherson made clear, completely hopeless. "I'm accused routinely of not promoting hope. But I've never suggested inaction because I'm hope-free!" he said. Later he added, "Hope is a four-letter word." And in his book *Extinction Dialogs: How to Live with Death in Mind* (coauthored with Carolyn Baker), it's mentioned he feels people are drugged by "hopium." "Climate change is a predicament, not a problem," McPherson told the audience in the church in front of him. "Problems have solutions. Predicaments do not."

As he tried to convey this message, some in his congregation were audibly shocked and dismayed, some were amused or skeptical, and some were angry. McPherson was unclear on this doomsday timeline but stressed that while it won't happen overnight, it will be an agonizing period of heat stroke, heat exhaustion, and starvation. In *Extinction Dialogs* he says humans won't exist on Earth "beyond the 2030s."

"We've triggered too many self-reinforcing feedback loops to prevent near-term extinction at our own hand," McPherson writes. But at the appearance at the Unitarian Church, McPherson seemed confident that the 2030s was a liberal guess and that the End was much closer. He mentioned that the 4-degree global temperature increase would be in the "very near future."

"And at 4 degrees Celsius hotter, all we can talk about is human extinction," McPherson said from the pulpit, explaining that lethal temperatures would be upon us "within four years, and probably much sooner. Could be as soon as fall or late summer." A couple audience members gasped at this information.

"If you think humans will adapt, think again," McPherson writes in his book. He cites a 2013 analysis by Malcolm Light, which suggests that "the temperature of Earth's atmosphere will resemble that of Venus before 2100."

"Worse than the media are the mainstream scientists who minimalize the message at every turn. Scientists almost invariably underplay climate impacts. In some cases, scientists are aggressively muzzled by their governments."

McPherson added that he believes the Pentagon knows that environmental, economic, and other crises could provoke widespread public anger toward government and corporations.

Live Here Now

McPherson lives between land he owns in New Mexico that he calls his Mud Hut, and a homestead he shares with several other people in Belize. From these locations he updates his blog, *Nature Bats Last*, plans speaking tours like the one that led him to Milwaukee, and hosts a workshop at his Belize homestead titled Only Love Remains. Part of McPherson's message seems to be an odd Doomsday Zen.

"I was asked to give a three-sentence synopsis of an hour presentation I had just done," Guy told the church congregation. "I said, how about a three-word synopsis? Live here now."

McPherson also revealed his three suggestions for living with extinction on the mind, which he outlined for his audience as they fanned themselves in the hot church. He also features them in his *Extinction Dialogs* book:[*]

1. Remain calm. Nothing is under your control. It doesn't matter what's going on around you. Act but do not be attached to the outcome.
2. Pursue excellence because at the end of the day you only report to the person you see in the mirror.
3. Pursue love. Do what you love. Get off the treadmill of just making a living.

McPherson's theory is not, of course, something that most mainstream climate scientists believe. McPherson asked his audience what they would do if they were given a terminal prognosis. In this case, I decided to get a second opinion. I met with Ankur Desai, who works for the Center for Climate Research at the University of Wisconsin–Madison in the Department of Atmospheric and Oceanic Sciences.

"I'm also affiliated with the Department of Climate Research, part of the Nelson Institute for Environmental Studies. Together the department and the center consist of both outgoing researchers who study climate change and climate change impacts from a whole variety of aspects, all the way from looking at past climates and how they

---

[*] McPherson has even published a children's book to help them wrap their head around the concept of the End. It's titled *Ms. Ladybug and Mr. Honeybee: A Love Story at the End of Time* (with Pauline Panagiotou-Schneider).

influenced vegetation patterns and distribution of animals, to people who do modeling of future climates," Ankur told me in his office on the fifteenth floor of the Atmospheric and Oceanic Studies building. "My particular research tends to focus on how ecosystems that exist on the surface of Earth are both influenced by changes in climate and weather, and how they then feedback on changing climates. So, how does a forest change the local weather patterns? And then, how does future climate change add to say . . . drought stress in the forest. We do that through a mix of field measurements we have in northern Wisconsin as well as other parts of the planet, and through a lot of computer-based simulations as well."

It's not always an easy line of work, since climate change research always seems to be under attack. "Scientists are not necessarily politically savvy enough to say my interest day-to-day is about doing basic research. I'm mostly trying to work with funding agencies to talk about what are the interesting scientific questions," Ankur said. "Then to have this whole second line of attack of, 'Well, because your research has negative political implications, we're going to find every possible thing that's possibly wrong with your science so we don't have to deal with the political implications.' It suddenly puts us in a limelight we didn't want to be in, and that's a battle that's hard to win."

Population Explosion

"I'm currently teaching a class on global change, and one of the things I try to get students to think about is this: Is change right now remarkable, or just part of what humanity has always experienced?" Ankur said. "Since the dawn of the Industrial Revolution, you can put civilization on this course of like basically hanging out with one hundred million people or so for thousands of years, civilizations coming and going primarily using local subsistence of resources, a few larger civilizations coming and going, agriculture really changing a lot of things but then the discovery and use of fossil fuels—coal, oil, and gas—along with a whole bunch of changes in education, vaccination, public health, birth control, modern agricultural use of fertilizers, pesticides—all these things basically coincide with this almost inflection point. You can basically look at this population as an L shape, and we suddenly go from maybe half a billion to seven billion in a hundred years after ten thousand years of not doing much at all. That's really remarkable, and what we focus on in that class is what are the consequences of that, because obviously we've gone from this perception of humans as one of many things that exist on this planet to the dominant driver of how the Earth system—the ocean, the atmosphere, the land is controlled."

So what effect has this huge population had on our environment?

"What we've seen over the twentieth century is that the climate has started to warm. It doesn't change year after year; it's not a monotonic increase, because you still have natural ability, and weather is kind of a chaotic thing. But you can basically attribute the relatively modest change, about a degree or so of warming, almost entirely to greenhouse gases. That's really—there's no debate on that. It's basic physics. It was first described in 1860 or so in a set of articles, and what we do now is mostly refine that, to understand how that happens across space, and how different drivers and feedbacks change.

"How does that change things? Well most of those changes have been relatively modest to date, but some things have been concerning. We have seen the advancement of spring and fall in the mid-latitudes. That's probably one of the most obvious examples here in Wisconsin. Spring's about a week or two earlier, fall's about a week or two later. Lake ice is losing about a day or so per decade, so it's about two to three weeks shorter—the length of snow cover season."

Ankur explained that if you want to see what the future climate-changed world is beginning to look like, take a trip to northern Alaska. "If you go up there, regardless of people's politics, no one doubts the climate has really changed. Arctic sea ice is at record lows. It's affecting foraging for large mammals. A lot of communities built on permafrost have basically started to move inland, and there's a few places where you're seeing wetlands starting to go away and forest coming in. We don't know what that type of change is going to look like."

Ankur said the other major change we've been starting to see has been sea level rising. "For the most part you're like half a foot or a foot. That's not a big deal. And that's true for most places, but there's a lot of low-lying areas where that makes a pretty big difference. It makes the biggest difference when you have extreme weather coupled to that. So, if you have a tropical cyclone that tends to push the ocean in, having an extra foot on top of that just allows you to get over the defenses that you had otherwise. That explains a lot of the extreme level of flooding we had during Hurricane Sandy, despite it being a modest-sized hurricane."

Drought is his final major concern. "Most of the impacts assessments say once you get about 2 degrees Celsius warming, that's when you start to see things like agricultural productivity in subsistence areas going down. We've built our entire civilization on the idea that food production always keeps up or goes faster than population growth. We've been successful with that so far with genetic hybridization, fertilizer, and pesticides."

Black Swans

"Some of the models do occasionally have outlier scenarios, and Hollywood loves these. *The Day After Tomorrow* took a physically implausible scenario or physically plausible element that didn't make sense," Ankur said, referring to the 2004 movie that features a sudden extreme weather change that creates a new ice age.

"There are a few of these outlier scenarios, most of which are discounted as very low-probability events, called 'black swans,'" Ankur explained. "There are a few of these I think, if they were to occur, that would be dramatic immediate impacts. One of these is that if you melt enough of Greenland into the North Atlantic, you slow down the ocean circulation so much that even in a warming climate you actually put Europe, that relies on that gulf stream, into a deep freeze. Remember, London's at 52 degrees north, the same latitude as Montreal. If you turned London into the same climate as Montreal, you'd have massive upheaval in Europe. You'd have crop failures, loss of life. There's some evidence that might have happened in the past."

Ankur said that unlike a crazy *Day After Tomorrow*–type of insane weather apocalypse, what we can more likely expect is that climate change will chip away in "little stories here and there." One of the little stories: increasing tree mortality in a harsher, drier world.

"One of the things people in the Southwest United States are really concerned about is tree mortality. We've seen a massive increase in forest fires, and these multi-decade-long droughts that seem to be occurring at a more greater frequency," Ankur said. "For example, in California, with their recent five-year-long drought, three to four million trees killed. A lot of the model predictions show that a lot of the Western United States gets drier, potentially the Amazon gets drier, and if that leads to widespread tree mortality, that has all sorts of cascading feedbacks on the ecosystems.

"There's also the outbreaks of pests. At the slow rate it's happening now it's probably adaptable, but even places like British Columbia, where 80 percent of business was shut down for a while because of an outbreak of a beetle that was driven by the heat and drought."

Climate Wars

Ankur said what is probably a bigger issue than the climate change itself is the repercussions it'll have on society. "I think the larger impact in these places I've just discussed were places that can essentially adapt to climate change. Insurance companies can change their risk pools, individuals can pay for things, towns can move.

"The places we worry about primarily in the future are areas where there is no capacity to adapt. So if you're thinking about flooding, places I would worry about would be Bangladesh, the Ganges basin. If you're thinking about access to fresh water, I'd worry about places dependent on the Himalayas glaciers, or what we'll see as the world gets drier in the future, especially in the Middle East. So, we might switch from wars of oil to wars of water, and in fact I think we're already starting to see some of that occurring."

This scenario is something explored in depth in Gwynne Dyer's book *Climate Wars*, which predicts impending disaster when the world's freshwater supply begins to shrivel up, including drought followed by famine, a huge flux of refugees, political instability, extreme weather, and rising sea levels. In between chapters offering data to back himself up, Dyer imagines future possible scenarios: In 2036 he imagines Pakistan and India going to nuclear war after drought has dried up all the rivers (which are fed by glaciers) and starvation has afflicted their populations. This starts a war fought over dams and canals. Dyer predicts an epidemic in 2042 of different ecoterrorists, both antinuclear extremists and agents from formerly oil-rich countries destroying solar power arrays, as well as major countries playing around with geoengineering, releasing sulfates into the atmosphere to cool the planet. The plan backfires when a super volcano eruption sends ash to the atmosphere, blocking sunlight and cooling the planet too much. This leads to a decline in crop production causing millions to starve.

In an alternative vision, Dyer paints a picture of 2045, when northern Europe blockades its borders from famine-stricken countries in the Mediterranean and North Africa.

"Climate change is not itself a harbinger of massive disruption, but it basically makes everything else that could cause disruption that much worse," Ankur said. "If what's going to lead to large-scale loss of life is going to be conflagrations of terrorists fighting in the Middle East, and suddenly water security is the thing they're fighting over because of climate change, that's going to make it more worse.

"Or if you have massive famine going in areas where you have some of the fastest-growing populations like Nigeria, that's going to lead to massive political instability.

"There are questions like, do we take in refugees from small island nations? We're already having a refugee crisis. Does that tip the balance even further to suddenly all of the developed world shutting their borders, saying there's no way we're taking anymore from the

Maldives or wherever. Those are hard to predict, the geopolitical aspects of it.

Politics as Usual

"The Paris agreement that was recently agreed to [in 2015] globally says that we would like to keep climate below 2 degrees Celsius. The idea is if we keep climate change less than 2 degrees Celsius, most of the really negative impacts are not fully born on us, and the cost of doing that is not as great as dealing with the cost of the potential future," Ankur said. "What that requires is a pretty large-scale decarbonization of the economy, or a massive technological change that will allow us to reduce carbon dioxide in the atmosphere."

That seems like a good start. To tackle the problem of climate change, we need strong leadership that takes the matter seriously in implementing change. Currently, that does not seem to be the case.

President Trump campaigned on withdrawing from the Paris Agreement, and on June 1, 2017, he said that the United States would withdraw from participating in the Paris Agreement's guidelines, saying it would "undermine the economy" and put American businesses and workers "at a permanent disadvantage." The agreement will at least stay in effect until 2020.

President Trump also picked well-known climate change denier Myron Ebell to lead the transition of power at the Environmental Protection Agency. "The whole case for global warming, I believe is silly," Ebell is quoted as saying. "I believe the vast majority of scientists think it's silly and therefore I'm a little bit embarrassed that I waste my time on a silly issue."

The clear majority of scientists do not think the issue is "silly." Consensus studies show that somewhere between 90 and 100 percent of climate scientists agree that humans are responsible for climate change.

"That quote is already false when he says the majority of scientists think it's silly, I don't even know where that comes from," Ankur said. "It's a pretty bad scenario for the US. Certainly, we've been here before, where we've had administrations hostile to environmental regulation bring in individuals who, at least in their public persona, are very negative. We saw this with Reagan and his choice of James Watt, who basically just told people to put on more sunscreen to deal with the ozone hole.

"Sometimes I wonder how much they say is essentially there just to get some points—getting points with either the industries that are funding their agenda, or getting points with the voters who have been made to believe that this is not a big deal. I do think there is inertia in the system, so even the Paris Agreement takes about three years to pull away from."

Speaking of growing alternative sources of energy Ankur added, "There's so much going on in the US in terms of an energy revolution, that our emissions might drop anyway regardless of our policy directions."

Despite Trump's 2018 State of the Union address, in which he boasted his administration had "ended the war on beautiful, clean coal," Ankur believes we are slowly moving away from fossil fuels.

"We're not going to get our coal miners working again, it's just not—there's maybe some demand for coal here and there, but natural gas is so cheap and the cost of solar and wind are going way down, nuclear is starting to show up again in places."

Ankur said one of the most frustrating things about his field is the ever-changing nature of climate change criticism. "It's a shifting target because it used to be, 'Oh, it's a hoax. It doesn't occur.' Then it was like, 'Oh yes, the climate is changing but it's natural variability.' Then it's been like, 'Oh yes, the climate's changing and it's humans causing it, but it's not that big of a deal or future generations can afford to pay for it.' And now it's like, 'Yes, it's happening, it's a big deal to some people and its influencing some parts of the world.'" Ankur said.

"The scientific community . . . is made of tens of thousands of independent actors who would love to win a Nobel Prize for showing that the whole thing is not happening at all, and there's some other mechanism. We've looked at every possible hypothesis out there, and we have a 98 to 99 percent certainty among the scientific community that this is the best explanation out there.

"Yeah there's been bad actors, political actors, environmental extremists that have taken a message and turned it into something much more dire." But Ankur also pointed to the book *Merchants of Doubt*, by Naomi Oreskes and Erik M. Conway, that documents scientists who are paid to cast uncertainties on science to avoid regulations.

Trump's eventual pick for leading the EPA was Scott Pruitt. Like many of Trump's cabinet picks, he was completely Orwellian, and Trump openly said his goal was to dismantle the EPA "in almost every form." Pruitt, the former attorney general of Oklahoma, was described by CNN as a "lightning rod" candidate. It went on to report, "As the hearing got under way, protesters criticizing Pruitt for his ties to the oil industry outside the room were clearly audible. A handful of protesters were escorted out of the hearing."

As Oklahoma attorney general, Pruitt filed at least twelve lawsuits against the EPA, targeting the program's clean power plan, which was designed to reduce carbon emissions from power plants and curb methane emissions from the oil and gas industry. The fox was now in charge of the henhouse.

Senator Tom Carper of Delaware, a Democrat on the Environment and Public Works Committee, nicknamed him "Polluting Pruitt" for his close ties to the oil and energy fields.

Like Trump and his secretary of state oil baron Rex Tillerson, Pruitt had adopted the line of saying he didn't believe climate change was a hoax, but didn't give any indication it was a priority for the administration. "The ability to measure and pursue the degree, the extent of that impact, and what to do about it are subject to continuing debate and dialogue," Pruitt stated at his congressional hearing.

In July 2018, Pruitt resigned after being dogged by months of ethics controversies, including misuse of travel expenses, building a $43,000 soundproof booth in his office, getting a discount on a condo rental using lobbyist connections, and requesting motorcade sirens to get him to an upscale French restaurant quicker, among other things. Pruitt's replacement, former coal lobbyist Andrew Wheeler, was not seen as an improvement by environmentalists. Jeremy Symons, vice president for political affairs at the Environmental Defense Fund, warned that Wheeler's likely deregulatory agenda "should scare anyone who breathes."

Trump's own statements have shifted somewhat, leaving a jumble of what his actual beliefs might be. He famously tweeted that he believed climate change was a hoax perpetuated by the Chinese during his campaign. After his election, he had an odd pair of visitors photographed in the lobby of Trump Tower, paying the president-elect and his daughter Ivanka a visit: Al Gore and Leonardo DiCaprio, directors of climate change documentaries *An Inconvenient Truth* and *Before the Flood*, respectively. Trump did later say he didn't believe climate change was a hoax and that there was "some connectivity." But it was unlikely Trump was going to change his mind or care much about the issue. On December 28, 2017, he tweeted, "In the East, it could be the COLDEST New Year's Eve on record. Perhaps we could use a little bit of that good old Global Warming that our Country, but not other countries, was going to pay TRILLIONS OF DOLLARS to protect against. Bundle up!"

"The best answer I can give you is rolling a die versus a loaded die," Ankur told me when I followed up with an e-mail asking about this tweet, and the common climate denial argument that climate change can't be real if it's still cold out. "A regular die you have equal chances to get any number from 1 to 6 (and an average across all rolls of 3.5). But if I loaded that die with some weights, I might get a few more 5s and 6s and less 1s and 2s (and an average closer to 4.5). But, because of the randomness of rolling a die, you will still get a few 1s and 2s. The same goes with climate, which is the average of weather. Cold stretches happen, just less often. Warm stretches happen, but now more often. We see that, for example, today we set more than twice as many record highs as record lows in the United States. Fossil fuel emissions is putting a thumb on the scale."

Ankur also told me that both denialist claims, like the Trump administration's, and alarmist claims (like Guy McPherson's proclamations that the world will be fried within a few years) are both based on best/worst case scenarios that have a low probability of coming true.

"I have found that both stem from a similar doomsday look at the world." On whether presenting these theories was harmful, Ankur wrote to me, "In my opinion, they do tend to paralyze people from taking steps to prevent the worst effects of climate change, in the same way that debates about what to do immediately after mass shootings tend to lead to inaction on gun safety or mental health."

Geoengineering

If we don't have the leadership to curb climate change, Ankur said one possibility was to try to fix our predicament by cooling off our planet. "There's a branch called geoengineering that says, 'OK, well it's hopeless to change policy on fossil fuels. We have way more fossil fuels than we think. We're not going to run out any time in the near future, but we can muck with the climate system,'" Ankur said.

"You can imagine all sorts of dystopian novels. For example, one of the ideas is to add a whole bunch of aerosol to the stratosphere. The way you do that is fly a whole bunch of planes and detonate nuclear bombs that send particles floating around the stratosphere blocking sunlight.

"In more realistic scenarios, . . . if we can reduce emissions by 2040 to 2050 at a rate that gets us back to something like the 1980s, that would actually work and keep climate change from harming human societies and most of the ecosystems we care about in the next hundred years. That's where the focus is.

"Every year that we wait seems like a year it becomes less hopeful, so there's a huge community that focuses on how you adapt to this future warmer climate. So there's a mitigation community that says global agreements are needed, and a whole group of communities within that focused on fossil-free energy developments. There's a lot of things on the horizon. I'm relatively optimistic. We're seeing even individual states without federal coordination reducing admissions. Places like California that are twice as efficient as the rest of the country on energy because of regulations they put into place decades ago. There's a lot of little stories. Just on the news today was India opening the world's largest solar power plant, produces power for a couple hundred thousand homes. The payback time based on what it cost to build is seven years. That's not bad. Nuclear power takes decades."

Ankur, unlike Guy McPherson, is not hope free. He believes the climate change problem can be dealt with. "I tend to be optimistic because I have children. I want to see them prosper and do well. I see a lot of exciting research developments going into place. I think it's very hard to predict humans and their ingenuity, and I think even in the twentieth century, where we suffered two major world wars, large-scale famine, and strife in parts of the world, we still managed to significantly reduce poverty, dealt with major environmental treaties like the ozone hole and others. Climate change is bigger, for sure, but I think if we get our act together in the next two decades, we might be able to deal with it. If we don't, yes, I think all of the efforts will have to go into adaptation for the vulnerable population."

10

BUGGING OUT

When the End happens, the first thing you'll need is a good bug-out plan, so you can escape society as it descends into madness. The most common and important prepper item you'll find is the bug-out bag, usually a backpack filled with survival gear that can be grabbed at a moment's notice. Building the perfect bug-out bag is a prepper art form.

To find out more about bugging out, I enrolled myself and my survival partner Kate into a Realistic Bug-Out Planning workshop, held in a conference room in the AmericInn in Elkhorn, Wisconsin. The class was taught by survivalist prepper Jim Cobb of Disaster Prep Consultants.

As a child, Jim would stockpile supplies (canned goods, his teddy bear, blankets, and pillows) and bug out to his basement when he would hear there was a tornado warning in the area. "I just thought it would be best to be prepared for life's little curveballs, so to speak," Jim told me.

In fifth grade he bought his own copy of *Life After Doomsday*, a book by Bruce Clayton published in 1980 that details how to survive in a postapocalyptic world. He was also taken with the 1977 book *Empty World* by John Christopher. "It was about a global pandemic that wipes out most of society," Jim explained, adding that he related to the teen protagonist who figures out how to survive in the postapocalypse.

Jim now lives in the upper Midwest with his wife and three children, teaches workshops, and has penned nine prepper guides like

Prepper's Home Defense and *Prepper's Long-Term Survival Guide* and his next is a sequel to the latter title. He runs a website, SurvivalWeekly .com, where he blogs about survival skills and links to his podcast, "Library at the End of the World," where he discusses postapocalyptic fiction in film and books, often interviewing the authors about their works.

"The media tends to portray us as fringe whackjobs, tinfoil beanie brigade type stuff—and make no mistake, there is, unfortunately, a good percentage of the prepper world that falls into those categories," Jim told me. "But the vast majority of us are just wanting to make sure that ourselves and our family and friends are going to be minimally impacted by any sort of emergency or disaster. If you look at situations like Hurricane Katrina or Superstorm Sandy, we don't want to be those people stuck in the Superdome, we want to be at home fending for ourselves with the supplies we have."

"It's completely self-serving," Jim told me about his role as a survival instructor. "Everyone who is prepared is one less person knocking on my door asking for a handout or help. Beyond that, it's just something I've been pulled to do, something I've been drawn to, the last few years in particular. I really enjoy teaching and I've always been a writer."

I knew we were near the right part of the hotel when we pulled up and spotted a jeep sporting the "Don't tread on me" Gadsden flag. Inside we found the usual prepper suspects including an elderly guy wearing a cowboy hat with a racoon tail hanging off of it. The class costs fifteen dollars (or two for twenty-five dollars).

"Buggin out is no one's idea of a rockin' good time," Jim told us. "Bugging out in almost every scenario is your absolute last option. Except for emergency situations, like a wildfire approaching or a hurricane. Bugging out, we're not talking about temporary evacuations, we're talking about packing your crap and heading for the hills."

Jim said that there were few situations that would be improved by grabbing your bag and heading for the forest. "One would be a pandemic situation where your goal is to avoid human contact cause that's where the threat is," Jim said. "The further you are from other people, the better off you'll be."

He breaks down the most important things to have in place for the art of bugging out and what your bug-out bag should be stocked with. He also reviews common bug-out bag mistakes, things like overpacking your bag, buying an uncomfortably fitting bag, or investing in cheaply made gear.

Some of the bug-out bag supplies, like a first aid kit, are obvious. Others aren't. Jim suggests packing a Jumpdrive with family photos and scans of important documents. It's a compact way to have a vital-info file folder and pictures of your family with you, in case the originals are lost in a catastrophe.

After my Escape the Woods weekend in Ohio, I spoke to Creek Stewart again on the phone to talk about his book, *Build the Perfect Bug-Out Bag: Your 72-Hour Disaster Survival Kit*. He told me that creating a bug-out bag was a good entry point for those interested in preparedness and survival.

"I think that's the easiest thing to start with, that people can wrap their head around," Creek told me. "Start with a bug-out bag that you can grab in case you have to evacuate in a hurry that has enough supplies to keep you alive for three days and has your needs—fire, water, tools, first aid, hygiene, important information. It's not going to break the bank, you can do it in a month or less, and you can experience a variety of survival skills while you put it together," he explained.

"I definitely have a plan that is variable in stages," Creek told me of his bug-out plan. He said he's more concerned about natural disasters than the various other doomsday theories.

Combining information gleamed from Jim's class, Creek's book *Build the Perfect Bug-Out Bag*, and other sources like an article in *Survivalist* magazine by Mark Bunch titled "Emergency Checklist," as well as a Zombie Squad pamphlet titled *How to Prepare Your Bug-Out Bag*, I put together a shopping list for common items to get your bug-out bag started:

Headlamp flashlight
Emergency blanket
Garbage bag

Socks and other extra clothes
Boonie-style jungle hat
Emergency rain poncho
Gloves
Water bottle
Water filter
MREs, power bars, trail mix, beef jerky
Fold-up utensils
Mylar blanket
Tarp
Hammock
Sleeping bag
Ferro rod
Cigarette lighter
Strike-anywhere matches in a waterproof container
PET balls (petroleum jelly mixed with dryer lint to use as
     tinder)
First aid kit
Hand sanitizer
Insect repellent
Travel toothpaste
Toilet paper
Knife
Paracord
Notepad and pen
Sunglasses
Sewing kit

Bug-Out Plans

"One of the things I stress in my classes is that everyone's plan is different because everyone comes to the table with different scenarios," Jim Cobb explained to me. "I have multiple children, multiple animals, that all comes into play with my plans. Somebody that's just a couple or one child is going to have a totally different plan. You have to look at the big picture."

With your bug-out bag slung over your shoulder, your next step is to have a bug-out plan, preferably more than one, that will lead to your bug-out location. You will hopefully have a bug-out vehicle to get you there, but you should have a plan to be on foot too.

Jim gave several suggestions about your possible route to your bug-out location. One is choosing a location you can reach within a tank of gas and planning multiple routes in case you run into road-blocks. He suggests you practice your routes so you are intimately familiar with them, and hiding caches made of PVC pipe along the route that can be filled with useful emergency supplies.

———

Many preppers practice bugging out, setting up exercises like a fire drill, sometimes timed to see how quickly the family can grab their bug-out bags and evacuate the house. When I was at Zombie Con, Cliff (from Chicagoland Chapter 020) told me about his group's annual mock bug-out hike. The chapter does two annual campouts in April and October, which are "pretty open and welcoming" at an actual campground, but in summer they do their "more hardcore trip," which is a mock bug-out hike.

"It's a weekend hiking trip, where you hike eighteen miles over the course of the weekend, broken up into segments—four and a half miles the first day, nine miles the second day, four and a half miles the third day, through Kettle Moraine State Forest in Wisconsin on the Ice Age Trail," Cliff explained. "The mock bug-outs are more arduous, intentionally. Those are the ones where you live out of your pack for the weekend. You filter water along the way and really are putting you and your gear to the test. We've done the route enough that we have a safety vehicle paralleling the route and keeping in radio contact, so if anything comes up or if someone needs to drop out for whatever reason, they can do that. There's cutout points along the route. We encourage people to push yourself but not kill yourself."

Bugging Out from Corporate America

"I hated my job. I hated my job as soon as I graduated," Jeurgen told me over the phone. He was telling me about his former job as an engineer for the oil industry. "I didn't do it because I had a love for it, I did it 'cause I made a shitload of money. I sold my soul to the highest bidder.

"What did I do? I was a corporate whore. It was very stressful, halfway through my career—my career was twelve years—I was down in Atlanta and I got really, really sick. I started developing all these ulcers, I couldn't eat for almost a week, lost lots and lots of weight. Went to a doctor and tried everything. He ran all these tests. He said, 'I can run some more, but I can't find anything.'

"So he started asking me some questions. 'How's everything going in your family life? Your romantic life? Your job? And I was like, 'I hate my fucking job,'" Jeurgen laughed.

"And he said, 'Well, you might want to work on that.'"

To add to Jeurgen's worry, he said that "a lot of my family members, especially the males, have passed away early because of one thing or another." His father and grandfather both died in their fifties.

So Jeurgen decided to mostly retire at age thirty-four. He walked away from a six-figure salary in corporate America in 2014 to go live on a homestead in the mountains of Virginia. He said a big appeal of bugging out from corporate America is seeing what he can build for himself instead of big oil companies.

"There was a group of us inside of our companies—I worked for two different companies—and they pretty much called us 'firefighters,'" Jeurgen said. "They would drop us in a problem project to get it up and running and then leave. So we never really saw anything to the finish and it was always a shitstorm. Here if I have a project to build a garage, I can see it get done and that garage will be here the next five, ten, twenty-five years. I'm still busting my ass, but I get to see the results. My to-do list is still nine-hundred-some items, and it'll always be nine-hundred-some items whether I'm in corporate America or on the homestead."

Jeurgen said he was part of a mind-set of "modern homesteaders who rely on society while it's still around, but if anything happens, we have the know-how and the resources that we could weather some storms."

His homestead is located on ten acres of land inside a five-hundred-acre private community made mostly of people with an interest in prepping or homesteading.

"There's about twelve of us that are full-time residents and another twelve that are weekenders," Jeurgen said. "What I like about it is I don't have to do everything. We have three families inside the community that have chickens, so that gave me a lot of freedom to not have to worry about getting livestock right off the bat. I got a sawmill and bees on the property—things our community didn't have already.

"I liked the community feel and aspect to it, the permanent residents predominately homesteaders with similar goals, with those here on the weekend being preppers. We are a homeowners' association, but not in the way like, 'Oh, your blinds have to be purple or your roof this color or whatnot.' Our fee goes mostly to putting gravel on the roads and plowing the roads. But having the community kind of creates a small town on the mountain. We barter with each other. One of the owners has twenty-some apple trees on his property, and he's not always around. So he's like, 'When I'm done picking, feel free to pick all the apples you want.' So we pick hundreds of gallons-worth of apples; we make apple butters, apple sauces, ciders, hard ciders. We all have different equipment to make that. I didn't realize how cool it was going to be to have good neighbors. That's one of the things I really enjoy. Hopefully by the end of the season we'll have six or ten hives going on," he added.

Time has a different pace out there. Jeurgen told me a story of being stuck on his mountain after he had some car problems. "A little while ago my Jeep took an unmanned journey down the mountain. The emergency brake popped and it ran down the mountain about thirty miles an hour into a tree with the engine running. We were shuffling cars around in my driveway," Jeurgen said. "I spent the next month fixing the Jeep. The benefit of having free time and not having to show up to work on Monday, it didn't affect me much. The garden was in full bounty at that time so I always had something to eat, it was interesting to be stuck in a location because of an emergency for three weeks and not be crawling out of my skin. Let's say I fell off a ladder and broke my leg and wasn't able to work six months or a year—that's when it helps to have that pantry full of reserves."

Juergen recalled the contrast with his working days. "Canadian oil sands, my first assignment, was four months on, ten days off. So I would be at work, living at camp. We were two and a half hours from the closest town and that town was a boomtown—casinos, bars, strip clubs, nothing fancy. You worked every single day, twelve-hour days. If you worked Sundays it was a half day, that was your day off.

"So much of my life was work. I didn't have to cook food, wash dishes. If I didn't want to do my laundry, I didn't have to. I would throw ten dollars to the cleaning lady and she'd do it. Coming out of that system and being so institutionalized, almost like a military individual where your focus is one specific task. That first year was psychologically challenging, because work wasn't in that equation anymore, and my brain kept wanting to identify back into that system.

"At the farm it could be kind of boring. I mean, my girlfriend comes down every other weekend. Yeah, I got my neighbors if I need their help, but predominantly you're by yourself. If you're getting yourself up at 4 or 5 AM, you are getting yourself up, there is no outside influence. That was really challenging. Most of that, it was like a glass of muddy water settling. The more the glass sits, the more the dirt settles to the bottom. So after the first year, most of the Earth has settled."

Jeurgen said preppers and homesteaders are similar but different and identifies as a homesteader. "I think if you looked at our pantries, they would look similar—lots of canned stuff. But preppers go to Costco to buy cans of tomatoes, where I grow the tomatoes, and can the tomatoes. So similar results, different approaches."

I asked him what he believed a likely TEOTWAWKI scenario looked like. "If you look at the statistics, I'd say a depression or long-term repression," Jeurgen replied. "I'm thirty-six right now, if I do live past my fifties any number of things might happen. If I have a full pantry, I won't experience as bad as some of my friends that live in the city that go out to eat every night. That was a big concern of mine."

You can watch some of Jeurgen's homesteading experiences on his YouTube channel, where he styles himself the "Badass Home-steader," and shares prep tips and updates on his projects like bee-keeping, planting garlic, and other projects around the farm. "It's to get news and information out there about trying to live a more regenerative and sustainable lifestyle," Jeurgen told me. It was not always an easy task. He documents how he was stung badly by a swarm of angry bees and scratched dangerously close to his eye by the farm cat.

Some of his videos show what he describes as a "Simulated Emergency Test" in which he spent a three-day long bug-out voy-age traveling through the woods to test his limits and the gear in his bug-out bag, including his emergency radio, fire starters, and his Lifestraw water filter, which you can see him demonstrate in a video titled "Simulated Emergency Test—Lifestraw—Drank My Own Piss."

Doomer Fatigue

If you're wondering if all this TEOTWAWKI prepping and worrying about the End can take a toll on you, the answer is absolutely yes. Tess Pennington, author of a guide called *The Prepper's Blueprint* and a three-hundred-recipe *Prepper's Cookbook*, has even coined a term for it: *doomer fatigue*. "I remember just wanting to sit on the couch and do nothing. My articles even reflected a very negative line of thinking and a bleak mental outlook. I was in a state of shock and allowed myself to go to the 'dark side.' Thinking that the world will end will do that to you."

While I was visiting Sheboygan, I was curious if James and Doug had ever experienced doomer fatigue, so I asked them about it while we traveled between their houses looking at preps. "If it starts to become an extremely violent thing, a state or national thing, then we're gone," Doug told me firmly. His fellow group member James nodded in agreement. "We've built all our things and practiced loading up. We will do it quickly and we will leave. We know a place we are going. There will be a few of us and we'll go from there. You can prep and worry, worry, worry. God doesn't want us to worry about things," Doug told me, then paraphrased Proverbs 22:3. "A wise man foresees trouble and hides, but a fool passes by and is destroyed."

"It happens to me sometimes, where you're constantly thinking about it," James admitted. "If it's always on your mind, it wears on you. So sometimes you got to let it go 'cause . . ."

"You can't control everything," Doug added.

"You can't control it, and you got to realize there's nothing you can do," James said.

But some people don't escape from doomer fatigue.

———

Tara looked at her husband, we'll call him Bob, who had taken some pain medication for his back, then lain down to take a nap. There were a million small thoughts in Tara's head and one huge one: now or never. It was a rare opportunity—for one, her husband was unarmed. They had flown to the East Coast from the Midwest and Bob had left his arsenal of weapons behind. Second, she had her bank card and cash, something Bob usually had on him and didn't allow her to touch. She waited until he started snoring, then quietly retrieved their son's birth certificate and her wallet. They were staying at Tara's grandmother's house; Tara pulled her aside and told her that she was going to the police.

At the police station, Tara outlined her husband's descent into deep paranoia—how he had made the family camp outside in a tent in the winter in the Midwest, so they could be better prepared for when the government came to herd masses of the population into FEMA camps. There was the fact that he didn't want their son to receive medical treatment for his autism, because he believed that the medical field had caused him to be autistic in the first place.

Bob became obsessed with conspiracy theory superstar Alex Jones of InfoWars. But the worst thing Bob did, Tara said, is hit their son.

Police picked up Bob, and at 9 PM that night they got a judge on the phone to issue a restraining order and Tara and her son were put into a safe house.

I first messaged Tara after perusing ads on a forum and site where preppers can post classified ad–style messages about land for sale, local meet-up groups and expos, and people trying to connect into a local network. I found an ad from Tara that was already a year old, but it caught my interest as it wasn't too far from me and she described wanting to start a "compound." That word frightened me a bit, but her ad was eloquently written and interesting. I thought I would try to e-mail and see how the compound was shaping up. But I got a surprising and disturbing reply.

Tara told me she first met Bob when she was still a teenager, working at a White Castle. "I was barely nineteen, naive and giddy with the taste of freedom I'd acquired during the year since I'd moved out of my childhood home. I remember loving how doting and attentive he was, how protectful and watchful."

They got married. Bob started to show an interest in prepping and Tara liked the idea at first. She had been a big fan of Laura Ingalls Wilder's Little House series, and the idea of living off the land, gardening, maybe having a pet goat, learning new skills, and bartering for goods instead of paying cash was an appealing fantasy.

"Can I make cheese? What a fun thing to learn!" Tara told me in an e-mail. "Ooh, how to turn a few pieces of wood, a bit of yarn, and an old window into a miniature greenhouse to help plants sprout . . . that's so cool, omg!"

But while Tara was entertaining her *Little House on the Prairie* fantasy, Bob was having a much darker vision: escaping the New World Order. They had major conflicts over their autistic son. "My husband went online and didn't emerge for a long time, but when he did it was all anti-vaccine and doctors are in league with the government and big pharmacy is poisoning our children, and I wanted to scream because I had done my homework, and I knew he was wrong.

"We were not allowed to say the word *autism* in our home. I don't know how the jump happened from vaccines cause autism, doctors in league with the government, big pharmacy is evil, to the government is going to round us all up and take us away to FEMA camps, but I blame a lot of it on Alex Jones and the InfoWars website. I can pick that man's voice out from across a house, and it's like nails on a chalkboard for me. He spews ignorance and fearmongering and my husband soaked it up like a sponge, absorbing every word and vomiting it back out whenever he saw an opening in a conversation."

They got rid of many of their possessions and moved from their home into an RV. Bob wanted to move to some property in Alaska, but after the land deal fell through he grew angrier and paranoid. "His eyes got wild when he talked about the government and FEMA camps and fighting to the death if they tried to take us. It was terrifying," Tara said.

Bob decided that to sharpen their survival skills, the family should move into a military tent on land Bob's father owned. "If there's one thing I would advise against, it's living in a tent in the middle of winter. It's a shitty idea. In fact, it's the shittiest idea in the world, trust me on that."

On a freezing night, their son, then five, began coughing, and Tara, fearing for his health, decided to defy Bob and took a spare key to bring her son to Bob's father-in-law's house to sleep indoors. After this move, Bob told her she was weak. Exhausted, she thought he might be right. "I promised to do better." But things got worse.

"Most days I was struggling to put food in our son's mouth, but my husband was buying guns and MREs and first aid supplies, filling boxes and plastic storage bins and bug-out bags with all sorts of things we just did not have money for." Most alarming was his growing collection of weapons, "guns and swords and knives, always within reach." One day Bob grabbed Tara and pressed the cold, sharp edge of a utility knife on her throat, near her jaw. He swore that if she ever tried to leave with their son, he'd kill her.

Tara describes this three-year period as an "ever-growing spiral of insanity." There were days she imagined Bob murdering her, and the thought was "a relief." But then their son would be alone with him, and that thought frightened her more than anything.

After being released from jail, Bob was escorted to pick up his possessions, then to the airport where he was ordered to return to Wisconsin. Tara woke up many nights in terror. "It didn't matter how far away he was, I was still scared. I think, in a lot of ways, I'll always be scared." Despite all the terrifying emotions, Tara marks the day she left as one of the best days of her life—it's the day she escaped.

Tara no longer considers herself a prepper. "I don't think all preppers are paranoid or crazy, like my husband. I refuse to stereotype an entire group of people just because I had a bad experience. But I do fear for those who are like I was—trapped, terrified, miserable. I worry about those who are convinced they are too weak to leave and too weak to stay and spend every day just fighting to stay alive. It's an intense lifestyle and requires a lot of sacrifice and a lot of hard work and dedication and no one, no one, especially a child, should ever be forced into it. It has to be a choice.

After a series of e-mails, Tara stopped replying to me, which is why the names have been changed and locations left vague. I don't have evidence to collaborate the story Tara told, but I've heard similar stories circulated. Based on my interactions, I agree that all preppers are not mired in paranoia or craziness. Some are people who don't want to suffer from lack of supplies in an emergency. But every social group like this has individuals who have descended into the deep end, in this case people with a bad case of doomer fatigue.

11

WASTELANDERS

It's the end of the world as we know it / And I feel fine.

—R.E.M.

"**D**id you seriously take a taxi here?" a volunteer asked me. It had been quite a journey—I had flown from Mitchell International Airport in Milwaukee to LAX in Los Angeles, took a bus from the airport to Union Station, took a train from there to Glendale, and a bus from there to California City. From there I called a taxi, who drove me six miles down a small highway, and then another six miles down a bumpy dirt road into the Mojave Desert (I tipped him extra for a car wash). Finally, we pulled up to the check-in point for an event called Wasteland Weekend.

"I had to be here!" I replied, lifting my giant hiking backpack out of the trunk of the cab. Inside it had everything I needed . . . I hoped. It was dark, but in the distance I could see lights and hear loud metal music. I signed a waiver with an emergency contact; a volunteer explained this was useful information. One year at Wasteland he accidentally lit his kilt on fire and had to be taken to the hospital. "But I'm back, I wouldn't miss it for anything!" he exclaimed.

The volunteers pointed me in the right direction, and I began walking past rows of parked cars and RVs, and eventually tents, through the sand toward Wasteland. A woman stumbled up to me as I struggled to push through the sand with my giant hiker's backpack.

"Hey, do you know where Vice Street is?" she asked.

"No, sorry, just got here," I said.

Wasteland Weekend is a place where people can party like the apocalypse has already happened. It's like a Burning Man of the damned or a Mad Max–themed Ren Faire. People look forward to the event all year and spend a lot of time, money, and ingenuity in making costumes and props, custom cars (and other vehicles), and tent structures with a gritty postapocalyptic theme.

There isn't a dress code, but if you show up to this thing dressed like Joe Schmoe, you are going to look like an idiot, so I contacted my friends who run a crafting business called Stinky Goblin Emporium as my Wasteland tailors. I visited Heather and Joe at their home studio and they dug through bins of army surplus gear, leather scraps, punk rock bracelets, pads and straps, and pieced together an apocalypse-cowboy-style outfit. The Stinky Goblins even made me a leather-bound notepad I could attach to my belt with a clip so I could take notes on the fly. They sliced into the leather cover the scrawled words "Observations of a Wasteland Madman."

After stumbling in the dark (I had forgotten my printout of the Wasteland layout, and couldn't connect with my smartphone), I found an empty-looking spot. A guy with a van was parked nearby. I asked if he minded if I camped near him. "Naw man, I don't give a shit."

I wouldn't even know where I was until I was oriented in the morning, but I had chosen a spot near the cross streets of Seven Sisters Boulevard and Buzzard Lane. Wasteland is set up in a giant grid, with areas with different names like Buzzard Patch, Old Town, the Ant Hill, and Rolling Thunder, divided by streets like Vice Street and Damnation Alley. Main Street and Fury Road are Wasteland's two main drags. My tent was in the corner of a small patch called Sanctuary. I set up my tent and put on my Wasteland costume.

California City

Isolated in the desert, the nearest city to Wasteland is California City, the state's third-largest city by area—a little over 203 square miles—but it only boasts a population of fourteen thousand. Mile after mile of dirt streets are named and gridded out, but there is nothing there—no homes, no electrical grid, nothing but an empty frame of a city that never happened. It was developed in the late 1950s with the unrealistic vision that California's population boom would make the land into a grand city to rival Los Angeles and San Diego. But while L.A. has Hollywood glitz and San Diego has beautiful beaches, California City has nothing going for it but lots of sand, tumbleweeds, and drought. The population started with about three hundred people and jumped to about seven thousand in the 1970s. My taxi driver told me people like him have moved to the desert here mostly because it's significantly cheaper than the rest of California. If he needs some big-city action, he makes the two-hour commute into L.A., or crosses the border to Las Vegas, about three and a half hours away.

The abandoned city that never was is a good backdrop for the Wasteland.

Main Stage Area

After setting up my tent in the dark and unloading my gear, I shuffled through the sand toward the lights and music into a Pleasure Island of apocalypse partiers. The main entertainment area features four main sections spread along the border of the festival. First there's a DJ booth set up next to a shipwreck. It's an actual ship that they were somehow able to haul out to the desert, and they've named it the Exxon Valdez. It's split in half and has platforms attached to it so people can gyrate and show off their bodies while DJs spin music on a smaller speedboat next to it. A firepit burns (the dance floor area is known as the Pit) and there's a suspended hoop nearby for aerial performances.

Next is the battle cage, which is a chain-link fence set up with a door that leads into a staging area behind it. The battle cage hosts gladiator fights nightly, and a daytime homemade robot fight. The main stage has musical performances each night. I was expecting nothing but blistering metal music for four days, but in addition to metal and punk there were DJs and a band with a traditional Irish sound, and other activities like a drag show and a Wasteland fashion show.

One of the most popular activities people signed up for was battling in the Thunderdome. After getting a crash course in fighting safely, people had the opportunity to be hoisted in a swing launched at their opponent. The two fighters would collide in the air, bashing each other with giant foam boffers, trying to knock each other out of their seats.

Wasteland Communication Corps

"I like helping make people's names," one of Wasteland's many colorful characters, Captain Fancypants, told me. "If they tell me their name is Bob, I'll say no, the hell it is! You are going to be Skullcrusher." Most Wastelanders, as the population of the event is known, have a Wasteland alias they adopt, so I altered my ego to Krulos the Terrible.

Krulos the Terrible takes a selfie in the Wasteland. *Tea Krulos*

Captain Fancypants had a role at Wasteland. He called himself "your official tour guide. I show folks the what's what, the who's who, and the where the fuck am I's in this brand spanking new Wasteland location. So if you're looking for something I can generally make something up about how to find it."

True to his name, Captain Fancypants had a sort of steampunk suit and overcoat and a goatee that made him look like a circus ringmaster. Being a guide appealed to him because "being a rabid egomaniac, I love the attention. Plus, some of the shops give me free stuff for bringing folks in."

He's been coming since 2012 to this "beautiful mecca, a gorgeous city of people that come out to play with three thousand of our closest friends. I don't have hard facts and figures, facts and figures don't interest me, I can barely read, but it feels like three thousand, tastes like three thousand."

After waking up I was eager to check out Wasteland in the daylight. I walked from the camp area through the giant gate that spelled out the word WASTELAND above it. Guards stood on either side of the gate keeping a silent, motionless watch, dressed as postapocalyptic warriors. The wall was made of sheets of corrugated metal and sheets of wood. Part of the gate wall was a beat-up cattle trailer with the back end of a car welded to it. Standing on top were a posse of War Boys. These are a clan of warriors adorned in outfits inspired by the 2015 film *Mad Max: Fury Road*, a major recent aesthetic influence on Wasteland Weekend. Covered in white body paint, gangs of War Boys were spotted throughout the fest.

My first stop through the gates was the Wasteland Communication Corps to meet my new editor. I found the building and stuck my head through a doorless entryway to find a group of Wastelanders sitting around a room with random chairs, a beat-up couch, and a minivan seat. A water fountain made from an oil barrel and a hubcap burbling precious water was the room's centerpiece.

"Is Deadline here?" I asked the group and was directed to a smaller back room separated with a beaded curtain. There I found Deadline, wearing dress pants and dress shirt, suspenders, and a

snazzy bow tie made from old typewriter parts. Deadline was the
editor of a daily newsletter called the *Wastelander*, produced and
printed right at the event. The paper reported on "current events,
daily happenings, tribe lore—whatever's cooking we try to keep an
ear on it, make sure everyone knows about all the fun that's going
on," Deadline explained.

A ragtag group of reporters handwrote reports and handed them
over to Deadline, who typed them up, assembled a double-sided
11 × 17 newsletter, and then printed editions on a parchment-colored
paper that slowly wheezed out of an old computer printer that fit-
tingly was found in a junk store. The *Wastelander* started as a quarterly
magazine in 2016 and this was the first year Deadline was producing
it as a daily. I had communicated with the *Wastelander* and said I'd be
up to take assignments as a stringer.

After I showed up in the office, Deadline gave me a rundown of
the Wasteland media group. "Wasteland Communication Corporation, started as a ham radio club, now a 501(c)(3) registered nonprofit organization, our mission is to support and spread knowledge
about amateur radio operation," Deadline explained. "We also run a
newspaper here at Wasteland, we also publish a quarterly edition of
the *Wastelander* as a magazine and the Wasteland Radio FM station
everyone gets to listen to at 88.3."

The shack-like buildings of Wasteland Communication Corps
included the newspaper office, the ham radio station, the radio tower
assembled in the desert every year that towered over the buildings,
and a small post office. People could actually buy and mail postcards
and send letters into outgoing mail. They also sold editions of the
Wastelander for fifty cents.

I asked Deadline to talk about our environment in general. "I
would describe Wasteland as an opportunity to kind of reinvent yourself to explore your potential. Out there in the real world, we're all
practically nobody. With billions of people on the planet it's impossible to feel anything but useless and insignificant, but in here you can
be anyone you want to be." I asked him why he thought the postapocalyptic theme in particular had resonated with all these people.

A Wastelander with the burning RV in the distance. *Courtesy of Cormac Kehoe*

"Personally, I think it's cause the world today is so fucked up. So completely, hopelessly lost and up its own ass I wouldn't mind if it ended tomorrow. I might survive, I might not, but I would consider it an improvement."

Deadline was in charge of processing incoming news going on around Wasteland, which was surprisingly plentiful. There were at least two weddings over the weekend, and on the first day an RV accidentally erupted into flames. Wastelanders passed the hat and put together emergency funds for the couple that lost their RV.

Deadline was an easygoing editor—he said I should write about whatever I was interested in. When I pressed him for an assignment, he said I should report on the evening's gladiator fights. "In the battle cage tonight at sundown, full contact fights. It's a basic sporting event story if you wouldn't mind attending and just give us the rundown, who beat who," Deadline instructed.

Exiting the Wasteland Communication Corps, I noticed the radio tower and remembered that in one of my utility belt ammo pouches I'd brought along a small portable AM/FM radio and earbuds, and so for the next couple hours I wandered around, listening to Wasteland

Radio and soaking in the sights of the apocalypse. "Keep it here on the dial . . . might as well, there's nothing else on," a station break on the radio announced.

I walked by Command Center, where volunteers were assembled. It was made of a porched-in area behind the giant cattle car where the War Boys stood guard.

Later, I approached the help desk, which was a truck tire in the middle of a fence with a hotel desk bell on it. I rang the bell and a Wastelander appeared on the other side of the tire. I asked if he knew where a certain camp was, and he pointed out something on a copy of a map of Wasteland. I asked if I could have a copy of the map.

He replied, "What do you have to barter with? Any caps?"

"What?" I responded. I didn't have a grasp of the currency of Wasteland yet—special coded bottle caps. These were traded and offered for services. (I even got paid for freelancing for the *Wastelander* in bottle caps, which is not the lowest pay I've received as a freelancer.) Many tribes of camps and Wasteland establishments had their own special bottle caps printed with their logos, which were traded and collected.

As I continued my tour of the camp, "We'll Meet Again" by Vera Lynn was playing on Wasteland Radio. The station played a good mix of classic World War II and Cold War–era songs about loneliness, novelty songs about the atomic age, vintage radio commercial ads, and more modern rock songs.

Next to Command Center was a salon section called the Body Shop where people could get their hair done with a list of options—a mohawk, messy feral look, and shaved head. I watched as an assembly line of War Boys got heads shaved and slathered in white body makeup while other makeup artists added detail.

"Just a Gigolo / I Ain't Got Nobody" crooned by Louis Prima filled my ears as I continued to walk under the hot desert sun. By late morning, Main Street and Fury Road were filled with Wastelanders with a wide range of styles. Some were dressed as Mad Max characters, and there were desert nomads and raiders, doomsday militias, cowboys from hell, Viking-influenced costumes, steampunks,

A Wastelander cruising around on his mechanical horse. *Tea Krulos*

postapocalyptic samurai, desert witches and warlocks, eccentric cult members, and even a league of Roman centurions, representatives of a camp called Legio X. Many people were smartly shielding themselves from the hot sun with umbrellas, often modified to fit their costumes—spray-painted, adorned with junk, ripped and restitched for apocalyptic effect.

Wasteland is not a place for prudes; some costumes show off a lot of flesh. I spotted one woman riding an ATV wearing nothing but an army helmet, boots, and a leather strap covering only a small party of her belly.

Vehicles slowly roll by in an endless parade, reworked to look as punk as possible. There's everything from flatbed army trucks loaded with Wastelanders enjoying a ride through the grounds, to old VW bugs covered in spikes, motorcycles, Jeeps, go-karts, and creative takes. I saw a man in a sombrero driving a motorized coffin, and a full-size

mechanical horse that moved its legs as its wheels turned while a
Wastelander cowboy in the saddle admired the view before him.

Camps

The real heart of the Wasteland experience are the various camps of
"tribes." These stretched around all the grounds and varied in size
and scope. The camps all had names that reflected their environment, like Skulduggers, Dukes of the Nuke, Dead Crows, Wasteland
Wolves, Guttersnipes, and Tooth n' Nail. Camps weren't simply an
array of tents. Large common space areas were often big tent structures made of shredded cloth or miniature geodesic domes; these
were surrounded by vehicles and tents and the area was festooned
with junk, skulls, tribe flags, and other decorations.

One day, my canteen was empty, I was parched in the desert sun,
and I happened to run across a camp called Rain Dogs, who had a
sign indicating that they had free water. I stopped in their army tent
and they kindly told me to fill up my canteen. I used the opportunity
to interview them in the shade.

There were four Rain Dogs and a friend visiting them who was
a prospect for Skulduggers. Much like a motorcycle gang, prospects
have to show their worth before being accepted into the tribe. Rain
Dogs had four members from the San Luis Obispo area of California
(and one from Las Vegas), but planned on having new prospects next
year, to make the tribe eight or nine strong.

One of the members, Jargon, said the group found out about
the event three years ago and got tickets. They found they were ill-
prepared, not bringing enough water for the event. One member got
ill and almost suffered heatstroke. "We're primarily a hydration tribe.
After coming out here our first year, seeing how many people need
water all the time, we just bring tons of extra water and make sure
people have it to drink. If you need shade, come on in," Jargon said.

The Rain Dogs told me that the event appealed to them because
they grew up with pop culture like the Mad Max movies. "I think all
of us dream about society collapsing," Jargon said. "I'm not saying I
want the world to collapse on itself . . ."

"But you've thought of it," the prospect friend chimed in.

"We keep coming back 'cause people are just amazing, every camp you go to is full of awesome people," Jargon said. "Everyone is weird here, so no one judges other people's weirdness."

Walking around the camps, I found people to be overwhelmingly friendly, respectful, and willing to share. With that large of a crowd, there were bound to be troublemakers and there were a couple of reports of theft at this year's event, as well as people who ended up in the medic's tent (easily located with a large neon Red Cross–style sign) for abusing drugs and alcohol. I heard a report of a man confronted by security because he was high on something and enraged that people were sleeping during the early dawn hours instead of partying with him.

Many of the camps have their own traditions or their own events, some open to other Wastelanders. I saw one camp that had made their own giant snakes and ladders board game, painted on a sheet of wood with Barbie dolls as playing pieces. Another camp had a miniature "Thumberdome" that combatants stuck their hands in to play thumb war. One camp set up an outdoor cooling station where passersby could handpump a shower sprayer to get a relieving sprinkle of water. Some camps offered special drinks, contests, and social mixers, and I heard of one camp that hosted their own dildo racing event. One of the biggest appeals of your tribe is that you get to walk around and represent as you check out Wasteland's wide range of entertainment.

Jugger Matches

One of the Wasteland spectacles is watching a Wasteland version of a sport called Jugger. Jugger evolved from a 1989 film called *The Salute of the Jugger*, with leagues popping up in Germany and Australia mimicking the sport portrayed in the movie. The sport now has a following around the world, including several leagues in the United States. The concept is kind of like playing football, but your team is armed for hand-to-hand combat.

Game play starts with two "qwiks" who attempt to be the first to grab a dog skull in the middle of the playing field. Whoever gets it falls back behind their line of defense—a group of enforcers armed with foam boffer weapons, including swords, chained weapons, and the double ended "Q-tip." The two teams collide to whomp each other with weapons while the qwik tries to make their way through the carnage to place the dogskull on a post on top of a traffic cone to score. I saw a nighttime and an afternoon match between the teams.

The Juggers of the Wasteland were divided into three teams: Red Team (a.k.a. Red City), Blue Team (also known as Feral Folk), and Gold Team (the Army of Los Angeles).

Like most sports events, there was a halftime show. The Molotov Mollies provided burlesque performances, shedding skull masks and combat gear, gyrating in the dust.

Wasteland added a dramatic backdrop for the sport, with Juggers being shoved and beaten to the desert ground in a cloud of dust while a quartet called the Badlands Savages lay down a primal beat on a row of bass drums propped on milk crates. The "Duchess" of the Badland Savages was Valkyrie, a fierce-looking Wastelander with a giant blonde mohawk, her face covered in war paint. She occasionally gleefully ululated a war cry.

It's a rough sport and often the field features half the players lying in the sand, writhing in pain. But the protective gear and padded weapons prevent serious injury.

Night Life

I found the answer to my questions of when things opened or got started was usually the same: "a little after dusk." After the blazing hot sun goes down, Wasteland lights up and comes to life. Bands start playing the main stage, Thunderdome battles begin, and the other Wasteland nightlife locations open up. These include a bar called the Atomic Café, nightclubs called Wasted Saints and the Mushroom Cloud Lounge, and the popular Last Chance Casino.

Atomic Café is a patched-together stand made of corrugated tin, old car doors, and a neon sign. People line up to get a drink. You need to bring your own cup (or in my case, canteen—they had a funnel to accommodate me). Alcohol is free, tips are expected, but you are kind of at the mercy of what happens to be in stock and on the menu at any particular time. You need to be drinking age, too, a spray-painted sign attached to the side of the building suggests that MINORS FUCK OFF. Like pretty much every entertainment structure in Wasteland, it has a platform where dancers gyrate to draw attention.

The Mushroom Cloud Lounge is a fun tent structure directly across from the bulletin boards where people gather to see the day's schedule. When I walked in they usually had '80s dance music spinning.

My favorite club was called Wasted Saints, which showcased a variety of burlesque and sideshow performance as well as DJs spinning goth/industrial and dark wave. The ground was cool sand and the structure was a loosely-constructed tent. A catwalk on the front of the building usually had a barker with a megaphone pitching the crowd outside to come in and check things out, usually accompanied by dancers. One of the funniest moments I had was walking into

Wastelanders on a go-kart cruise by the Atomic Café. *Tea Krulos*

Wasted Saints one afternoon without seeing the schedule and witnessing a line of people onstage wiggling and shaking their exposed buttocks. One even had giant googly eyes adhered to her butt cheeks. It turns out this was the "Rump Olympics," with awards going to Wasteland's best butts. Other listed activities that day at Wasted Saints included a "Ritual Offering" and "Jazz Brunch."

There are small things hidden around Wasteland that you stumble upon, like the Nuclear Bombshells stage, where I saw people learning swing dance steps, and a small movie theater I wandered by called the Nuke Review Theater. A chalkboard marquee on Damnation Alley listed three movies that night: *Steel Dawn*, *Waterworld*, and *Sinbad of the Seven Seas* starring Lou Ferrigno.

While walking by the Last Chance Casino one day, their catchy Wasteland Radio jingle—"at the Last Chance Casino . . . *we'll take your money!*" popped into my head. I saw some of the employees hanging out and asked if I could come in to talk to them. I was let in by a casino worker named Sweetpea and we sat down by the casino's bar.

When Sweetpea wasn't working out in the Wasteland he worked at a theater in Irvine, California, and was going to school for biochemistry. Spread out in tents and the open space were a number of casino games. Sweetpea explained how it all worked. "You come up to the bar and entertain the bartenders in whatever way they see appropriate in exchange for a handful of caps and a drink," Sweetpea said. Sitting near him was his coworker Big Disco, wearing a suit covered with shards of CDs and a colorful umbrella hat. "You can then use our special caps to play at any of our games. We got a spinning wheel over here, a slot machine, craps and roulette, and two card tables—gin, hold 'em, and blackjack."

Players win more caps.

"At the end of each night there is an auction and store that occurs between 11:30 and midnight and they can exchange their caps for valuable prizes. Higher-value things get auctioned off," Sweetpea said. The casino evolved from "a group of friends fucking around" to a Wasteland establishment with about thirty-five to forty-five people working the event.

"Our member Markansaw was a Jugger and went to the very first Wasteland Weekend and sent out a big message to the rest of us saying we need to get together so I can tell you about this thing. He gives this whole presentation on what Wasteland Weekend is and we should do this thing. So, I'm like, 'OK, shit, if we do this thing we obviously have to have a schtick.' We spent the rest of the day drinking and figuring out what to do. Turns out to be a casino, which is fucking great."

I return to the casino after sunset and earn a drink and some caps by reciting a dirty limerick about a man from Toledo to a bartender. I lose at both the slot machine (three bike tires hand-cranked by a casino worker) and roulette (the wheel is made out of a hubcap), and when I spin the wheel of prizes I don't win caps but land on the "get chromed" triangle, which earns me a spray on the mouth with some silver makeup spray paint, a reference to how the War Boys get a buzz in *Mad Max: Fury Road*. Other wheel landings include a consensual spanking or sharing a safe-sex tip.

Post-Apocalyptic Swimsuit Contest

One of my most exciting assignments from the *Wastelander* was covering Saturday's Post-Apocalyptic Swimsuit Contest. A large crowd gathered in the scorching sun at the Exxon Valdez. The show was emceed by Big Disco of the Last Chance Casino. Scantily clad women sprayed the audience with water pump blasters and threw out boxes of candy cigarettes. Soon a parade of Wastelanders was strutting their stuff, showing off costumes made of bottle caps, barbed wire, leather thongs, bazookas, gas masks, rubber eggs sunny side up, goggles, and combat boots. Dust blew through the air, but the contestants got relief as each one of them was blasted with the water sprayers as they stepped out on deck. Several awards were announced. A Wastelander named Fathom won "most entertaining" for her outfit that included a bikini top made out of bottle caps and a boa made of VHS cassette tape ribbon. Best craftmanship went to Rope, who made her mermaid costume out of bottle caps. "They're all scraped out, burned, and hammered by me." Judge's choice went to a sexy rodeo clown outfit worn by Slapjacks.

After the swimsuit contest, I headed over to the battle cage to catch a robot cage match, where builders pitted their remote-controlled robotic creations against each other. Equipped with buzz-saws and pinchers, the machines wheeled around each other, trying to thrash each other out of commission.

Bartertown

A stretch of Main Street in front of the Wasteland gates is called Bartertown, named after a location in the 1985 movie *Mad Max: Beyond Thunderdome*. It's a row of shops with Wasteland-appropriate names like War Mart, the Grotto, Six Finger Discount, Midnight Mercenary Supply, and the Junksmith that sell and barter army surplus gear, weapons, jewelry, and junk. The Bartertown Trade Bazaar is an area with long tables where people can show up with items they want to trade. Bartering is a favorite pastime at Wasteland Weekend.

Bartertown also has two food stands, Golden Bamboo and Dinki Di, which sells wild boar chili (served in a Dinki Di dogfood can, a reference to *Mad Max 2: The Road Warrior*), gator nuggets, fries, water, and Gatorade.

LARP

There are also live action role-play (LARP) games that go on at Wasteland. I was walking down Main Street when an ATV with two people pulled up. "Have you seen this person?" a woman wearing an army helmet and thick black makeup circles around her eyes asked me, holding up a wanted person flyer. WANTED DEAD OR ALIVE: PICKLES.

I looked at it and shook my head. Throughout my time I witnessed other LARPers searching for other wanted characters, and learned they originated from a camp called Rust Devils, who operated the bounty hunter LARP. Their website explains, "Hunt and be hunted. Explore the wastes, meet new people, and kill them."

Other Wastelanders relish staying in character for the event, especially Wasteland celebrities. These are mostly the people playing famous characters like Immortan Joe, along with his harem and gang of War Boys; Aunty (*Mad Max: Beyond Thunderdome*); and Lord Humungus (*Mad Max 2: The Road Warrior*). I witnessed Lord Humungus leading a caravan down Main Street to the Wasteland gates and got to see a gate opening ceremony, a small skit that kicks off the day.

"The Gates!" Lord Humungus yelled into a megaphone as his caravan approached. "Open the gates!" Arriving at the closed gates, he addressed the guards outside.

"I am greatly disappointed. Again you have made me unleash my Dogs of War. Why? Because you are selfish. You horde your alcohol. You will not listen to reason. Now they say you plan to spend the whole weekend partying in the Wasteland." The crowd roared approval. His speech was parodied from a scene from *Mad Max 2: The Road Warrior* where Lord Humungus, the "ayatollah of rock 'n' rolla," demands a settlement hand over their oil.

"Look around you. My dogs like to party too," Lord Humungus continued. "There has been so much drinking, so much partying there are none here without a hangover. But I have an honorable compromise. Just open the gates! Share with us the gambling. The live bands. The DJs. The whole event! And I'll spare your lives. Just open the gates! We promise to take selfies with the whole Wasteland. Just open the gates and witness Wasteland Weekend!" The crowd cheered again.

"Wastelanders! Shall we let them in?" a guard on top of the gate called out. The crowd cheered wildly and began to chant, "Let them in! Let them in! Let them in!"

"Open the fucking gates!" a spectator screamed. The giant rusty doors slowly swung open and Lord Humungus and his Dogs of War rolled in. I would later see Lord Humungus officiating a wedding by the gates and later still having a DJ battle with Immortan Joe.

Another gate opening ceremony saw the Queen of Wasteland confronted by a dystopian police force that threatened to shut down Wasteland, only to be chased away by the Queen's guards.

Lord Humungus. *Tea Krulos*

Apocalypse Culture

On Sunday I packed up my tent and met up with a Wastelander named Favorite, who was part of the Dead Crows and Ace Hole, a worker at the Last Chance Casino. We carefully stuffed Favorite's car with gear and headed back to civilization, somewhat of a letdown after a fun fantasy weekend.

Wasteland, like Burning Man, has its own culture. I think the Wastelanders could qualify as a subculture. They produce their own media—Wasteland Radio and the *Wastelander*. Some Wastelanders write their own fan fiction. They have their own customs, they've adopted their own sports, like the Wasteland Jugger matches. They even have their own currency of bottle caps.

Is this what happens when the world ends? The party here would definitely be short-lived. The cruel Mojave Desert would kill someone quickly—water and food are extremely scarce. But what a hell of a way to ride out the end of the world—death by partying.

12

ONE-WAY TICKET TO MARS

Rise to Mars, men and women
Dare to dream! Dare to strive!
Build a home for our children
Make this desert come alive!
There are challenges before our eyes
That nature never knew
But the power of human enterprise
Shall take us through and through
Rise to Mars! Men and women

—"RISE TO MARS!," COLLABORATION BETWEEN OPERA SINGER
OSCAR DOM VICTOR CASTELLINO AND MARS SOCIETY PRESIDENT
DR. ROBERT ZUBRIN, WHO HOPES IT WILL BECOME
"THE NATIONAL ANTHEM OF A FREE MARTIAN REPUBLIC"

One day, Yari Golden-Castaño was crossing the street in Boston when she spotted a familiar face in the walkway, Chris Patil.

"Chris?" she said.

The man stopped walking. "Yari?" Then they shared an embrace in the middle of the street.

More improbable than this chance meeting was the membership Yari and Chris shared in a highly selective group, a hundred people out of the 7.4 billion on Earth who were chosen for a shot at the trip of a lifetime. These people, fifty males and fifty females, are from thirty-two countries around the world, range in age from twenty to sixty-one, and come from a wide variety of backgrounds. Narrowed down from an initial two hundred thousand applicants, these one hundred will be whittled down to forty and then twenty-four candidates. These final applicants will spend ten years of their lives together in teams of four to train to become the first humans to colonize the planet Mars.

Four of these candidates will be selected to blast off from Earth, travel millions of miles during a nine-month flight, and become our first Martians. Yari and Chris might be two of the people on that ride. This is the vision of Mars One, a Dutch company founded in 2011 in Amersfoort by wind-energy entrepreneur Bas Lansdorp. His vision is to send the first Mars colonists on a one-way trip projected to launch in 2031, a voyage estimated to cost over $6 billion (and some Mars One critics think this is a naively cheap estimate).

A one-way ticket to Mars seems drastic, but Mars One has had the goal of a permanent colony from the start. A one-way trip "reduces the mission infrastructure," as there won't be a need to bring along a return vehicle and fuel, which makes the price tag smaller—NASA's plan for a round-trip Mars mission is quintuple the price at $30 billion.

After the tricky landing on Mars's surface, the first four Martians will find a small structure made of connected pods waiting for them, assembled by robots sent ahead of time. It'll be cramped quarters (but spacious compared to the last nine months or so they would have spent in a small space capsule). After settling in and hanging up the HOME SWEET HOME sign, the settlers will get to work trying to grow their own crops, get a functioning water supply rolling, explore the planet, and start expanding the building of their colony. Another group of four Martians will land about a year later, followed by more and more. Mars civilization will be born.

Crashing Mars

The settlement of Mars has long been a human dream, mostly relegated to science fiction stories. The red planet stood silent and unvisited except for dust storms for millions of years until November 27, 1971, when the planet received its first visitor in the form of the Soviet Mars 2 lander crashing into the planet. The earthlings had arrived!

Mars 3 stuck the landing a few days later and joined the junked Mars 2, but only transmitted for twenty seconds before stopping for unknown reasons. For the following decades occasional satellites or landers would head to the red planet, with some successes and some failures. Things steadily became more advanced over the years. The Mars 2 and 3 orbiters transmitted data for a few months, but NASA's Spirit rover was active on the planet from 2004 to 2010. As of this writing the NASA Opportunity rover (which landed in 2004) and Curiosity rover (which landed in 2012) are still functioning on Mars, exploring and sending back images of a harsh, red world.

Sending actual astronauts to the surface of Mars to study and explore has long been a goal of most space agencies, but with the space race settled, Mars and the huge price tag attached to it became less of a priority. The Nixon space doctrine encouraged development of NASA's space shuttle program for military purposes, but not in exploration projects like sending astronauts to Mars. If Nixon had chosen otherwise, it's likely we could have already been on Mars.

Private companies like Mars One and Elon Musk's company Space X are likely to reach Mars first. A government agency is tied down by bureaucratic red tape, budget, and pressure for results. A private company can do whatever the CEO and shareholders want. Whether it'll be successful is another question.

The Mars 100

The idea of packing up and leaving family and friends permanently behind on a blue marble getting smaller and smaller in the rearview window is a challenge not everyone is up for, so the Mars One candidates are composed of a group of people willing to leave their current lives behind to become pioneers. Curious to learn more about these people, I asked Mars One for contacts, and got info for several of their hundred candidates and began e-mailing them around the world. I found a hundred great short stories.

"A lot of people have told me this is a crazy dream, to which I usually reply, 'All dreams are crazy until they become real,'" said Sabrina Surovec. She is a good example of a Mars 100 candidate—adventurous and bold, Surovec has led the life of a nomad, traveling to more than twenty-five countries. Born in the United States, she went to school for a while in Germany before becoming a permanent resident of Japan. She's studied music and theater in Asia and, inspired by her favorite band Erasure, hopes to someday be the first musician to play a concert on Mars.

I talked with Natalie Lawler, an Australian schoolteacher. Raised in a small town in Australia, Lawler's life was altered when she got in a car crash when she was sixteen that killed her boyfriend. She overcame her injuries and had a newfound passion for school. She got a bachelor's degree in business and became a property evaluator and entrepreneur but switched careers in her thirties after she reevaluated her life. She got divorced, sold her businesses, and went back to school to become a math and science teacher, a career she finds more rewarding. She told me she volunteered in part because she would like to inspire students everywhere to study math and science.

"We can't stand around saying 'Why didn't someone go to Mars?' because we are someone!" Lawler told me in an e-mail. "If I have the right profile to represent humanity to live on Mars, why wouldn't I go? I will inspire more students than I could ever imagine to invest in the knowledge of science and the wonder of space."

I also spoke to Hannah Earnshaw, a student at Durham University in the United Kingdom who is pursuing a PhD in X-ray astronomy ("black holes and the like," she explained) and documents her thoughts on going to Mars via a Tumblr page called "Hannah Goes to Mars." I spoke to a few more—Dr. Bhupendra Singh of New Delhi, the only candidate from India, and Laurel Helene Kaye, a physics student from Long Island. Going through the list of candidates, I noticed something curious—the highest percentage of Mars One candidates (by city) came from Boston, with five out of the hundred candidates. So when I began arranging East Coast travel, I decided to see if I could make some contacts to talk about Mars One in person.

The Martian Dinner Party

"I call us the Bahstan Mahsians," Peter Degen-Portnoy, the first Mars One candidate I get to meet, shortly after I got off a train in Back Bay Station, told me in his best Boston accent.

Peter is a software engineer and manager and found out about the Mars One program as it began to circulate online. Immediately after my train arrived in Boston I walked to meet up with him at a coffee shop, where he told me he'd been fascinated by space since he was a child. "Learning about stars and planets has been a consistent theme in my life and a secret dream had been to live on another world. So much so that early in our relationship my wife and I talked about colonizing another world. She said she loved the idea of being a colonist or pioneer but would not ever leave the Earth even if it were possible in our lifetime, while I said that I wouldn't hesitate. After learning about Mars One, I read everything I could to assess whether this idea had any merit and decided that it was a serious, albeit optimistic, endeavor. At that point I knew that I would apply. I had to. This is my one opportunity to pursue a lifelong dream. I realized that there is only a tiny fraction of a tiny fraction of humanity who would be willing to consider an idea such as Mars One, who are capable of participating because of their aptitude, education, and skills, and would actually thrive in such a challenging and uncertain environment and mission. I feel that I am one of that tiny fraction, that I have a responsibility to try and do everything I can to help it succeed."

After meeting with Peter, I moved on to a restaurant called the Salty Pig in Boston's Back Bay area. Peter wanted to join along to meet his fellow Bahstan Mahsians but couldn't because he needed to attend his daughter's recital—his time with her on Earth is precious. Meeting me at the restaurant were three more candidates: Yari Golden-Castaño, R. Daniel Golden-Castaño, and Sara Director. Dr. Chris Patil, the fifth Boston candidate, was unable to make it.

Boston Martians (left to right) R. Daniel, Yari, and Sara. *Tea Krulos*

Sara was first to arrive. "Some of my first memories are of watching *Star Trek: The Next Generation* with my parents when I was three or four," Sara said. "My mom tells a story about holding me up in front of the TV during a shuttle launch, when I was a very young toddler, just saying to me 'This is really, really important; pay attention to this.' The house was full of sci-fi novels and movies and artwork . . . so really it's just always been there. It's actually completely unrelated to my occupation—I'm doing part-time copyediting at the moment, after a long stretch of unemployment. The fact is, I've been unemployed or underemployed for the majority of my time after getting my BA in biology, and I think that actually is connected. Specifically, my interests and skills are very varied—I consider my versatility to be my greatest strength—and that's not what employers want to see, nor is it something that many jobs require. Going to Mars would really be my dream job in this sense, in that it would truly challenge me in *every* way that I want to be challenged, not just hit on a few things I'm interested in."

When she saw the Mars One call for applicants, she said she would have regretted it forever if she didn't take a shot. "I've just been figuring I'm going to take this as far as I can. And if I don't go, I gave it my best shot. And if I do go, I'm going to go down in history forever, and I'm really cool with that."

One thing she would like to contribute is to possibly be the first Mars artist. "It seems that an art school would not be one of the first priorities in a new colony, but maybe something simple such as stone carvings that tell the colony's history, like ancient cave paintings on Earth. Or maybe just a really big abstract piece that I start and future teams add to it. Or maybe contributing decoration to whatever structures we build out of Martian materials. I have a million ideas."

Yari and R. Daniel arrive, an engaged couple who will be married in a few weeks. As we settle in at our table and examine the restaurant's pork-heavy menu, I am told the story of how R. Daniel and Yari became the first Mars One couple, brought together by their love of the program.

"I grew up interested in human space travel and looked at becoming an astronaut when I was sixteen," R. Daniel told me. "That led me into the US Army communications field, where I've been a specialist covering computer, radio, phone, and satellite systems for fifteen years, including my current position in electronic warfare with the Massachusetts Army National Guard. I'm also working on a degree in mechanical engineering with an interest in robotics and remote sensing."

Yari is an engineer and said she never believed the adage "the sky's the limit." "The idea of becoming an astronaut was planted in my head since I was a baby. My mother dressed me up in a baby astronaut onesie that she found at a thrift store. My grandmother taught me to read using an encyclopedia, and the story I remember most is that of cosmonaut Yuri Gagarin.

"I took my first steps for this journey when I was six. I left my mother and siblings in Mexico City to move to California, where I was born, to live with my aunt. I loved my immediate family and knew I would miss them, but I was excited about the prospect of living in a different place and learning a new language. Throughout my childhood, I had many ups and downs from moving back and forth between my two families and not having a space of my own—the only thing I held on to was my desire to see Earth from another world.

"As an engineer with a degree in engineering science, I have been prepared to take on any problem—mechanical, electrical, systems control, etc. I have the skills to succeed, and I am committed to learning. My ideal job is to be a hands-on engineer, conducting research and developing new space technologies. What better setting is there than Mars to contribute to NASA's research and perform all the tasks that Mars rovers cannot currently do? I want to get my hands dirty with Mars's regolith, become an expert on the planet, and directly contribute that knowledge to the development of leading-edge technologies to support and enable humankind's mission in Mars and our future in space exploration."

After applying, Yari received an e-mail from Mars One and misread it at first as a rejection letter. "But then I kept reading down and it said congratulations. And I was like, *What? Wait a minute! Aaaaah.* I'm like screaming my guts out. It was the happiest day of my life. Meanwhile my cousin is in the driveway saying, 'What's happening? What's happening?' She grabbed me and we just started jumping and screaming our guts out."

Mars One is almost a micro subculture that includes not only the Mars 100, but former candidates who applied for the program and fans optimistic about the program's potential. They communicate in Facebook groups and forums and attend regional meet-ups. R. Daniel is a moderator of one of these Facebook groups. The Mars One—Aspiring Martians group has over thirteen thousand members who share news and discuss the latest developments in Mars colonization plans, everything from technology to philosophy.

It's in one of these online forums that R. Daniel and Yari met. R. Daniel had initially applied and didn't make the cut, but after another potential Martian dropped out, he took his place. He was an admin for the group, well known for his blunt advice for the Mars 100, particularly on the topic of media appearances. Mars One candidates are minor celebrities right now, often featured on local news stations in typical flavor-of-the-day pieces.

"I saw his comments and he was just like a smartass telling people how it is, and I was like, *Oh, I actually like this person*. He's straight to the point, no bullshit. I suck at being in front of a camera, and it was right around the time people started asking me for interviews. I remember I did my first interview with a giant camera in my face and I just froze in the spotlight. They ended up using five seconds of me saying I was going to bring Flamin' Hot Cheetos to Mars," Yari laughed.

WHAT ARE YOU BRINGING TO MARS?

Yari has mentioned she's planning to stuff every available bit of extra cargo room with Flamin' Hot Cheetos to Mars if she can. Here's what some of the other Mars 100 candidates said they would bring . . .

R. Daniel Golden-Castaño: "I need a shovel/pickax on Mars. You can discover and build a lot of things with that ancient tool."

Sara Director: "One thing to take to Mars. This is probably the most commonly asked question, and I still don't have a good answer. Most things I'd want can either be sent digitally like books/music/movies, or wouldn't be allowed, like my cat."

Dr. Chris Patil: "Every cubic centimeter that I can fill with something that's nonessential I would fill with spices because they're very efficient. You don't have to use a lot of them; years' and years' supply of spices fit into a kilogram of mass; and it would be hugely psychologically beneficial to be able to flavor our food in interesting ways."

"I started asking him how I did in this interview. A lot of people were like, 'You're fine, you're fine,' but he had honest feedback," Yari said. She was living in Somerville, a suburb of Boston, and R. Daniel was living in El Paso, Texas. They continued to talk online and then began exchanging texts to talk about how their P90X workouts were panning out. Then, realizing she would be alone in Boston during the holidays (she visits her family in California and Mexico before or after the holiday rush), Yari decided to be bold and ask R. Daniel on a long-distance date.

"I said, 'Hey, come over, we'll go beer tasting in Boston.' And he was like, 'OK,'" Yari laughed. "I was like, 'Wait . . . OK? Are you sure? Like, complete stranger . . . ' But then it was cool. And we met. And it happened."

The Martians fell in love and decided to get married. Yari thought it would be most appropriate to get married when the stars were aligned in their favor, meaning the time of year when planet Mars was closest to planet Earth (known in astronomy as a Mars close approach). After some Internet searching, they found that alignment was coming up quickly—May 30 would be the closest the two planets had been to each other in ten years. They settled on a date of May 22, Mars opposition—the day the Earth is directly between Mars and the sun. As the sun is setting, Mars is rising. To celebrate the date, R. Daniel and Yari beamed as they held their hands across our table to show off their wedding rings—tattoos on their ring fingers, a miniature depiction of the Mars opposition lineup of a yellow, blue, and red trio of circles.

Ten days after I met them, the wedding took place. Bride and groom both wore Mars One T-shirts and galaxy-print canvas shoes, with R. Daniel wearing a star-print bowtie. Their friends and family and Mars One colleagues joined them on a Boston bar crawl to celebrate that first date the Martians went on together.

Which made me feel like a bit of a mood killer when I said, "It kind of breaks my heart to ask this, but what if one of you makes the cut and the other doesn't?" R. Daniel and Yari glanced at each other.

"If only one of us gets to go, we'll decide what we're doing at that point," R. Daniel explained thoughtfully. "We have at least ten years before anybody would leave."

Sara, who is engaged to get married, said the conversation with her fiancé was pretty smooth. After her dad sent her a link to a story about

Mars One, she decided to apply. "When I first brought it up it was so far-fetched, like, 'I'm going to apply to this thing, there's no way I'm going to get it, but just for funsies,' and he said, 'Great, sounds like fun.'"

But after she made it through the first round, it became clear that the odds of her being selected had descended from the atmosphere into the realm of possibility. "Why worry about it until it's something we need to worry about? I mean, he's comfortable with me going to Mars. It's not his plan A, but he's like, 'There's way more reasons a relationship will end that are a lot shittier than someone leaving to colonize Mars.'"

"Why'd you get divorced?" R. Daniel cracked across the table. "My wife went to Mars."

As for missing family, the candidates say it will be difficult, but our plugged-in social relationships will make the distance easier. Mars One will be able to exchange messages and videos with loved ones back home. For many modern technology-based relationships, one might as well be on Mars.

When I spoke to Peter, it seemed he faced the biggest challenge, leaving a wife and five kids behind. He speaks of his wife with nothing but the most glowing admiration. He cites the beauty of her eyes as one of the earthly things he would miss on Mars. "We will have e-mail and video exchanges and be able to constantly be part of one another's lives. It means that I will be physically distant, but we will be always present in each other's lives," Peter said. "I've told my children I won't ever stop being their daddy. I'll be their daddy who lives and works on Mars."

Both Sara and Peter mentioned that we have no idea where we might be technology-wise in ten or more years, so there is a possibility the Martians could receive visitors in the future. Just jump on the space Greyhound for a Mars vacation.

"Actornauts"

After dinner Sara, R. Daniel, and Yari also pass around a college-ruled composition notebook with a Mars One sticker on the front. This notebook has been traveling the world as a sort of international (or maybe intergalactic) slam book where the candidates have been leaving short messages and signing their name. There is also a T-shirt being passed around that reads, BAS IS SENDING ME TO MARS, that all candidates are posing in. Someday, when the round is complete, the slam book and the pictures will be delivered to Bas Lansdorp as a gift. Lansdorp and his program are well admired by his Mars 100, but he has a field of critics, too, who say his program is more science fiction and fantasy than a coherent plan.

Critics have called Mars One everything from being too ambitious to being a scam. One factor that makes the program ripe for criticism is their plan to do major fundraising by filming and packaging the astronaut selection and training process as a reality TV show—imagine *Big Brother* goes to space, complete with a vote from the home audience. It's this emphasis on showbiz and an unclear plan of overcoming scientific challenges that has opened Mars One up to blasts of criticism. One online commenter on the Mars One Facebook page even jeered the participants as not trained astronauts but "actornauts."

Mars is an incredibly harsh environment to survive in, one that will eventually have to be terraformed (artificially changed to be more like the Earth's atmosphere), since Mars's atmosphere is 95 percent carbon dioxide and a hundred times thinner than Earth's. A warm day might get up to 20 degrees Celsius (68 degrees Fahrenheit) near the Mars equator, but the average temperature is −60 degrees Celsius (−76 degrees Fahrenheit). And then there's the radioactive solar flares and dust storms, which can blanket the planet for months.

Critics, including scientists and the media, say the technology simply will not develop sufficiently to match the Mars One timeline.

"Mars One Torn to Shreds in MIT Debate," reported IFLScience .com. The report covers a debate between Bas Lansdorp and one of his key technical people against two scientists at the Massachusetts Institute of Technology in a debate titled "Is Mars One Feasible?" The scientists' examination of Lansdorp's plan led them to believe the Mars One astronauts would all be dead within sixty-eight days.

"You'd be hard-pressed to find anyone in the space industry who thinks they can do what they've claimed. They lack any of the technology needed to send humans to Mars (including a heavy-lift rocket, spacecraft, habitat, life-support system; the list goes on) and have shown no shred of development since they burst onto the scene in 2010," IFLscience reports.

Other critics have included Business Insider, which published an article titled "Mars One Plan Is Totally Delusional," and especially harsh criticism from Gizmodo.com, whose articles on the program include "Mars One Is Broke, Disorganized, and Sketchy as Hell," and "Mars One Is Still Completely Full of Shit."

Both publications argue that the program's estimated $6 billion budget is way too low, but even this too-low budget is a long way from being met. As of this writing, Mars One's attempts at fundraising have gotten them nowhere near the $6 billion mark, and no reality show deal has panned out. The program lacks the technology to get to Mars, let alone sustain human life there.

When I brought up the lack of funding and unrealistic budget and timeline as dinner conversation with R. Daniel, Yari, and Sara, they seemed unfazed by the armchair critics. "Anyone that has ever worked in anything knows that every project in the history of mankind has gone overbudget and over the original timeline, but they still get done and when they get done they are still considered a success if they perform as intended," Sara said. "So there's critics that say this budget and this timeline is absolutely ridiculous, but even if it takes longer than expected or costs more, it's still a good thing if it happens. And having an aggressive timeline and an aggressive budget is a great way to keep the amount of time and money you're spending under control."

Even if Mars One does fall short and can't fund the mission, or has a later timeline than expected, they aren't the only organization looking to get boots on the ground on Mars. With problems on Earth like overcrowding and dwindling resources, colonizing Mars will be a necessity sooner than later. In the United States, NASA hopes to send a manned crew to Mars and back by the 2030s, and the Russian and Chinese space agencies have a strong interest in visiting Mars as well.

However, Mars One's biggest challenger in this space race is probably not a government-backed space agency weighed down by red tape, but a private company contender. The biggest name in the private sector is Space X, the California space transport company backed by billionaire entrepreneur and Tesla Motors CEO Elon Musk. Space X has been developing some of the most innovative technology to make a Mars trip a reality. Their rockets haven't been able to comfortably stick the landings, but they are getting more and more accurate all the time. Mars One hopes to buy Space X technology to make their mission a success, but although they haven't announced a clear timeline Space X might choose to develop their own mission first.

Selecting the Mars 40

Mars One announced they were preparing for the next selection stage—narrowing the Mars 100 down to 40, sometime in 2017. However, as of this writing, that step has yet to happen. Eventually, although an exact timeline hasn't been announced, the Mars 40 will be whittled down again to the Mars 24. The final two dozen candidates will spend a decade training in fields like "medicine, dentistry, agronomy, electronics, political science, law," as well as scientific exploration, according to the Mars One website. To help prepare, the final candidates will be trained in remote locations to simulate Mars. A variety of harsh terrains, like Iceland and Antarctica, have been looked at as potential training spots.

During this ten-year training period, Mars One hopes the proper technology will fall into place to launch cargo (including robots that will assemble a series of pod-like homes as an outpost) to the red planet in 2029. After a 2031 launch and a projected nine-month voyage, the first four Martians will be followed by another group in 2033, and more to arrive at the growing colony every two years after that. These groups of four will not only need to be our best representatives, but they'll need to work well as a team. Imagine being stuck on a commute for nine months strapped next to someone who pushes all your buttons, and then spending the rest of your life in an enclosed space on a faraway planet with that person.

"I think we're all hoping we identify the assholes as quickly as possible, before we even get teamed up, but definitely before we leave," Sara said.

"We'll have ten years of living together, working together, including time in isolation," R. Daniel explained. "You can only keep your rude tendencies or bad behavior hidden for so long. Eventually it all comes out."

A New Chance

On their way out of Earth's atmosphere, these potential Martians might reflect on some things they will and won't miss on Mother Earth behind them.

When polled on what earthly things the Mars One candidates might miss, they mention a lot of small things we take for granted, like our landscape and weather. Sabrina and Sara both mentioned they'll miss their pet cats. Peter Degen-Portnoy mentioned things like the still of a spring morning, the sound of an orchestra filling a music hall. But what is more profound is the things the candidates say they won't miss.

"War, prejudice, violence," said Dr. Bhupendra Singh.

"Money and everything around the expectations of earning it, spending it, and deserving it," added Sara Director.

"Religious and political squabbling," said Sabrina. "It's my hope we can get away from all that and start with a clean slate on Mars."

And that is perhaps the most exciting aspect of Mars: to start a new civilization removed from our worldly problems, a new chance to start over, far away in the stars.

Who knows? Maybe this time we'll get it right.

EPILOGUE

I Twisted My Ankle and Watched Four Documentaries on Nostradamus

In the days that followed the shock of 9/11, one man got more Google hits than Osama bin Laden and George W. Bush. That would be a Frenchman who died over five hundred years ago, prognosticator Michel de Nostredame—better known as Nostradamus—who died in 1566. After 9/11 books about the prophecies of Nostradamus skyrocketed on Amazon, catching the number one spot and several more spots in the top twenty-five. Could the famous soothsayer have predicted this terrible day? Nostradamians, as those who study his work are sometimes called, believe he did.

Nostradamus's work consists of ten sections. Each section contains a hundred short poetic quatrains (except one section that has just forty-two), and each quatrain makes a prediction. Toward the end of his life he would write one of these each night, walking up the stairs to his study on the top level of his house after his children had gone to bed so he could look into the future undisturbed. He would place a bowl of water on his desk next to his astrolabe and stare into it until visions formed in his head, which he'd write down with a quill pen. Like the Bible and works by William Shakespeare, Nostradamus's prophecies have never gone out of print.

Here's the famous quatrain Q 6-97 that allegedly predicts 9/11:

At forty-five degrees, the sky will burn,
Fire approaches the great new city,
Immediately a huge, scattered flame leaps up,
When they want to have verification from the Normans.

Winter is a brutal time in my Wisconsin home. Walking home one day, I slipped on the ice and badly twisted my ankle. After using my new survival skills to wrap my ankle and put ice on it, I decided I would rest and watch documentaries (four in total) on Nostradamus to find out more about the mystical Frenchman.

Nostradamus became famous during his lifetime in France after his first greatest hit occurred in his lifetime, when it appeared one of his quatrains, Q 1-35, predicted the death of France's King Henry II.

The young lion will overcome the older one,
On the field of combat in single battle:
He will pierce his eyes through a golden cage,
Two wounds made one, then he dies a cruel death.

The prophecy shocked the queen and made her a Nostradamus believer when King Henry II did indeed die in an accident during a friendly jousting match. A lance splinter pierced the eyehole of his helm and gouged into his eye, and he did die a slow, cruel death.

From then on, Nostradamus's reputation grew throughout Europe and the world. His 942 mysterious quatrains began to be applied to world events, and it would seem in hindsight that Nostradamus predicted everything. Quatrain Q 2-51 seemingly foretells the Great Fire of London of 1666:

The blood of the just will be demanded at London,
Burnt by lightning fire in twenty-three the sixes:
the ancient lady will fall from her high place,
And many of the same sect will be killed.

Quatrain Q 2-24 is said to predict the advancement of the Nazi Party across Europe. It mentions a "Hister" (an antiquated Latin name for the Danube River). Hitler himself believed the prediction was about him and used it as propaganda.

> Beasts ferocious with hunger will cross the rivers,
> The greatest part of the battlefield will be against Hister.
> Into a cage of iron will the great one be drawn,
> When the child of Germany observes nothing.

Other quatrains supposedly predict the assassination of JFK, the bombing of Hiroshima and Nagasaki, space travel, Napoleon's army, and much more. Skeptics say that his followers are misinterpreting his word salad to retrofit historic happenings. The quatrains are extremely vague metaphors that can be applied to any number of world events over the last five hundred years. And then there's quatrain Q 10-72, which appears to be Nostradamus striking nothing but air:

> In the year 1999 and seven months,
> A great King of Terror will come from the sky.
> He will bring back the great King Genghis Khan.
> Before and after Mars rules happily.

This quatrain caused panic in some people. Between this and the Y2K bug, retailers must have been happy with the amount of food, water, and emergency supplies that were clearing off the shelves. But July 1999 witnessed nothing out of the ordinary.

History has no more famed prognosticator than Nostradamus. Proponents of the all-seeing Frenchman say his poetic quatrains have eerily predicted many of history's great turning points that have occurred since his death in 1566. Did Nostradamus really predict the 9/11 attacks or the election of President Trump?

Surely the person whose various adherents say he has predicted all these key tragic events must have an explosive finale predicted for planet Earth, right? Well, yes, but not as impending as you might think. Nostradamus actually predicts the world will end in the year 3797 AD after the sun expands and destroys the Earth. "Nostradamus tells us plainly in one of his writings that the world will more or less end in the year 3797, due to burning stones from heaven bombarding the surface of the Earth. He refers to this as the 'final conflagration.' Furthermore, he states that our sun will burn out in the year 7000," Victor Baines told me in an e-mail. Baines is the president of the Nostradamus Society of America.

So that's the good news. If this book is still in print in 3797 (or as a file in your brainchip, or however people read books then), you might be reading this on Mars or a different solar system far away from Earth and reflecting on how primitive and quaint the Mars One program and AI like Rose are. Because Nostradamus predicted that even as the Earth was destroyed in a solar firestorm, humanity would live on. He predicted that they would find a home among the stars and inhabit new worlds. Hopefully these new worlds have moved forward and learned some things from this divisive, destructive Earth. We can only hope.

You know what? Even though he failed with that 1999 quatrain, whatever that was about, I'm going to be optimistic and say I hope the world makes it to 3797.

My money is on Nostradamus.

ACKNOWLEDGMENTS

I don't fear the end of the world because I have met enough wonderful people to fill several lifetimes. These include my supportive mom and dad and my sisters Megan, Margot, and Rita, and the rest of my family. I'd like to thank my editor Jerome Pohlen and all the great people at Chicago Review Press. Jan Christensen, as always, helped me review my work. Thanks to my fellow road warriors Alex Groh, Paul Kjelland, Bridget, Sean, Drea, and Beth, Tracy, Joe, and Russ of Zombie Squad 053 who joined me in my adventures. Additional people who helped me in some capacity: Kate Humphreys, Lee Gutowski, the *Wastelander* editor Deadline, *Pop Mythology*, Risto Pakarinen, my excellent tailors Heather and Joe of Stinky Goblin Emporium, Tracey Collins, Maggie Reed, all my friends at the Riverwest Public House, and all the people who have participated in the Apocalypse Blog Book Club.

And of course, thanks to Rose for all the interesting conversations.

APPENDIX A

Congratulations! A List of Apocalypses in This Book You've Survived

Here's some good news for you: you've already survived the apocalypse several times. Here's a list of apocalyptic predictions—and these are just the ones mentioned in this book!

OCTOBER 22, 1844 (MILLERITES)
Apocalypse, a.k.a. the Great Disappointment.

DECEMBER 21, 1954 (DOROTHY MARTIN)
Great flood and arrival of the Clarians.

FEBRUARY 4, 1962 (JEANE DIXON)
Planetary alignment destroys Earth.

1982 (PAT ROBERTSON)
Apocalypse.

1988 (HAL LINDSEY)
Apocalypse.

SEPTEMBER 6, 1994 (HAROLD CAMPING)
Apocalypse.

1995 (HAROLD CAMPING AGAIN)
Apocalypse.

1999 (NOSTRADAMUS)
King of terror comes from the sky.

JANUARY 1, 2000 (VARIOUS)
Y2K computer malfunction causes widespread disaster.

2003 (NANCY LIEDER)
Planet X causes major pole shifts and other disasters.

2008 (VARIOUS)
Hadron collider causes black hole disaster.

MAY 21, 2011 (HAROLD CAMPING AGAIN)
Apocalypse.

OCTOBER 21, 2011 (HAROLD CAMPING YET AGAIN)
Apocalypse.

DECEMBER 21, 2012 (VARIOUS)
Mayan apocalypse.

2015 (MICHAEL SNYDER)
Economic collapse.

SEPTEMBER 27, 2015 (MARK BLITZ AND VARIOUS)
Blood Moon apocalypse.

2015 (RICARDO SALAZAR)
Asteroid explosion.

JUNE–OCTOBER 2016 (NORA ROTH)
Apocalypse.

MAY–OCTOBER 2016 (RICARDO SALAZAR)
Giant asteroid, ice age, World War III.

2017 (DAVID MEADE)
Planet X cataclysm.

APPENDIX B

The Apocalypse Blog Book Club

After the election of Donald J. Trump as president, his appointment of cabinet members, and perceived use of "doublespeak," an old favorite was soon riding high on Amazon's bestseller list: George Orwell's dystopian novel *Nineteen Eighty-Four*, which he wrote in 1949. Soon sales were brisk for another classic dystopian novel. Margaret Atwood's *The Handmaid's Tale* (written in 1985) saw a boost from a Hulu show adaptation.

I decided that to get my mind into the dystopian premise of this book, I should start reading some of these classics. Then I thought I'd invite people to join me, so I started the Apocalypse Blog Book Club, in which members vote on a different dystopian title to read each month. The club has members from around the world. A group of locals meet in Milwaukee and Racine and discussion takes place in our Facebook group. We've occasionally written reports on our selections for the site Pop Mythology.

Our selections for our first year are as follows:

FEBRUARY 2017

Parable of the Sower by Octavia Butler.

MARCH 2017

The Handmaid's Tale by Margaret Atwood. Read the Pop Mythology report by Ryder Collins at www.popmythology.com /apocalypse-blog-book-club-march-handmaids-tale.

APRIL 2017

The Man in the High Castle, by Philip K. Dick. Read the Pop Mythology report by Tea Krulos at www.popmythology.com /apocalypse-blog-book-club-april-selection-the-man-in-the-high-castle.

MAY 2017

The Sirens of Titan by Kurt Vonnegut Jr. Read the Pop Mythology report by Jacqui Castle at www.popmythology.com /the-apocalypse-book-club-may-selection-the-sirens-of-titan.

JUNE 2017

The Dispossessed by Ursula K. Le Guin. Read the Pop Mythology report by Katie Jesse at www.popmythology.com /apocalypse-book-club-dispossessed.

JULY 2017

Woman on the Edge of Time by Marge Piercy.

AUGUST 2017

Borne by Jeff VanderMeer.

SEPTEMBER 2017

Who Fears Death by Nnedi Okorafor.

OCTOBER–NOVEMBER 2017

Fall break.

DECEMBER 2017

Ready Player One by Ernest Cline.

JANUARY 2018

Wastelands: Stories of the Apocalypse, anthology edited by John Joseph Adams.

FEBRUARY 2018

Parable of the Talents by Octavia Butler.

Our full list of selections is also available online at https://teakrulos.com/the-end/

APPENDIX C

Dispatches from the Wasteland

As you read in chapter 11, I worked as a stringer for the *Waste-lander*. I would handwrite a short article each day in my notepad and then hand it over to Deadline to type up. My byline was Krulos the Terrible and I tried to capture a sort of "Wasteland AP" style in character of a postapocalyptic reporter. Here are the three articles Krulos the Terrible penned at Wasteland Weekend 2017.

"Bash in the Battle Cage," *Wastelander* I, no. 3 (Friday, September 29, Year Eight)

"Ready to see a fuckin' fight?" The announcer on top of the Battle Cage shouted.

"Fight! Fight! Fight!" The audience, pressed against the cage, chanted back. And what a fight the Wastelanders got! History will not talk about the sad losers, but let's talk about the glorious winners!

First up, Murder Crow. This gladiator is quick and nimble, and bested three scumbucket foes in a row, as the audience roared and the ladies of The Wastes gyrated sweet meat above the cage. Murder Crow swung his sword quickly and on target, but eventually he was worn down.

Two more victorious fan favorites were the mighty Beast and newcomer The Chef. Beast was solid as a rock, but he had helmet issues and needs to adjust to be more suitable for the Wasteland.

Next up, Chef showed off slice n' dice skills, swinging his sword with brute force.

"Open him up like a can of tuna!" a spectator ecstatic with bloodlust shouted. At one point, Chef bashed his opponent to the ground—another opponent wasted. It looked like the night was going to Chef—but then a surprise opponent—Smash!

Smash is about the size of 5 War Boys put together, a total brute. Chef had fought bravely, but his order was up. Smash threw him into the cage wall and was victorious!

Can anyone in the Wasteland possibly defeat Smash, or will they all fall like sacks of potatoes? We will see at the next Wasteland Gladiators match. Fight! Fight! Fight!

"Fire Good!," *Wastelander* I, no. 4 (September 30, Year Eight)

What a glorious Friday night in the Wasteland! Everywhere you turned there were cage fights, Thunderdome matches, ripping bands, and Wastelanders reveling.

Survivors know you need these things to survive: food, water, shelter, and fire. Wastelanders don't just need fire to survive. They need to play with it. Bring out the Wretched Embers!

This crew of 10 hypnotized the audience, spinning staffs, fans, and hula hoops burning with flame. The air smelled heavily of kerosene as Wastelanders howled their approval. The Wretched Embers spun like dust devils of fire under the starry apocalyptic sky. Burn it down!

"Wet N Wild at the Post-Apocalyptic Swimsuit Contest," unpublished

Wastelanders were sprayed with precious spare water from the decks of the ruins of the Exxon Valdez and then witnessed a parade of Wasteland's best looking meatbags showing off their bods. These crafty dogs fashioned sexy swimsuits from bottle caps, leather straps, barbed wire, horns, skulls, tattered rags and more. About 50 men and women strutted their stuff while babes sprayed them down with delicious water.

The judges bestowed three awards. "Most entertaining" went to Fathom, who made a sultry boa out of VHS cassette ribbon and a bikini decorated with bottle caps. Va-va-voom! "Best craftmanship" went to Rope for her mermaid inspired suit, the scales made of bottle caps. "I scraped them out, burned and hammered them myself," Rope explained. "Judge's choice award" went to a sexy rodeo clown inspired outfit worn by Slapjacks. And how did she win the judge's favor?

"Definitely with some slutty dancing, middle splits, and ass shaking," Slapjacks said with a wink. Well done!

Let's all throw up the horns for these swimsuit clad warriors for keeping the Wasteland sexy!

NOTES

Introduction: Two Minutes to Midnight

"Timeline," *Bulletin of the Atomic Scientists*, https://thebulletin.org/timeline.

John Mecklin, ed., "It Is Two and a Half Minutes to Midnight: 2017 Doomsday Clock Statement," *Bulletin of the Atomic Scientists*, https://thebulletin.org/sites/default/files/Final%202017%20Clock%20Statement.pdf.

John Mecklin, ed., "It Is Now Two Minutes to Midnight: 2018 Doomsday Clock Statement," *Bulletin of the Atomic Scientists*, https://thebulletin.org/2018-doomsday-clock-statement.

1. Blood Moon Prophecy

Adam Gabbatt, "'Blood Moon' Brings Prophecies of End Times—but NASA Says Not to Worry," *Guardian*, September 27, 2015.

John Hagee, *Four Blood Moons: Something Is About to Change* (Brentwood, TN: Worthy Publishing, 2013).

Associated Press, "Mormon Church Issues Call for Calm as 'Blood Moon' Sparks Apocalypse Fears," *Guardian*, September 26, 2015.

David L. Rowe, *God's Strange Work: William Miller and the End of the World* (Grand Rapids, MI: William B. Eerdmans, 2008).

Nora Roth, telephone interview with the author, May 2, 2016.

Nora Roth, "About," 7Trumpets.org, accessed April 19, 2016, www.7trumpets.org/about.htm.

Nora Roth, "2016: The Time of the End—Are 6,000 Years of Sin Almost Over? Will Jesus Come in 2016?," 7Trumpets.org, March 10, 2016, www.7trumpets.org/print/70Sevens.pdf.

Bob Thiel, *Hillary Clinton, Prophecy, and the Destruction of the United States: Is Hillary Clinton Fulfilling Biblical, Islamic, Catholic, Hopi, and Other America-Related Prophecies? What About Donald Trump?* (Arroyo Grande, CA: Nazarene Books, 2015).

Lawrence R. Moelhauser, *The Fourth Beast: Is Donald Trump the Antichrist?* (self-pub., 2016).

2. When the SHTF

Lynda King, *Preppers: History and the Cultural Phenomenon* (Prepper Press, 2014).

William R. Forstchen, *One Second After* (New York: Forge, 2009).

Ted Koppel, *Lights Out: A Cyberattack, A Nation Unprepared, Surviving the Aftermath* (New York: Random House, 2015).

"James" and "Doug," interviews with the author, Sheboygan, WI, August 10, 2017.

Jason, interview with the author, Harlem, NY, May 9, 2016.

Kathy, e-mail interviews with the author, 2016–2018.

3. Rose

Rose, discussion with the author, May 10, 2016.

Seth Baum, interview with the author, New York City, May 10, 2016.

Anthony M. Barrett and Seth D. Baum, "Risk Analysis and Risk Management for the Artificial Superintelligence Research and Development Process," in *The Technological Singularity: Managing the Journey,* ed. Victor Callaghan, James Miller, Roman Yampolskiy, and Stuart Armstrong, Frontiers Collection (Berlin: Springer-Verlag, 2017), 127–140.

Bruce Wilcox, e-mail interview with the author, November 24, 2015.

John Austin, "Will Large Hadron Collider Destroy Earth? CERN Admits Experiments Could Create Black Holes," *Daily Express,* July 28, 2016.

Richard Waters and Tim Bradshaw, "Rise of the Robots Is Sparking an Investment Boom," *Financial Times,* May 2, 2016.

Clip of Android Philip K. Dick from PBS's *Nova,* YouTube, www.youtube.com/watch?v=ot0Fuy34xN0.

Hanson Robotics' Sophia has her own website, which has a clip of her *The Tonight Show* appearance, at http://sophiabot.com/.

Shona Ghosh, "Facebook's AI Boss Described Sophia the Robot as 'Complete B——t' and 'Wizard-of-Oz AI,'" Business Insider, January 6, 2018, www.businessinsider.com/facebook-ai-yann-lecun-sophia-robot-bullshit-2018-1.

James Walker, "Researchers Shut Down AI That Invented Its Own
      Language," Digital Journal, July 21, 2017, www.digitaljournal
      .com/tech-and-science/technology/a-step-closer-to-skynet-ai-invents-a
      -language-humans-can-t-read/article/498142.
Gil Fewster, "The Mind-Blowing AI Announcement from Google That You
      Probably Missed," freeCodeCamp, January 5, 2017, https://medium
      .freecodecamp.org/the-mind-blowing-ai-announcement-from-google
      -that-you-probably-missed-2ffd31334805.
Daniel Victor, "Elon Musk and Stephen Hawking Among Hundreds to
      Urge Ban on Military Robots," New York Times, July 27, 2015.
Paul Ratner, "AI Experts Make a Terrifying Film Calling for a Ban on Killer
      Robots," Big Think, November 18, 2017, https://bigthink.com/paul
      -ratner/watch-slaughterbots-a-terrifying-new-film-warning-about
      -killer-robots.
"AI: 15 Key Moments in the Story of Artificial Intelligence," BBC, accessed
      May 15, 2016, www.bbc.co.uk/timelines/zq376fr.

4. My Zombie Con Journal

Zombies: A Living History, directed by David V. Nicholson, aired October 25,
      2011, on History Channel.
Mark West, "Correlation of the Week: Zombies, Vampires, Democrats, and
      Republicans," Mr. Science Show, May 23, 2009, www.mrscienceshow
      .com/2009/05/correlation-of-week-zombies-vampires.html.
I met Zombie Squad Chapter 053 at their meeting on January 20, 2017.
My Zombie Con journal entries and interviews with Zombie Squad
      members took place at Zombie Con, June 20–25, 2017.

5. Apocalypse Apple Pie

Michael Snyder's Economic Collapse blog is at http://theeconomiccollapseblog
      .com/.
Jon C. Ogg, "Industries Making the Most Money on Doomsday Preppers,"
      24/7 Wall St., August 19, 2013, https://247wallst.com/special
      -report/2013/08/19/
      industries-making-the-most-money-on-doomsday-preppers.
Micah Maidenberg, "For Doomsday Preppers, the End of the World Is
      Good for Business," New York Times, August 11, 2017.

Leanna Garfield, "Trump Has Caused a Growing Number of Liberals to Start Prepping for an Apocalypse," Business Insider, March 5, 2017, www.businessinsider.com/liberal-doomsday-preppers-trump-2017-3.

Lindsey Rae Gjording, "US Bomb Shelter Industry Booms as Trump Stokes Fears of Nuclear War," DW.com, September 22, 2017, www.dw.com /en/us-bomb-shelter-industry-booms-as-trump-stokes-fear-of-nuclear -war/a-40636649.

Survivalist, nos. 24 (September/October 2015), 25 (November/December 2015), and 26 (January/February 2016).

I attended the National Survivalists and Preppers Expo, Richmond, VA, May 8–9, 2016.

Joseph and Amy Alton, The Ultimate Survival Medical Guide: Emergency Preparedness for Any Disaster (New York: Skyhorse, 2015).

Alexandra Sifferlin, "The Zika Threat," Time, May 16, 2016.

The referenced episode of the Survival Medicine Hour can be found at www .doomandbloom.net/survival-medicine-hour-zika-death-reporters-and -prepper-events-more/.

Matt Kempner, "Kempner: Cobb Survivalists Gathering Preps for Doomsday," Atlanta Journal-Constitution, April 28, 2016.

I attended the Chicagoland Survival and Preparedness Expo, March 19, 2017.

6. Monster Planet

Tricia Talbert, ed., "Planetary Defense Frequently Asked Questions," NASA, last updated August 30, 2017, www.nasa.gov/planetarydefense/faq.

Leon Festinger, Henry W. Riecken, and Stanley Schachter, When Prophecy Fails: A Social and Psychological Study of a Modern Group That Predicted the Destruction of the World (Minneapolis: University of Minnesota Press, 1956).

Benjamin E. Zeller, "Anatomy of a Mass Suicide: The Dark, Twisted Story Behind a UFO Death Cult," Salon, November 15, 2014, www.salon .com/2014/11/15/anatomy_of_a_mass_suicide_the_dark_twisted _story_behind_a_ufo_death_cult/.

Michael Hafford, "Heaven's Gate 20 Years Later: 10 Things You Didn't Know," Rolling Stone, March 24, 2017.

The website for Heaven's Gate is still active at http://heavensgate.com/.

Susan Palmer, Aliens Adored: Raël's UFO Religion (New Brunswick, NJ: Rutgers University Press, 2004).

"Luc," Skype interview with the author, March 23, 2016.

Nancy Lieder, *ZetaTalk: Direct Answers from the Zeta Reticuli People* (Columbus, NC: Granite Publishing, 1999).

David Meade, *Planet X: The 2017 Arrival* (self-published, 2016).

Alejandro Rojas, "New Survey Shows Nearly Half of Americans Believe in Aliens," *Huffington Post*, August 2, 2017, www.huffingtonpost .com/entry/new-survey-shows-nearly-half-of-americans-believe-in _us_59824c11e4b03d0624b0abe4.

7. Survival

Jarema Drozdowicz, *The Symbolic Dimension: Anthropological Studies in Culture, Religion, and Education* (Zurich: Lit Verlag, 2014).

Kurt Saxon, "What Is a Survivalist?" 1980, available at www.textfiles.com /survival/whatsurv.

I attended Escape the Woods, July 28–30, 2017.

Creek Stewart, "Creek's Bio," personal website, www.creekstewart.com /about.

Creek Stewart, follow-up interview with the author, February 27, 2018.

8. Doomsday Bunkers of the Rich and Famous

I took a tour of the Survival Condos, September 19, 2017.

Jane Poynter, *The Human Experiment: Two Years and Twenty Minutes Inside Biosphere 2* (New York: Thunder's Mouth, 2006).

Samantha Cole, "The Strange History of Steve Bannon and the Biosphere 2 Experiment," *Vice*, November 15, 2016, https://motherboard.vice.com /en_us/article/qkjn87/the-strange-history-of-steve-bannon-and-the -biosphere-2-experiment.

Garrett Graff, *Raven Rock: The Story of the U.S. Government's Secret Plan to Save Itself—While the Rest of Us Die* (New York: Simon & Schuster, 2017).

9. The Sixth Extinction

To take notes on the *Third Planet* exhibit, I visited the Milwaukee Public Museum, February 1, 2018.

Elizabeth Kolbert, *The Sixth Extinction: An Unnatural History* (New York: Henry Holt, 2014).

Mark Lynas, *Six Degrees: Our Future on a Hotter Planet* (Washington, DC: National Geographic, 2008).

Guy McPherson, "Abrupt Climate Change" talk, First Unitarian Church, Milwaukee, WI, July 12, 2017.

Carolyn Baker and Guy McPherson, *Extinction Dialogs: How to Live with Death in Mind* (San Francisco: Next Revelation, 2015).

Ankur Desai, in-person interview with the author, November 30, 2016, and follow-up e-mail interview with the author, February 18, 2018.

Gwynne Dyer, *Climate Wars: The Fight for Survival as the World Overheats* (London: Oneworld, 2011).

Justin Mikulka, "Insights into the Thinking of Trump Advisor Myron Ebell's Competitive Enterprise Institute on Climate Change," *DeSmogBlog*, November 27, 2016, www.desmogblog.com/2016/11/27 /insights-thinking-trump-advisor-myron-ebell-s-competitive-enterprise -institute.

"The 97% Consensus on Global Warming," Skeptical Science, accessed September 22, 2018, www.skepticalscience.com/global- warming-scientific-consensus-intermediate.htm.

Jerry Diamond, Eli Watkins, and Juana Summers, "EPA Chief Scott Pruitt Resigns Amid Scandals, Citing 'Unrelenting Attacks,'" CNN.com, July 5, 2018, www.cnn.com/2018/07/05/politics/scott-pruitt-epa-resigns /index.html.

Eric Wolff, "Environmentalists: Pruitt's Replacement 'Should Scare Anyone Who Breathes,'" *Politico*, July 5, 2018, www.politico.com/story/2018 /05/05/scott-pruitt-epa-andrew-wheeler-570641.

10. Bugging Out

I attended Jim Cobb's Realistic Bug-Out Planning workshop, January 20, 2018.

Jim Cobb, phone interview with the author, March 2, 2018.

Creek Stewart, *Build the Perfect Bug-Out Bag: Your 72-Hour Disaster Survival Kit* (Cincinnati, OH: Betterway Books, 2012).

Jeurgen, phone interview with the author, February 24, 2016.

Jeurgen's Badass Homesteader videos can all be found at http://bah.farm.

Tess Pennington, "Another Doomsday Prophecy Come and Gone. Finding Meaning When the World Does Not End," Ready Nutrition website, September 28, 2015, http://readynutrition.com/resources